Princeton Theological Monograph Series

Dikran Y. Hadidian

General Editor

42

JESUS CHRIST AND CREATION IN THE THEOLOGY OF JOHN CALVIN

JESUS CHRIST

And

CREATION

In the Theology of

John Calvin

PETER WYATT

PICKWICK PUBLICATIONS
ALLISON PARK, PENNSYLVANIA

Published by

Pickwick Publications
4137 Timberlane Drive
Allison Park, PA 15101-2932
USA

Printed on Acid Free Paper in the United States of America

Library of Congress Cataloging-in-Publication Data

Wyatt, Peter
Jesus Christ and Creation in the theology of John Calvin /
Peter Wyatt
p. cm. -- (Princeton theological monograph seriers ; 42)
Originally presented as the author's thesis (Th. D.)--Toronto School of Theology
Includes bibliographical references (p.).
ISBN 1-55635-030-9 (alk. paper)
1. Jesus Christ--History of doctrines--16th century. 2. Creation--History of doctrines--16th century. 3. Calvin, Jean, 1509-1564.
I. Title. II. Series
BT198.W83 1996
230' .42' 092--dc20 96-799
CIP

CONTENTS

PREFACE

This essay in historical theology attempts to provide a new perspective on the remarkable quality of internal tension in Calvin's theology. This tension has been attested often enough by interpreters, either explicitly through critical comment, or implicitly through the considerable effort required to sustain exposition of Calvin's theology as a consistent whole. The thesis advanced in these pages is that Calvin combined two distinct approaches in theology, one which could be called "existential" or evangelical, and the other "sapiential", and that as a practitioner of sapiential thought, Calvin was not only a critic, but also an inheritor, of medieval theology.

On the one hand, it was Calvin's reforming intention to affirm the pre-eminence of Jesus Christ as the proper focus of faith and theology, and in so doing to underscore the sole authenticity of knowledge of God which is knowledge of God's disposition toward us as fallen creatures. On the other, he makes room in his thought for a broader view, and for reflection on the implications of this redemptively focused knowledge, particularly with respect to the original divine purpose in creation and to knowledge of God the Creator.

As originally conceived, these pages were a dissertation for the Th. D. degree in the Toronto School of Theology. More than a dozen years ago, the position I took was that this tension amounted to incongruity and was evidence of a failure on Calvin's part to express his theology on as thorough-going a christological basis as his evangelical vision mandated. In effect, a Barthian template was laid on Calvin and he was found wanting. Today, I still encounter moments when the tension between the evangelical and the more philosophical Calvin approaches dissonance. However, when Calvin is seen as the mediating theologian that he strove to be, the "incongruity" in his theology can be recognized for what it usually is—the expression of a relatively inclusive theological interest, and of healthy tensions, if not complementarities. Though he was capable of intransigent and polemical behaviour, Calvin was not an either/or, but a both/and thinker. It is not surprising, then, that he did not regard the existential and the sapiential as mutually exclusive ways of going about the theological venture.

The interpretation advanced here may have a certain controversial character. However, my intention in presenting it is to add to the repertoire of interpretive perspectives, not to displace or deny others. We have portraits of the christocentric Calvin, the Lutheran Calvin, the catholic Calvin, the revolutionary Calvin, the pneumatic Calvin, the pastoral Calvin, the rhetorical Calvin, the Calvin of metaphysical anxiety, the eucharistic Calvin, and so on. Each of these portraits offers insight vital to our understanding of the Reformer; none can claim to be a complete or uniquely correct appreciation of his work. To this ongoing work of interpretation I wish to add another portrait, that of the mediating and sapiential Calvin.

In order to allow Calvin to speak for himself as much as possible, the text is saturated with quotations, and end-notes abound. The standard English translations are used, namely, the McNeill-Battles edition of the *Institutes*, the New Testament commentaries edited by the brothers Torrance, and the Old Testament commentaries of the Calvin Translation Society. To facilitate ease of reference, simple citations of the *Institutes* will appear bracketed in the body of the text, rather than in end-notes. References to the commentaries will follow the generally accepted convention of citing the relevant Scriptural book, together with indication of the chapter and verse under discussion, as, for example, "*Comm. Rom.* 8.5". The major repeated abbreviations employed are as follows:

CO	*Calvini Opera*
Inst.	*Institutes of the Christian Religion*
ST	*Summa Theologiae of Thomas Aquinas*
LW	*Luther's Works* (American Edition)

In undertaking the work of revision, I found myself responding to the worthy imperative of inclusive language, and an attempt has been made to honor it in my own prose. However, with regard to quotations, respect for the sources leads me to present them as they were penned. As well, the complexity of carrying on a dialogue with Calvin, Aquinas, Luther and others, especially with respect to the intimate nature of Trinitarian relationships, means that my own references to the deity do not always achieve the goal of inclusivity.

I express appreciation to David Demson of Emmanuel College, the supervisor of the thesis in its original form, to the late John Gilchrist of Trent University, who read the original with a view to making the "cuts", and to my wife and colleague, Joan Wyatt, whose encouragement has sustained me through many ventures. I dedicate the work in its present form to the memory of the Rev. Dr. P. P. Miedema, courageous pastor and faithful exponent of evangelical truth.

Peter Wyatt
October, 1995

INTRODUCTION

The character of any theologian's work is rarely shaped by a single determinant but rather by a complex of factors. In Calvin's case, at least three major influences of a spiritual-intellectual nature were formative in his theology. The first and most obvious is his conversion and commitment to the cause of reform and to the task of the restatement of theology on an evangelical basis. In this regard, his chief mentors were Luther and Bucer. The second is the matrix of humanism whose influence upon Calvin is signalled by the appearance of his first published work, the commentary on Seneca's *De clementia*, and by his continuing dialogue with Cicero on "natural" knowledge of God. The third factor is Calvin's inheritance of the overall theological tradition of Christendom. With respect to patristic authors, most notably Augustine, this influence could scarcely go unnoticed. Among the earlier medievals, the influence of Bernard of Clairvaux is especially evident, especially his teaching on the spiritual union of believers with Christ.[1] However, it is with respect to the ordering of Christian doctrine for the purpose of a comprehensive understanding and instruction in Scriptural faith that insufficient notice has been taken of the medieval influence on Calvin.

This influence is easily overlooked precisely because of his adversarial stance toward the unreformed church and its dependence on scholasticism. However, in criticizing inherited tradition, even the most radical reformer inevitably assumes a portion of the standards of the preceding intellectual ethos, and may ultimately learn to distinguish between its chaff and its grist. The aim of this study is to take into account the influence of the theological frame of intelligibility which Calvin inherited from "the sounder schoolmen" and to trace its usually complementary relationship to Calvin's evangelical presentation of the incarnate, mediatorial Christ. In particular, this complementarity will be explored through consideration of the relationship between Jesus Christ and creation in Calvin's theology.

THE HISTORY AND STATE OF THE QUESTION

Not long after the close of the First World War, Hermann Bauke posed the problem of widespread, apparent contradictions in the theology of Calvin and characterized the work of the Reformer as a *complexio oppositorum.* Bauke argued that previous scholarship had been mistaken in seeking to interpret Calvin's theology on the basis of a single controlling doctrine. He asserted that this approach was typically German and assumed a "material principle of interpretation." The key to understanding Calvin was to be found, however, in a formal principle, an approach typical of the French mind. He argued that, in the case of Calvin, we have an example of "formal rationalism" in which opposing and equally important principles are set in dialectical relation to each other. Bauke attributed this dialectical method not to any speculative tendency but to the Reformer's "Biblicism," that is, his strategy to limit theology to the exposition of the authentic themes of Scripture.[2]

Bauke's perceptive eye and ingenious argument heralded a rebirth of critical scholarship. "Bauke's study was a genuine step forward," observes John H. Leith, "for it made plain that every attempt to interpret the *Institutes* must consider form as well as content. He dealt a devastating blow to the notion that Calvin was a speculative systematizer who deduced a system of theology from one or two principles."[3] The continuing validity of Bauke's phrase, *complexio oppositorum*, is evidenced, furthermore, by the remark of François Wendel that "the paradoxes of Calvin," "the dialectical opposites," remain. "Calvin's is not a closed system elaborated around a central idea, but . . . draws together, one after another, a whole series of Biblical ideas, some of which can only with difficulty be logically reconciled."[4]

Scarcely any contemporary commentary can be found which does not draw attention to this "antithetical structure" in some way, though its significance is interpreted variously. Viewed in a thoroughly positive way by F. L. Battles, it is evidence of the way that Calvin sought to approximate ever more closely to truth, steering a middle way "between the Scylla of aberrant Romanism and the Charybdis of the radical tendencies of his time." With reference to Aristotle's concept of a spectrum between defect and excess, Battles asserts that for Calvin "every fundamental notion of his thought is defined as a field of tension —a true middle between false extremes."[5] On the other hand, J. H. Leith sees the antitheses as evidence of inconsistency, deriving "from Calvin's intense concern to maintain the glory of God in Geneva" and resulting in the obscuring of divine grace through "speculative theological abstractions, laws and ecclesiastical discipline."[6]

Bauke's recognition of this internal tension in Calvin's theology forced interpretation to a reconsideration of the fundamental coherence of his work. In the past fifty years, two major approaches have been taken. Wilhelm Niesel's *Theology of Calvin* well represents the first approach in which it is argued that competing and apparently contradictory emphases in the Reformer's thought can be resolved successfully around his doctrine of the person and work of Jesus Christ. For Niesel, this means that the Chalcedonian definition of the two natures in the person of the Mediator—union but not fusion, distinction but not separation—was employed by Calvin as a principle of method throughout his theology. Among other examples, he cites that of the relation of the living Word to the written Word: "The relation between the words of Scripture and the incarnate Word is analogous to that between the human nature of Christ and the Logos. The written word is not interchangeable with the one Word, but neither is it separable from the latter."[7] It is Niesel's summary insight that "Jesus Christ controls not only the content but also Calvinistic thought."[8]

Niesel properly credited Karl Barth with a revolution in interpretation based on the principle that theology must be determined by its object, Jesus Christ. In the decade of the thirties, marked by the ascendancy of the Nazi ideology in Germany, interpretation of Calvin's theology became a flashpoint of bitter controversy. Emil Brunner of Zürich had published an essay on the place of a revelation from the creation in Calvin's thought and Barth replied to his fellow national with some heat, regarding Brunner's argument as a potential buttress for the "German Church" movement. In "No: Answer to Emil Brunner," Barth denies the possibility of attributing any kind of natural theology to Calvin since the expression *si integer stetisset Adam* brackets and qualifies everything the Reformer ever said about natural knowledge of God.[9] Thus, the notion of a knowledge of God from nature is purely hypothetical because of the noetic blindness occasioned by human sin. The only way one can ascribe to Calvin a revelation in nature distinct from the revelation in Christ is by taking advantage of "that little corner which has been left uncovered in Calvin's treatment."[10] Peter Barth joined his brother in taking this approach, and, in the English-speaking world, T. F. Torrance and T. H. L. Parker are among those who have affirmed that Calvin is an unequivocal progenitor of christocentric theology. Parker echoes Barth in saying, "Calvin always follows what appear to be generous concessions to natural theology by denying any religious validity to them at all."[11]

Emil Brunner and E. A. Dowey are representative of the other major approach, based on the conviction that Calvin's position is more complex than a strictly christocentric interpretation will allow. Neither wishes to deny the centrality of Christ to Christian faith and knowledge, but they maintain that Calvin also has a special place in his theology for a knowledge of God from creation which is distinct, while not separate, from the knowledge given in the redemptive event of Jesus Christ. In the very essay to which Barth so angrily reacted, Brunner argues that we must speak of a double revelation and face the challenge of discovering how the revelation in creation and that in Jesus Christ are to be related.[12] As a consequence of the existence of this special sphere of the knowledge of God in creation, he holds that there may be found in Calvin evangelical definitions of natural revelation, natural theology, and natural law.[13] Brunner argues that in contrast to the Roman Catholic concept of an "unrefracted *theologia naturalis*," the Reformers espoused a dialectical one, one that could not be correct "unless Christ be taken into account."[14]

It is the singular contribution of E. A. Dowey to have attempted an explanation of the complex relationship obtaining between the knowledge of God the Creator and the knowledge of God the Redeemer in the *Institutes*. Dowey characterizes the knowledge of God the Creator as pertaining to "the orderly universal inclusiveness of law," while that of God the Redeemer to "the special-gratuitous quality of God's mercy." The relationship between the two orders of knowledge is one of "mutual presupposition."[15] Knowledge of God's redemptive activity logically presupposes knowledge of God the Creator, since only the providential world-Ruler has the power to bring about the event of salvation. On the other hand, knowledge of God the Redeemer is the epistemological presupposition of the knowledge of God the Creator, since God the Creator cannot be known naturally by sinful humanity, but only through the regeneration wrought in Christ through the power of the Spirit.[16] According to Dowey, "The believer can never build a continuous thought structure relating the creating and redeeming work of God because of . . . the noetic effects of sin."[17] These two aspects of the divine work belong together because of God's own unity, who is both Creator and Redeemer, but this coherence can only be known from the perspective of faith.

While maintaining a christological center to Calvin's theology, Dowey is prepared to defend Brunner's use of the term, "Christian natural theology." Even if, because of the fall, the revelation from creation has a pre-eminently negative function (in rendering humans universally inexcusable before God), nevertheless it thereby possesses "eristic" potential: it offers no positive foundation to faith but it is "a battering ram against false 'faiths'."[18] Moreover, after the regeneration of believers through faith, the revelation from creation occupies "a subsequent and subsidiary, but nonetheless essential, place," amplifying the knowledge of the one, triune God first gained in Christ.[19] Thus, natural theology may be seen to complement, rather than undermine, evangelical truth.

The polarization of mid-century gave way to studies which, while profiting from the insights generated out of the Barth-Brunner controversy, attempted to achieve fresh perspectives. Especially notable are works by David Willis and Benjamin Milner to which reference will be made in the body of this work. However, the present interpretive moment is characterized by an emphasis on Calvin's humanism and its pervasive impress on his theological vocation.

THE "RHETORICAL" CALVIN

Almost lost in the controversy over natural theology was the importance of pioneering work by Quirinus Breen, who, over sixty years ago, proposed that Calvin's humanism was the precipitate of his vocation as a reformer. Breen went so far as to say that "the Reformation is largely a defence of the new age that the Renaissance had ushered in."[20] Thirty years later, he saw fit to revise that remarkable opinion, but still managed to argue that in Calvin's doctrine of common grace is to be found "a post-conversion defence of secular studies, particularly the pagan classics" and a "charter of liberties" for these same studies.[21] More recently (1971), Egil Grislis has suggested that, with respect to the question of natural knowledge of God, "Calvin's argument is essentially a restatement of Cicero's insight" and that "comparisons of Cicero have indicated both a literary dependence as well as a basic general agreement."[22] In response to this position, Charles Partee adjudges that Grislis has made an over-interpretation of the evidence. Arguing that the parallels are clear but the dependence is not, he maintains that Calvin uses the resources of antiquity, and of classical philosophy in particular, "not as a source of truth but as a learned adjunct to the explanation of the Christian faith."[23] What especially characterizes Calvin's use of pagan writers is the selectivity by which he accepts some of their views and rejects others. "Calvin's use and evaluation of the classical philosophers is instructive not only as an illustration of his Christian humanism but as an important part of his theology." [24]

The renewal of interest in Calvin's humanism in the eighties and nineties has focused not so much on the philosophical as on the philological and literary aspects of the classical legacy. Alister McGrath observes that the renaissance of the sixteenth century was "remarkably heterogeneous"; nonetheless, "if there is any common theme to humanist writings, it is the need to promote spoken and written eloquence." Ancient texts were read in the original tongues "as a means to an end, rather than as an end in themselves."[25] "Humanism was concerned with *how ideas were obtained and expressed*, rather than with the precise nature of the ideas themselves.[26] In almost every field there was a concerted attempt to escape the strangulation of the medieval glossators and thus to free the texts for fresh encounter and renewed uses.[27]

"Humanism" has the present-day connotation of a world-view

developed without reference to the deity. However, far from being an enemy of theology, the humanism of the sixteenth century meant to "tap the pure, clear founts, overgrown with the thorny disputes of scholasticism . . . A piously learned examination of Scripture would release a golden stream of eloquence where only muddied rivulets of schoolish debate had trickled."[28] Thus Erasmus believed that an increasingly accurate philology would spark the renewal of theology and serve the cause of Christ. For this cause he was willing to endure the storm occasioned by the publication of his critical edition of the New Testament in which he corrected the translation of *logos* from *verbum* to *sermo*.[29]

Quirinus Breen calls Calvin "par excellence the orator of the Reformation era":

> He actually used his voice most of the time; he preached several times a week, and much in his commentaries was prepared for class lectures. His audiences represented a general cross-section of society, with no specific preparation for theology through years of drilling in a technical vocabulary, as was usual in a theological faculty at the universities. When he spoke, he addressed the whole man: mind, will, feeling. In all this he observed the canons of classical rhetoric. These canons also said that he must expound with clarity (i.e., clarity to the general run of men), with agreeableness (so that he would not put his hearers to sleep), and in such a manner as to move. All this was required for persuasion. The orator does not appeal to the mind alone, as the philosopher does, so as to convince; he intends to persuade for change of faith, and for action. [30]

Calvin's exposure to humanism came through his legal studies under luminaries like de l'Estoile and Alciati, where the goal of eloquence was approached through the Ciceronian way of "dialogue, interrogation, and persuasive speech."[31] The legal provenance of Calvin's humanism, however, should not suggest images of dialectical jousting or manipulative technique. Quoting C. S. Baldwin, David Willis distinguishes between two different conceptions of rhetoric. In the Sophist sense excoriated by Socrates, it means the best possible presentation of a case, without regard to the truth or falsity of the argument, for the purpose of persuading one's hearers. "The other conception of rhetoric concentrates not on making the speaker effective, but the truth effective." On Aristotle's definition, rhetoric is "the energizing of knowledge, the bringing of truth to bear upon men."[32] Willis concludes that Calvin's rhetorical formation led him to define knowledge of God in a highly experiential way: faith is a matter of being *persuaded* of God's goodness in Christ; truth is measured by its power to change those whom it grasps; and divine revelation is the accommodation of God to human weakness for the sake of our persuasion.[33]

A number of important corollaries may be drawn from the recognition of Calvin as essentially a rhetorical humanist. One is the critical importance that can be assigned to the concept of "accommodation" in understanding God's will and work in Calvin's thought. God now may be seen as the unsurpassable practitioner of the rhetorical gifts of informing, delighting and moving human minds and hearts. From beginning to end, revelation is the loving condescension by which God crosses the chasm between divine and human capacities. Here, if ever, *Infinitum capax finiti*,[34] or, as Willis puts it, *Humanitas capax divinitatis per accommodationem.* "That is, God begins with our incapacity, makes himself small to adjust to it, and by his gracious action of strategic self-limitation, transforms us so that we are increasingly united to God himself in Christ."[35] While others give important accounts of the principle of accommodation, it is F. L. Battles who argues most clearly for its programmatic significance:

> Calvin makes this principle a consistent basis for his handling not only of Scripture but of every avenue of relationship between God and men. Thus the starkest inconsistencies in Scripture are harmonized through rhetorical analysis, within the frame of divine accommodation to human capacity . . .; this method unlocks for Calvin God's beneficent tutelage and pedagogy of His wayward children.[36]

While the concept of divine accommodation to human capacity functions to underscore God's parental goodness, it may also raise questions about the relationship between the *deus revelatus* and the *deus absconditus*. On Calvin's definition, "the mode of accommodation is for [God] to represent himself to us not as he is himself, but as he seems to us."[37] Does "accommodation" then imply discontinuity between God known in a tempered revelation and God's unknown essential being and character? Could it mean that God's ways, even God's disposition toward creatures, may change in response to diverse human situations and a changing creation? Calvin resolutely denied change in God, although his doctrine of accommodation might have led him in that direction, and seems to have made others suspicious that it did.[38] And while he maintained that speculation about the divine essence opened upon an inconceivable abyss, God's "naked divinity" is at least a boundary concept for him; moreover, a "hidden God" (God unrevealed) is presupposed logically by the notion of God revealed. Thus, there is latent ambiguity in the concept of accommodation and, as we shall have occasion later to note, it becomes a knife-edge in Calvin's account of the atonement.

A second major corollary is derived from the recognition of Calvin's vocation as a Christian humanist. For some interpreters it serves as corroboration of the fact that Calvin never was what later tradition made him out to be—the great systematizer. It was as a humanist committed to letting the text speak for itself—in other words, as a Biblical theologian—that Calvin proscribed speculative theology and came to regard system as the enemy of faith. According to William Bouwsma, the systematic Calvin is an "historical artifact: the artificial construct of his followers of the later sixteenth and seventeenth centuries, when human insecurity and the yearning for social and political order received symbolic expression in a great wave of system building of the kind Calvin sought to avoid."[39] The sixteenth century was too fragmented an age for the construction of grand, coherent systems of thought.[40] "A systematic Calvin, as that term is usually understood, would be an anomaly and an anachronism."[41]

David Willis observes that if Calvin is recognized as a reforming humanist, then the tensions in his thought may be seen as "instances of rhetorical correlation rather than dialectical diastasis" and as "more cohering in an order of teaching and persuasion than in a formally systematic way."[42] Humanist *persuasio* is the contrary of system and, as a rhetorical humanist, Calvin's aim (like that of Marx!) was to change the world, not understand it.[43] In general agreement with the humanist interpretation of Calvin, but from the point of view of political philosophy, Michael Walzer sees Calvin as a "practical man of ideas," not so much a theologian or a philosopher, as an "ideologist." The practical task of bringing people "into the obedience of the gospel" was the engine driving his antispeculative *animus* and his can be called a "theology antitheological."[44] In summing up, Bouwsma says, "It is hard to understand how anyone who has read Calvin could maintain the systematic nature of his theology."[45]

But not everyone seems to agree. "System" can mean many things. If it means the kind of logical exposition presented in Beza's *Sum of All Christianity*, in which a comprehensive account of the successive divine decrees determining the destiny of the elect and the reprobate is set forth in the form of a diagram, then Calvin has no system.[46] If it means the derivation of a selfconsciously complete account of Christian faith from a single principle or pre-eminent doctrine, then Calvin was no systematizer, though there are still moments when interpreters find themselves prepared to hazard the opinion that a certain doctrine or theme is central to the spirit and organization of Calvin's thought. Thus, for example, Brian Gerrish identifies the correlative theme of "grace and gratitude" (God's free adoption of believers and their thankful response) as aptly descriptive of a complex of images that shape Calvin's theology.[47] But the day is gone when an abstract concept, such as absolute will or divine sovereignty, could be thought to control Calvin's thought and to be a canon according to which the varying themes of Scripture would be measured and incorporated into his theology.

It *would* be an anachronism to think of Calvin as a systematic theologian in our contemporary sense. Above all, Calvin was a pastor and a public lecturer in the Scriptures, who also published much of what he thought and said. But, as Melanchthon adjudged, in these roles he was also a theologian, "the theologian." That he was a Biblical theologian and strove to make his thought an expression of the authentic themes of Scripture is beyond debate. But this did not mean that he avoided weighing the relative importance of these themes or ignored the need to relate them to one another in a coherent whole. Indeed, the existence of the *Institutes* in its varied and growing editions is the incontrovertible evidence that he regarded some expression of "the sum of religion" as essential to his vocation.

In his preface to the *Institutes* of 1559, Calvin says that he "was never satisfied until the work had been arranged in the order now set forth." His claims the office of "a teacher in the church" and declares (beginning with the 1539 edition) that his purpose in this labour has been "to prepare and instruct candidates in sacred theology for the reading of the divine Word":

> For I believe I have so embraced the sum of religion in all its parts and have arranged it in such an order, that if anyone rightly grasps it, it will not be difficult for him to determine what he ought especially to seek in Scripture and to what end he ought to relate its contents.

He goes on to remind readers of what he first said in the second edition of 1539, namely, that in any future published interpretations of Scripture "I shall always condense them, because I shall have no need of long doctrinal discussions, and to digress into commonplaces." In the final edition, the French of 1560, his preface promises the work to be "first, a sum of Christian doctrine, and, secondly, a way to benefit greatly from reading the Old as well as the New Testament." The *Institutes* are meant to be both an introduction to the themes of Scripture and a compendium of what they teach.

To be a Biblical theologian is to be more than an exegete or an expositor. Edward A. Dowey notes that when Calvin is commenting on Scripture "the choice, sequence, disposition and interrelation of the elements are determined not by Calvin's mind but by his intent to express the mind of the writer." However, in his treatises, and particularly in the *Institutes,* "Calvin's own ways of thinking, farther removed from any given Biblical text than in the commentaries and sermons, are freer to express his own mentality."[48] As theologian, the Biblical theologian's task is to set forth the Scriptural narrative in a way that its recurrent themes, underlying unity and doctrinal significance can be grasped. And surely it is the case that even as an exegete and expositor Calvin's own drumbeat can be heard. In remarks on Calvin's sermons that could be extended to his commentaries and letters, John H. Leith observes "that they fit into a theological framework with certain unifying perspectives that influence all doctrines....His theology is an organic whole not a machine put together with different parts."[49]

It is noteworthy also that there is a difference between Calvin's finished work in the *Institutes* and the topical method employed by Erasmus and Melanchthon.[50] Unless one persists in treating "system" as a shibboleth, the utility and widespread influence of the *Institutes* can be seen to derive from a quality that one naturally would call systematic. Gerrish notes that the O. E. D. defines "systematic" as "arranged . . . according to a system, plan, or organized method." He goes on to observe of Calvin: "He was a systematic theologian in exactly the same sense as Schleiermacher; he looked assiduously for the interconnections between doctrines, the way they 'hang together' (their *Zusammenhang*)."[51] Calvin's quarrel with scholastic theology did not concern its organization but its entanglement in abstraction, speculation and contorted reasoning.

Sooner or later we all manage to fall under the ban of our own indictments and Bouwsma is no exception in his essay on "Calvinism as a Renaissance Artifact." Having argued that it is anachronistic to think of Calvin as a systematic thinker, he later asserts that his theology "was directed not to all time, but to his own."[52] Ascribing this viewpoint also to humanism in general, he concludes that "an understanding of the historicity of theological discourse may be essential to a proper interpretation of its substance."[53] Is it not anachronistic to suppose that sixteenth-century authors, living on the farther side of the nineteenth-century historiographical revolution, could have conceived of their discourse as historically conditioned in the radical sense that we do? While Bouwsma is right to underline Calvin's insistence on achieving practical results through galvanizing his hearers, did this emphasis on action and utility exclude passion for truth, and for stating it in a precise and coherent way?

Bouwsma's assertion that Calvin rarely made truth claims[54] is surprising, particularly in light of a quotation cited near the end of his essay, in which Calvin begins by saying, "Let us hold this as an undoubted truth which no siege engines can shake..." This particular passage, in which Calvin asserts the complete vitiation of human powers in graphic and virtually scatological terms,[55] is a salient example of a recurring characteristic in Calvin's prose, that is, the coincidence of his passion to persuade with his intellectual conviction. Rhetorical purple underscores the intensity with which he holds "undoubted truth." One might be forgiven for thinking that making claims about the truth of the Christian religion, in both rhetorical and intellectual senses, is something Calvin did virtually non-stop throughout his career.

THE SAPIENTIAL CALVIN

The re-apprehension of Calvin as a sixteenth-century humanist is a breakthrough in the work of interpretation and functions to inform, delight, and almost persuade. The difficulty is that the proponents of the rhetorical Calvin seem committed to an oppositional approach of either/or. Either Calvin was a humanist or a rationalist, a contextual thinker or a systematizer, a proponent of rhetorical persuasion or discursive truth. Is it possible that Calvin was both?[56] Bouwsma's gripping portrait of Calvin as a human being caught between the labyrinth of selfconfining order and the abyss of chaotic freedom suggests as much. In *John Calvin: A Sixteenth-Century Portrait* he speaks of "Calvin's struggle to reduce the incompatible impulses in himself" and of Calvin's Calvinism as "composite," acknowledging that while there is one Calvin who was a rhetorical humanist, there is another who "was a philosopher, a rationalist and a schoolman in the high scholastic tradition represented by Thomas Aquinas."[57] There are moments when the duality of Calvin's thought appears to be an either/or alternative of incompatibility. However, there is another and more positive way of looking at the relationship between the rhetorical and the intellectual Calvin, that is, on a both/and basis: often enough the dual interests evident in his thought can be seen also to complement and presuppose each other.

Calvin seems not to have conceived that his goal of evangelical restatement would preclude sapiential discourse and systematic considerations. In his treatise, "The Necessity of Reforming the Church," for example, he indicates that the reforming mandate is not without certain limits: "All our controversies concerning doctrine relate either to the legitimate worship of God or to the ground of salvation."[58] Again, in a Confession of Faith, he writes:

> Wherefore all our differences relate to the following points: on what our confidence of salvation should rest, how we ought to invoke God, and what is the method of well and duly serving him. And there are points depending on these, viz., what is the true poli-

> ty of the Church, the offices of prelates and pastors, the nature, virtue and use of the Sacraments.[59]

As viewed by Calvin, the great issues between the Reformers and Rome concerned soteriology and ecclesiology (especially liturgy). It is no surprise, therefore, that it is in these contexts that we find him most adamant about the all-encompassing need of humanity for God, and the radical initiative of God in reaching out to us in Jesus Christ. But care must be taken not to assume an attitude of total rejection on Calvin's part to medieval theology, thus imposing on his thought an unwarranted opposition between evangelical humanism and sapiential breadth. In fact, a proper definition of the sapiential approach will show it to be inclusive of the fundamental humanist dynamic. The *animus* of sixteenth-century humanism was directed at the convoluted speculation of later nominalism and the scandal of ecclesiastical abuses, not against the broad stream of Augustinian tradition.What the humanists opposed was an obfuscating theology, not theology itself.

The meaning of humanism is not exhausted under the heading of rhetoric or eloquence: the passion of humanism includes wisdom and prudence also, and in this sense it is sapiential. While the humanism of the sixteenth century had a particular focus on persuasive eloquence, it had in common with the earlier renaissance of the twelfth century an openness to truth arising from ancient (and therefore mostly pagan) sources. Humanist non-theological sources susceptible of adoption and adaption by the theologian belongs to the definition of the sapiential. Integral to the high scholastic vision was a resolve to overcome the initial challenge of the philosophical revolution of the twelfth and thirteenth centuries—the recovery of Aristotle through Muslim provenance —by co-opting the dynamic of this revolution. What was true of the Aristotelian renaissance is arguably true of the later, more philological and literary, renaissance of the sixteenth century. Thus the degree to which Calvin continued to employ the resources of his humanist erudition reflects also the degree to which he was an inheritor of the medieval tradition and a practitioner of sapiential theology.

Defining the Sapiential

In an essay in the genre of "ecumenical theology," Otto Pesch has set in relation to one another the signal contributions to theology of Thomas Aquinas and Martin Luther. He proposes that the real source of opposition between the two is found not in differing thought content or even differing thought forms (*Denkformen*), but in two distinct "intellectual styles of performance" (*Denkvollzugsformen*).[60] Such a difference in intellectual style arises out of "a basic concern and interest which is prior to all theological reflection, which may not even be conscious, but which produces the diverse structure of the questions each asks."[61] Pesch describes the style of Luther as "existential," and that of Aquinas as "sapiential": "While Luther thinks in the categories of relationship Thomas thinks in ontological categories of nature."[62] Luther's approach is illustrated by his understanding that "the proper subject of theology is man guilty of sin and condemned, and God the Justifier and Saviour of man the sinner. Whatever is asked or discussed in theology outside this subject is error and poison."[63] In contrast, Aquinas views theology as "like an imprint on us of God's own knowledge"[64] and as the wisdom of "understanding reality in terms of ultimate causes, as we learn in faith the very thoughts of God himself."[65] Pesch adds this compendious definition:

> Existential theology is the way of doing theology from within the self-actualization of our existence in faith, as we submit to God in the obedience of faith. Its affirmations are so formulated that the actual faith and confession of the speaker are not merely necessary presuppositions but are reflexly thematized. Sapiential theology is the way of doing theology from outside one's self-actualization in the existence in faith, in the sense that in its doctrinal statements the faith and confession of the speaker is the enduring presupposition but it is not thematized within this theology.[66]

Pesch's distinction between "existential" and "sapiential" theology provides helpful insight and is a valuable tool for understanding the composite character of Calvin's thought. However, to employ these words is not to subscribe to his thesis in its entirety. It is possible, for example, that the identified theological styles arise also from the theological content and scope with which they deal. Intellectual style reflects the manner in which a theologian actually works, and derives from his or her conception of the nature of the theological task as it is engaged. Luther is "existential," i.e., thinks in the categories of relationship, not only because he may be predisposed to, but also because he encounters in Scripture a theological mandate to deal with one issue pre-eminently, namely, the personal, or covenantal, relationship obtaining between sinful humanity and God redemptively revealed in Jesus Christ. Likewise, Aquinas is "sapiential," i.e., thinks in the categories of being, not only because he may be so predisposed, but because the texts of Scripture and Aristotle provide him with a theological mandate of broader scope, namely, created being as it is ordered to its final end and as it is intelligible on that basis.

On this basis, the sole use of the term "existential" would have limited value in serving the present task. As has been noted, there is good cause to describe Calvin's approach as evangelical (in its focus on the mediatorial Christ) and also as experiential (in its emphasis on persuasion and practical results). The use of the three terms offers something like a comprehensive description of Calvin's style as a passionate Christian humanist and all three will be used in this study, though, for the sake of convenience, "evangelical" will predominate. "Sapiential," however, appears to be an apt descriptive in referring both to a style and to a content and scope. In brief, the evangelical approach begins with Christ as "God manifest in the flesh," whose mediatorial existence becomes the crucial litmus for all theological statement. The sapiential approach begins with creation and values most highly the vision of God the Creator who is the beginning and end of all things, and whom Jesus Christ serves primarily as a redemptive agent, providing the way for creatures to return to their Exemplar.

CALVIN'S KNOWLEDGE OF THE SCHOLASTICS

In this study, the theology of Thomas Aquinas, particularly the *Summa Theologiae*, will serve as a bench-mark for our definition and understanding of the sapiential approach to theology. This use of Aquinas is justifiable theologically since Aquinas is the author of the culminating work in the genre of the *summa theologiae* and is arguably the epitome of the medieval theological mind. If Calvin indeed has a sapiential dimension, then it is appropriate to test this dimension in his thought against the soundest schoolman. It is justifiable historically because Aquinas was not unknown in the sixteenth century, as sometimes has been alleged. Karl Barth once maintained that Calvin never read St. Thomas, arguing that one cannot find in Calvin an explicit rejection of the nature-grace schema because the Reformers were not aware of the great synthesis of Aquinas. "They did not feel themselves called upon to clarify the problem of the formal relation between reason with its interpretation of nature and history on the one hand and the absolute claims of revelation on the other" because of "the practical non-existence of St. Thomas in the sixteenth century."[67]

Of course, Calvin did know St. Thomas. It is noteworthy that Bucer, Calvin's mentor in much, had been a Dominican and therefore would have known the work of Aquinas even if his work were largely unknown at the time of the Reformation. Through Bucer, if not through the University of Paris, Calvin had a plausible avenue of access to Thomistic ideas. However, it is scarcely likely that without this special link Calvin would have had no substantial acquaintance with Aquinas. Though the theology of Aquinas was in eclipse during the fourteenth century, the revival began in the fifteenth through the effort of Capreolus (1380-1444), who wrote a major commentary and defence of Aquinas' work and became known as "*princeps Thomistarum.*" [68] It is also worth recalling that the papal legate who examined Luther at Augsburg in 1518 was none other than Cajetan, another Dominican, who, during the years 1507-22, wrote successive commentaries on the parts of the *Summa Theologiae*. It is difficult to believe that either Luther or Calvin would have been ignorant of the theological position of which Cajetan had made himself a champion. Furthermore, there is recognition today that the decrees of the Council of Trent (1545-63) largely reflect Thomistic doctrine.

Due to Calvin's reticence to speak about himself personally and also to the doubtful reliability of his biographers, questions about his intellectual formation are notoriously difficult. In the late middle ages three schools of thought were part of the curriculum in the faculty of arts at Paris, the *via sancti Thomae*, the *via Scoti*, and the *via Nominalium*. Thomism and Scotism were the alternatives of the *via antiqua* and nominalism was known as the *via moderna*. As well, it is now known that there existed two schools of nominalism, the *via moderna* as such, and the *schola Augustiniana moderna*. While both schools espoused an "anti-realist" philosophy (in which it is denied that class names or universals have any existence independent of particulars, that is, a "real" existence), they differed considerably on matters theological. The Augustinian school maintained a radical divine initiative in human salvation, while the *via moderna* was characterized by the conviction that "God rewards those who do their best." Calvin's thought shows similarity with the theological positions of the Augustinian school, especially as exemplified by Gregory of Rimini.[69]

That Calvin knew the later, nominalist scholastics who were the mentors of his own teachers in Paris is beyond doubt. It was to the doctrines of the *via moderna* that he reacted with the greatest vehemence. In Calvin's opinion, the chronology of medieval theology is one of progressive deterioration.[70] What Calvin rejected so adamantly in the scholastics was the attempt to give humans some role to play in their own salvation. It is in contrast to "the more recent sophists" that Calvin can extend a backhand compliment to "the sounder schoolmen."[71] Among these earlier, "sounder schoolmen" are Peter Lombard and Thomas Aquinas, both of whom Calvin quotes by name in the *Institutes*.[72] The McNeill-Battles edition of the *Institutes* lists over one hundred references to the teaching of the scholastics which can be traced to the writings of Peter Lombard. In the case of Aquinas, there are approximately one hundred and thirty which are attributed to the *Summa Theologiae*. It is the case, then, that Calvin knew the scholastics, and Aquinas among them, well enough not only to be a judicious and sometimes intolerant critic of their doctrines, but also to be an inheritor, in part at least, of their sapiential frame of intelligibility.

THE SHAPE OF THE STUDY

The aim of this study is to present an account of Calvin's understanding of the relationship between Jesus Christ and creation as this relationship is seen to reflect a tension fundamental to the Reformer's theology. This tension arises from the interaction of Calvin's evangelical intent with his acceptance and utilization of the medieval frame of theological intelligibility. These two approaches, the evangelical and the sapiential, show their greatest potential for both complementarity and conflict at that point where Calvin's profoundest insights about the activity of God in redemption must be related to the divine work in creation and providence. In what way, then, does Calvin articulate his doctrine of creation, where he must treat of issues that can involve extrapolation or abstraction from salvation history and from the redemptive office of Christ? Does he find a way here also to assert the mediatorial pre-eminence of Jesus Christ for faith? In successive chapters the following aspects of the relationship between Jesus Christ and creation will be addressed:

1. The methodological aspect. Definitions of Calvin's evangelical aim and of the medieval frame of intelligibility are offered, with specific reference to the *Summa Theologiae* of Thomas Aquinas and to the ordering of sacred doctrine in the 1559 edition of Calvin's *Institutes*.

2. The christological aspect. The relationship between Jesus Christ and the majesty of God is explored. The question is raised as to how Calvin relates his teaching on the transcendence of Christ as eternal Word (beyond the limitations of his incarnate existence) to his insistence that God can be known only in "the flesh of Christ."

3. The ontological aspect. Calvin's doctrine of Christ as the mediator of creation is explored, with particular reference to the doctrines of creation, providence and human nature, and to the overall question of the divine purpose in creation.

4. The epistemological aspect. Raised here is the controverted question of the nature and status of the knowledge of God from creation. Is there, strictly speaking, a revelation in creation distinct, but not separate, from the revelation in Jesus Christ? The relationships of Scripture, reason, and experience to the divine self-revelation in Christ are also considered.

5. The ethical aspect. Consideration is given to the nature and status of the *lex naturae* in relation to Jesus Christ, and to the relationship obtaining among natural law, the moral law and conformity to Christ as ethical norms.

In our discussion, both the *Institutes* and Calvin's Biblical commentaries will be treated as major sources, with occasional reference to sermons and treatises. The attempt will be made to avoid using characteristic emphases of one of these sources simply to "correct" those of another. Nonetheless, given our interest in the "sapiential Calvin," the 1559 edition of the *Institutes* will provide a crucial starting point and a repeated point of reference.

NOTES

1. Bernard was known as "the last of the Fathers" because "he is the last to write on the great theological issues with no apparatus of dialectic." David Knowles, *The Evolution of Medieval Thought,* 147. Articles by A. N. S. Lane and Jill Raitt on the influence of Bernard on Calvin have recently been complemented by a University of Chicago dissertation by Dennis E. Tamburello, "Christ and Mystical Union: a Comparative Study of the Theologies of Bernard of Clairvaux and John Calvin," as noted by Brian Gerrish, *Grace and Gratitude: the Eucharistic Theology of John Calvin*, 96.

2. Hermann Bauke, *Die Probleme der Theologie Calvins*, 13-20.

3. "Calvin's Theological Method and the Ambiguity in His Theology," in Franklin H. Littell, ed., *Reformation Studies; Essays in Honour of Roland Bainton*, 107.

4. *Calvin: the Origin and Development of His Religious Thought,* 358.

5. Ford Lewis Battles, "Calculus Fidei," in Wilhelm Neusner, ed., *Calvinus Ecclesiae Doctor*, 85, 107.

6. John Haddon Leith, *John Calvin's Doctrine of the Christian Life*, 17, 217. Leith lists six antitheses at 217f.

7. Wilhelm Niesel, *The Theology of Calvin*, 248. Niesel goes on to list nine more instances of a tension which is essentially salutary because it is derived from the reality of the hypostatic union.

8. Ibid., 247.

9. Karl Barth and Emil Brunner, *Natural Theology*, 71.

10. Ibid., 103.

11. T. H. L. Parker, *Calvin's Doctrine of the Knowledge of God*, 110.

12. Emil Brunner, "Nature and Grace," in Karl Barth and Emil Brunner, *Natural Theology*, 26.

13. Ibid., 36-50.

14. Ibid., 46.

15. E. A. Dowey, *The Knowledqe of God in Calvin's Theology*, 46, 147, 238.

16. Ibid., 221, 239f.

17. Ibid., 238.

18. Ibid., 85.

19. Ibid., 138.

20. Quirinus Breen, *John Calvin: A Study in French Humanism*, 108.

21. Ibid., 164f.

22. Egil Grislis, "Calvin's Use of Cicero in the Institutes I.1-5: A Case Study in Theological Method," *Archiv für Reformationsgeschichte*, 62 (1971), 10, 14.

23. Charles Partee, *Calvin and Classical Philosophy*, 91.

24. Ibid., 15.

25. Alister E. McGrath, *A Life of John Calvin*, 53.

26. Ibid., 54.

27. Ibid., 51f.

28. Marjorie O'Rourke Boyle, *Erasmus on Language and Method in Theology*, 69.

29. Ibid., 30.

30. Quirinus Breen, "St. Thomas and Calvin as Theologians: A Comparison," in John H. Bratt, ed., *The Heritage of John Calvin*, 35f.

31. Thomas F. Torrance, *The Hermeneutics of John Calvin* , 101.

32. E. David Willis, "Rhetoric and Responsibility in Calvin's Theology," in Alexander J. McKelway and E. David Willis, eds., *The Context of Contemporary Theology; Essays in Honour of Paul Lehmann*, 45f.

33. Ibid., 50-4.

34. Heiko Oberman argues that the phrase, *Infinitum capax finiti*, not *finitum non capax infiniti*, is characteristic of Calvin's christology. "The 'Extra' Dimension in Calvin's Theology," *Journal of Ecclesiastical History*, xxi, 1, 61f.

35. E. David Willis, "Rhetoric and Responsibility in Calvin's Theology," in op. cit., 58. Alister McGrath provides a further account of the principle of accommodation at op. cit., 130-2.

36. Ford Lewis Battles, "God Was Accommodating Himself to Human Capacity," in Donald K. McKim, ed., *Readings in Calvin's Theology*, 22.

37. *Inst.*, I.17.13.

38. E. David Willis, "Rhetoric and Responsibility in Calvin's Theology," in op. cit., 55.

39. William Bouwsma, "Calvinism as a Renaissance Artifact," in Timothy George, ed., *John Calvin and the Church; a Prism of Reform*, 31. Alister McGrath provides an instructive account of the survival of Aristotelianism at the Paduan school and its impact on the second-generation Reformed in op. cit., 212-4.

40. William Bouwsma, "Calvin and the Dilemma of Hypocrisy" in Peter de Klerk, ed., *Calvin and Christian Ethics: Papers Presented at the Fifth Colloquium on Calvin and Calvin Studies*, 1f.

41. William Bouwsma, "Calvinism as Renaissance Artifact," in op. cit., 32.

42. E. David Willis, "Persuasion in Calvin's Theology; Implications for his Ethics," in Peter de Klerk, ed., *Calvin and Christian Ethics: Papers Presented at the Fifth Colloquium on Calvin and Calvin Studies*, 83f.

43. William Bouwsma, "Calvinism as a Renaissance Artifact," in op. cit., 36.

44. Michael Walzer, *The Revolution of the Saints: A Study in the Origins of Radical Politics*, 24. Ralph C. Hancock agrees with Walzer's phrase but observes that "an antitheology is still something more than the absence of a theology." *Calvin and the Foundations of Modern Politics*, 13.

45. "Calvinism as a Renaissance Artifact," op. cit., 35.

46. See Heinrich Heppe, *Reformed Dogmatics*, 147f., or Alister McGrath, op. cit., 215, for Beza's table.

47. B. A. Gerrish, op. cit., 20, 123.

48. Edward A. Dowey, "The Structure of Calvin's Theological Thought as Influenced by the Two-Fold Knowledge of God," in Wilhelm Neu-

sner, ed., *Calvinus Ecclesiae Genevensis Custos*, 136, 137.

49. "For example, the way Calvin understood the transcendence and immanence of God, the distinction between Creator and creature, gives a unity to his doctrines of the person of Jesus Christ, of the presence of Jesus Christ in the sacraments, and of the church as a human work and a divine work." John Haddon Leith, "Calvin's Doctrine of the Proclamation of the Word and Its Significance for Today," in Timothy George, ed., *John Calvin and the Church: A Prism of Reform*, 219.

50. Observed by Brian Gerrish, op. cit., 16, and Alister McGrath, op. cit., 139.

51. Brian Gerrish, op. cit. 15,16.

52. Op. cit., 38.

53. Op. cit., 39.

54. Op. cit., 35.

55. Interestingly, Bouwsma elsewhere describes Calvin's use of such scatological language as "an almost obsessive pollution imagery." *John Calvin: a Sixteenth-Century Portrait*, 36.

56. "Is it possible both to attempt to determine a 'structure' to Calvin's theology and to understand him within the context of renaissance humanism?" Richard C. Gamble, "Calvin's Theological Method: Word and Spirit, A Case Study," in Robert V. Shnucker, ed., *Calviniana: Ideas and Influence of John Calvin*, 63.

57. Op. cit., 230f.

58. *Calvin: Theological Treatises*, ed. by J.K.S. Reid, 187.

59. From Article 6 of "Confession of Faith, in the Name of the Reformed Churches of France," in *Tracts and Treatises*, ed. by T. F. Torrance, II, 141.

60. Otto Hermann Pesch, "Existential and Sapiential Theology," in Jared Wicks, ed., *Catholic Scholars Dialogue with Luther*, 65.

61. Ibid., 64.

62. Ibid.

63. *Luther's Works* 12, 311, quoted in Pesch, ibid.

64. *ST, Ia*.1.3 ad 2, quoted in Pesch, op. cit., 65.

65. Pesch, ibid., 73.

66. Ibid., 76.

67. Karl Barth, "No! Answer to Emil Brunner," in op.cit., 101.

68. David Knowles, op. cit., 330.

69. See Alister McGrath, op.cit., 41-7, for a summary of the opinions of the two different schools. McGrath lists seven characteristics of the Augustinian school as exemplified by Gregory of Rimini and maintains that all are echoed in Calvin's thought. (45.) "Calvin, far from breaking totally with medieval tradition, actually adopts many theological and philosophical positions of an impeccable medieval pedigree." (47.)

70. *Inst*. II.2.4, 6.3

71. *Inst*. II.2.6; III.14.11; IV.18.1.

72. E.g., Lombard at II.3.7 and Aquinas at II.2.4.

I

INTELLIGIBILITY AND THE TRUE CHRIST

"The most important work that the Reformation accomplished was to restore the true Christ to his rightful place....The true meaning of the Reformation is that it was a widespread and intensive witness to Jesus Christ."[1] These words of T. H. L. Parker underscore the fact that the revolutionary character of Reformation theology derived from its recovery of a proper christological basis. It was not that the scholastics failed to proclaim Christ but that they did not proclaim him as the uniquely availing Mediator.

Like Luther before him, Calvin has no quarrel with the orthodox formulae of the divinity of Christ in the preceding tradition. The problem with these definitions, however, is that they do not deal with the point of the Incarnation:

> And indeed, faith should not cling only to the essence of Christ, so to say, but should pay heed to his power and office. For it would be of little advantage to know who Christ is unless the second point is added of what he wishes to be towards us and for what purpose. He was sent by the Father. Hence it has come about that the Papists have nothing but an esoteric Christ, for all their care has been to apprehend his naked essence; his kingdom, which consists in the power to save, they have neglected.[2]

"For what purpose": in Calvin's thought finality usually takes the shape of effectual results. "Why" is always a more pertinent question than "how."[3]

Calvin's insistence on effectual finality and on a "literal" reading of Scripture issues in hermeneutical consequence. Thus, Scriptural references to the relationship between Jesus Christ and the Father are to be regarded not as occasions for speculation on the "immanent Trinity" (that is, on relationships internal to the Godhead) but rather for evangelical apprehension of Christ's indispensable mediatorial role:

> "Even as the Father hath loved me"...Those who imagine that he here speaks of the secret love of God the Father which he always had towards the Son phil-

> osophize beside the point. Rather it was Christ's design to place, so to say, in our bosom a sure pledge of the divine love towards us. Therefore that subtlety as to how the Father always loved himself in the Son has nothing to do with this passage. The love mentioned here must be referred to us, because Christ declares that the Father loves him as head of the Church—a thing extremely necessary for us. For he who seeks to be loved by God without the Mediator gets imbrangled in a labyrinth in which he will find neither the right path nor the way out.[4]

Calvin is not denigrating Trinitarian theology in such comments, but is choosing rather to affirm what seems to him to be the literal meaning of the text, although this unvarying determination earned him, posthumously, the epithet of "Judaizer" from the theologians of Wittenberg. It almost goes without saying that for Calvin authentic Trinitarian thought is related to the "economic" Trinity, that is, to the differentiated work of the persons of the Godhead *ad extra*.

Scripture is fundamentally concerned not with God's nature or being *(deus in se)* but with God's disposition toward us (*deus erga nos*). "We ought therefore to put these titles of Christ to our own use, inasmuch as they have a relation to us...His intention was not to describe the likeness of the Father to the Son within the Godhead, but, as I have said, to build up our faith fruitfully, so that we may learn that God is revealed to us in no other way than in Christ."[5] In the case of texts presenting difficulty by reason of their susceptibility to Arian interpretation, Calvin is able to ascribe the apparent inferiority of the Son not to his nature but to the voluntarily assumed role of Mediator.[6]

The true Christ must be the "whole Christ" (*totus Christus)*,[7] for to fail to emphasize his redemptive office is to maim him:

> So today the Papists choose to have half a Christ and a mangled Christ and so none at all and are therefore removed from Christ. They are full of superstitions which are directly opposed to the nature of Christ. Let it be carefully observed that we are removed from Christ when we accept what is inconsistent with his mediatorial office.[8]

The true Christ is always Christ "clothed with his gospel," the Christ who includes within his person the office of Mediator. (*Inst.* III.2.6.)

The actual phrase, *Christus verus*, occurs in Calvin's writing in two places. Commenting on John's Gospel, Calvin observes that Philip "foolishly calls Jesus the son of Joseph, and ignorantly makes him a Nazarene; but all the same, he leads Nathanael to none other than the Son of God who was born in Bethlehem."

> Many argue acutely about Christ, but so obscure and wrap him up with their subtleties that he can never be found. For this way the Papists will not say that Christ is the son of Joseph, for they know precisely what his name is; but they empty him of his power and so exhibit a phantom in his place. Would it not be better to stammer foolishly with Philip and yet keep the true Christ than to introduce a fiction in clever, impressive language?[9]

In "The Theme of the Epistle to the Colossians," Calvin notes that the Jewish interpreters at Colossae "by urging their ceremonies, had enveloped everything in mists and hidden Christ."[10] He goes on to identify the schoolmen of his own day as guilty of the same shameful obscuring of Christ:

> For in this especially we differ from the Papists, that while we are both called Christians, and profess to believe in Christ, they invent for themselves one that is torn, disfigured, emptied of his power, denuded of his office, in fine, such as to be a spectre rather than Christ himself . . . This epistle, therefore, to express it in one word, distinguishes the true Christ from a fictitious one.[11]

This theological distortion functions to despoil Christ of his proper lordship in the life of the Church. While, in fact, Christ's work is to transfer us from the kingdom of darkness to the realm of light, the scholastics "after confessing Christ to be Son of God, transfer his power to others and scatter it hither and thither, and thus leave him next to empty."[12] Christ's power is given instead to saints who are invoked as intercessors in prayer[13] and even accounted mediators of salvation;[14] or is restricted only to the forgiveness of original sin through the sacrament of Baptism;[15] or is ignored when it is said that he died to attain merit for himself,[16] or is minimized by maintaining that humans cooperate with God's saving grace[17] and that there is a universal grace inhering naturally in humanity.[18] In sum, all these detractions from Christ's mediatorial power constitute a denial of God's eternal counsel, since it is by God's appointment that "Christ is all things to us: apart from him we have nothing."[19]

It is vital to note that Calvin is not in any danger of allowing his christology to be dissolved into soteriology. Dietrich Bonhoeffer once observed that the dictum of Melanchthon, "to know Christ is to know his benefits" (*Hoc est Christum cognoscere, beneficia eius cognoscere*), led to such a dissolution and, ultimately, even to "a repudiation of any christology."[20] Whether or not Bonhoeffer is fair to Melanchthon, Calvin's treatment of human salvation everywhere assumes as its foundation the incarnation of the Word. To express the underlying, indispensable relationship of the deity of Christ to the work of salvation, Calvin readily adopts as a summary of the Christian faith, the unifying phrase, "God manifested in the flesh" (*Deus manifestatus in carne*).[21] Soteriology rests upon a sound understanding of the two natures united in the person of Christ:

> It is impossible for us to trust in Jesus Christ aright without understanding his human nature; as also it is necessary to have comprehended his majesty before we can put our trust in him for salvation. Moreover, it is not sufficient to understand that Jesus Christ is God and that he is man unless we add also that there is in him but one person.[22]

Calvin's concept of *Christus verus* is not aimed at limiting the incarnational basis of theology but rather at grasping its full significance in its intended result.

"Christ is the beginning, the middle, and the end," writes Calvin; "it is from him that all things must be sought; nothing is or can be found outside him." [23] Christology is the basis of Christian theology because it is Jesus Christ who alone reveals God to us. It is through Christ that we come to a knowledge of what the Reformers thought so compelling exhibited in him—God's fatherly goodness. It is only because of human sin that this knowledge of God as a father could come as an astounding revelation. Calvin comments on this radical change in our perception of God as he grapples with a difficult question at *Comm. Jn.* 15.13, "Greater love than this hath no one":

> But it may be asked how Christ died for his friends, since we were enemies before he reconciled us. For, having expiated our sins through the sacrifice of his death, he abolished the enmity between God and us. . . . In reference to us there is discord between us and God until our sins are blotted out by the death of Christ; but the cause of this grace which was manifested in Christ was the everlasting love of God, with which he loved even his enemies. In the same way, Christ laid down his life for strangers, yet he already loved them: otherwise he would not have died for them.

Here is the open disclosure of God's disposition toward us which the Reformers believed to be so clearly shown in Christ. "It is indeed a wonderful commendation of the Gospel that we have the heart of Christ opened in it, so that his love is not doubtful or obscure ....God has entirely given himself to us in his Son."[24] As Paul van Buren observes, "This means, then, that for Calvin the gift of reconciliation reveals the true nature of God. In Christ God establishes himself and reveals to men what he is in all eternity."[25]

The focus of Reformation thought is reflected in a summary recognition: the proper object of faith is Jesus Christ. Calvin does subscribe to the scholastic definition that God is the object of faith but only with qualification (*Inst.* II.6.4.), and not at all, if the definition concerns God *simpliciter*.[26] The target (*scopus*) of faith is missed unless aim is more carefully taken, for "Christ is the one and only goal of faith."[27] Thus he presents his case:

> All acknowledge that we should believe in God; it is indeed a settled axiom to which all assent without contradiction. But there is scarcely one in a hundred who really believes; not only because the naked majesty of God is too distant from us, but also because Satan interposes all sorts of clouds to block our sight of God...Therefore Christ holds out himself as the object to which our faith, if it is directed, will easily find where it may rest. For he is the true Emmanuel who, as soon as he is sought by faith, responds within us... When the Papist divines dispute (or rather, prattle) about the object of faith, they make a bare mention of God only and have no interest in Christ. Those who have a taste for their notions must be shaken by the slightest breath of a breeze.[28]

Alternatively, Calvin will define the proper object of faith as the divine promise of mercy. This is merely another way of expressing the same christological truth in differing contexts. Thus, for example, Calvin makes mention (at *Inst.* III.2.29,30) of what in the Schools is called "the common object of faith," that is, God's truth, "whether he threaten or hold out hope of grace." It is in contrast to the idea that faith could rest secure in this "first truth" of divine trustworthiness that Calvin speaks of the promise of mercy as the proper object of faith. To commend God's goodness to human beings compromised and corrupted by sin is always to invoke the specificity of redemption in Christ and to recognize the indissoluble unity of Christ's person with his mediatorial ministry. "Faith looks at nothing but the mercy of God and Christ dead and risen."[29]

Although Calvin, unlike Luther, never argued for a canon within the canon, Christ's unique place as the proper object of faith is confirmed in the Reformer's doctrine of Scripture. He invites the readers of the New Testament translated by his cousin, Olivetan, to a single-minded purpose: "This is what we should in short seek in the whole of Scripture: truly to know Jesus Christ and the infinite riches that are comprised in him and are offered to us by him from the Father."[30] Again, he writes:

> First, then, we must hold that Christ cannot be properly known from anywhere but the Scriptures. And if that is so, it follows that the Scriptures should be read with the aim of finding Christ in them. Whoever turns aside from this object, even though he wears out all his life in learning, will never reach the knowledge of the truth. For how can we be wise apart from the wisdom of God?[31]

Those who are obstinate enough to desire more knowledge than what has been given in Christ, are arraigned by Calvin on a charge of ingratitude. They are "not content with Christ," although it is true that "whoever obtains Christ wants nothing, and hence that whoever is not satisfied with him alone strives after something beyond perfection."[32] "The whole of God is found in him, so that he who is not satisfied with Christ alone, desires something better and more excellent than God."[33] "Those therefore, who do not rest in Christ alone injure God in two ways; for besides detracting from the glory of God, by desiring something above his perfection, they are also ungrateful, in as much as they seek elsewhere what they already have in Christ."[34] In the face of this, there is only the conclusion to be drawn that "all the errors that are in the Papacy, therefore, must be reckoned as proceeding from the ingratitude that, not resting in Christ alone, they have given themselves up to alien teaching."[35]

With this account of the rich and emphatic quality of Calvin's teaching on *Christus verus* we have in view the intent of his theology as evangelical, that is, as determined in its aim by a Christ of existential consequence.

THE FRAME OF INTELLIGIBILITY

It was Calvin's reforming vision to set faith upon its proper christological basis anew, according to his concept of *Christus verus* and its consequences for the practical life of the Church in government, liturgy and sacraments. Caustic and even abusive as he could be about scholastic distortion in the areas of christology and ecclesiology, he nonetheless was also an heir to the overall theological legacy of Christendom. This is true not only with regard to individual doctrines, but also, and especially, with regard to the organization of sacred doctrine for the purpose of teaching in the *Institutio*. At the same time as he sought to assert the pre-eminence of the mediatorial Christ for faith, he was also relying upon an inherited methodological pattern to express his restatement. A possible result is that the revelation in Christ could appear to be bounded and controlled by a principle of systematization external to that revelation. Christ himself might even be regarded as an instrument, albeit a unique and absolute instrument, in a divine cosmic plan whose importance transcends the very incarnation of the Word.

The frame into which Calvin set his portrait of *Christus verus* is derived from the *summae theologiae* of high scholasticism and from their concern for a universal intelligibility. In order to see how this may be true of that *summa theologiae et pietatis* which came from the pen of Calvin, some account of the pattern against which the *Institutio* is to be measured must be given.

By definition, "intelligibility" refers to the relationship between subject and object, specifically as it is based on intellectual rather than sensory apprehension, or in so far as the intellect abstracts from sensory data. Intelligibility consists in the correlation between the comprehensibility of an object and the comprehending mind. For medieval thought, including both philosophy and theology, intelligibility had special reference to the concept of finality, or of the ultimate purpose of the cosmos. "Born of a final cause, the universe is saturated with finality, that is to say, we can never in any case dissociate the explanation of things from the consideration of their *raison d'être*."[36]

Intelligibility as a specific goal of theology also involves human reason in understanding the content of revelation "from within," that is, on the basis of its logical necessity or appropriateness. In this regard, the events of salvation history are viewed as not unlike a species of sensory data: the mind must attend to the "phenomena" of revelation so as to perceive the underlying noumenal structure deriving from the divine intelligence and purpose. The *summae theologiae* of the thirteenth century set the high-water mark in the attempt to fulfill this mandate of theology.

The appearance of the *summae theologiae* constituted the telos of a process that spanned a century and a half. At the beginning of the twelfth century, various masters of the cathedral schools compiled anthologies called *sententiae*, containing brief formulations of doctrine from patristic and conciliar sources. Peter Abelard's *Sic et non* gave a more systematic and dialectical cast to the anthology, organizing the opinions cited under specific headings and as they gave evidence of apparent contradiction. Throughout the third and fourth decades of the century, the comparatively undialectical *sententiae* were becoming more complete and schematic and in so doing earned the appellation "*summae sententiarum.*" In another idiom entirely, a comprehensive if ponderous curriculum of theology was set out by Hugh of St. Victor in *De sacramentis christianae fidei.*

The synthesis of all these approaches was achieved by Peter Lombard in his *Four Books of Sentences* published at mid-century. He dealt respectively with:

> (1) God, (2) creatures, that is, with the history of the world before Christ, (3) the Incarnation and Redemption, and (4) with the Sacraments and the *Novissima*, that is, death, judgment, hell and heaven. His method was to propose a doctrinal thesis or question, to bring

> forward authorities for and against the thesis, from Scripture, the Councils, the Canons and the Fathers, and then give judgment on each issue.[37]

Lombard thus combined the comprehensive scope of Hugh, the dialectical method of Abelard, and the wide-ranging reference of the sententiae in a single resource.

The eminent medievalist, H. O. Taylor, asserts that the detailed arrangement of the *Four Books* derives from the opening chapters of Genesis, following as it does the pattern: God, creation, redemption, new life. He attributes Lombard's inspiration for this "historical order" to a work of Augustine, *De Genesi ad litteram*.[38] He goes on to exhibit the main divisions of the summae of both Aquinas and Bonaventure as conforming to this overall schema.[39] What Taylor neglects to observe, however, is the degree to which Aquinas treated this schema not so much as the proper order of teaching according to salvation history but as the expression of theological truth according to an intelligibility derivable from God, the first Cause.

M.-D. Chenu observes the following about the method of St. Thomas:

> In order...to understand the *Summa Theologiae* as well as the purpose of its author, it is important to perceive the *ordo disciplinae* that is worked out in it—not only the logical plan of the work, with its divisions and subdivisions, but also that inner flow of movement giving life to the structure after having created it . . .The theologian strives to discover and elaborate reasons ("necessary" reasons as St. Anselm calls them) within a series of contingent facts. The whole edifice of demonstrations and theological conclusions which he builds, rest on a datum, whose appropriateness, but in no way its necessity, the human mind can discover. [40]

The *ordo disciplinae* is the ordering of sacred doctrine for the purpose of teaching, as this order, supplied by the theologian, actually brings out the dynamic of the divine plan. It is in respect of its *ordo disciplinae* that one could regard theology as "scientific." To express the intelligibility inherent in nature and revelation, Aquinas invoked the neo-platonic paradigm of *exitus-reditus*, which commentators later identified as the "golden circle."

In the Prologue to Question Two of the *Summa*, Aquinas outlines the pattern of his work as a whole:

> Because, as we have shown, the fundamental aim of holy teaching is to make God known, not only as he is in himself but as the beginning and end of all

> things, and of reasoning creatures especially, we now intend to set forth this divine teaching by treating, first, of God, secondly, of the journey to God of reasoning creatures, thirdly, of Christ, who, as man, is our road to God.[41]

The major divisions of the *Summa* are reflected in this threefold statement, though it only hints at the range and depth of what is to follow. In *Pars prima,* Aquinas deals not only with the nature and *personae* of the deity, but also with the procession of creatures from God, the *exitus* constituting creation. As the Creator, then, God is our Beginning. God is also our End. Accordingly, *Pars secunda* treats of the *reditus*, the journey back to God.

For the Protestant reader, a surprising feature of this second part is the absence of eschatological focus. Where we might have expected God's own epochal acts in redemptive history to be to the fore, the focus is anthropological and falls on the human capacity for the spiritual and moral life as it is actualized through grace. Aquinas' point in proceeding thus is that by nature humans are unique among returning creatures and stand in a special relationship to the Creator. As made in the image of God, a human "is the principle of his actions, as having free-will and control of his actions."[42] "Thus human acts (and through them, the whole cosmos they order and develop) are now rightly viewed as so many steps by which human nature, on its journey back to the source of its being, realizes its end, thereby achieving happiness and perfection."[43]

It remains for *Pars tertia* to speak of the actual historical means which God has employed to effect humanity's return and reconciliation, namely, the Incarnation of Christ and his obedience on our behalf, as well as the sacraments of the new law. By an implied metaphor, the creation and return of creatures constitute the visual statement of a circle. The circle is "golden" because in its simplicity the whole of existence is rendered intelligible, as possessing an eternal foundation in God, the Beginning and End of all things.

What is most striking about the golden circle is that *Pars tertia* does not belong integrally to it. The specifically christological dimension lies outside the logic of the circle. Only the movement away from God (*Pars prima*) and the movement homeward (*Pars secunda*) are essential to open and close the circuit. What constitutes *Pars tertia* are the historical conditions actually enabling the return such that the Incarnation is viewed as a contingent event. "The transition from the *IIa* to the *IIIa Pars* is a passage from the order of the necessary to the order of the historical, from an account of structures to the actual story of God's gifts."[44] If, then, we were to locate, in as accurate a way as possible, the events of *Pars tertia* on a diagram of the circle, this might best be achieved by the superimposition of a second circle (the actual historical way of salvation) upon the original one (the purely intelligible structure).

Chenu reflects on the fact that, in Question 109 of *Ia IIae*, for example, Aquinas discusses the necessity for grace without substantive reference to Christ.

> Indeed, the object of theology is properly and primarily not the economy by which man is the recipient of faith and of grace through Christ but rather it is God in very reality . . . Grace is studied in itself as a sharing in the life of God, and the adjective Christian is not added to it. This is because grace, as such, has its own nature, its own structure, its own laws, beyond the temporal conditions of its realization; in due course, filial adoption by Christ will follow.[45]

Although the golden circle originated in the non-Scriptural speculation of Plotinus, it is clear that its adaption and use by Dionysius, and then by Aquinas, was meant to express, and not deny grace. In fact, Thomas employs the *exitus-reditus* schema to expound a concept of grace which is prior to nature, that is, the providential grace by which God authors the creation. It is a commonplace of theology to say that with Aquinas nature is prior to grace, and this is evidenced clearly enough, as at *Ia*.2.2 *ad* 1: "The existence of God and similar things which can be known by natural reason as Rom., ch. 1 affirms, are not articles of faith, but preambles to the articles. Faith presupposes natural knowledge just as grace does nature and as perfection presupposes what can be perfected." Yet it is also true that the very act of creation, the procession of creatures from God, together with the return to their source as implied in the logic of the circle, manifests a grace that derives from the very nature of deity.

It is to this absolutely prior, uncreated and creative grace that the principle, *bonum diffusivum sui*, may be seen to have reference in Aquinas' theology of creation. Inherited, as was the circle, from Dionysius, this principle according to which "it is the nature of goodness to communicate itself" is not without ambiguity. It betrays the suggestion that in the act of creation God may have acted from some necessity. Henri de Lubac, however, describes well the gratuitous character of divine creativity:

> God's goodness—"goodness, that supremely august word!"— is a "willed goodness," a goodness which is also a benignity. God is love in person, love which freely, and not because of any law or inner determination, creates the being to whom he wills to give himself, and gives himself freely. "Not that neutral *bonum*, but that living flame of charity: *Bonus*."[46]

The existence of creation in its procession from God is an

event just as contingent upon God's will as the Incarnation. But while the creation conceivably might never have existed, it could not have been other than it is with respect to its nature. Creation is essentially the imitation of the eternal ideas which God thinks; these ideas actually constitute the objectifiable dimension of God's own intellect. The intelligibility of creation therefore derives directly from what belongs to God's own reality, specifically, the divine self-knowledge. Contingent upon the will of God for its existence, the creation is nevertheless necessary in its nature. The Incarnation, by contrast, is contingent as respects its very nature: God could have chosen quite another means to effect the homecoming of humanity.

It is clear that in Thomas' programmatic use of the golden circle as a metaphor for creative and providential grace we have to do with a majestically theocentric theology. It is clear also that with Aquinas nature is prior to *redemptive* grace, and accordingly, that creation rather than redemption is the fundamental category of his thought. But in his mind, this is not the case so as to restrict the sphere of grace so much as to enlarge it; to acknowledge that created nature is a "gift outright," sprung from that primal grace which is God's own plan to share the divine being and goodness with creatures. It is this plan which is the underlying dynamic of creation and redemption and which confers upon both their intelligible order. And it is with respect to this plan that the *ordo disciplinae* of the golden circle is an appropriate expression of theological methodology.

In the foregoing, an attempt has been made to portray the sapiential character of medieval theology as expressed by Aquinas. It is important now to make explicit that this sapiential orientation is not simply the equivalent of either "scholasticism" or "rationalism."

In the case of scholasticism, one is confronted with a stereotype whose connotation is, at least in the Protestant ethos, primarily negative. David Knowles observes the difficulties which even those well disposed to scholasticism have had in arriving at an acceptable definition of it, and concludes that, although scholasticism can be described, it cannot be defined. He notes three essential characteristics. First, there is the close connection of philosophy with religion, in which, originally, philosophy was regarded "as no more than an instrument, or means of understanding or 'extending' revealed truth." Secondly, there is a close dependence upon ancient philosophy, "and this philosophy is regarded as a corpus of rational, natural truths which are as ascertainable and valid in their degree as in the body of revelation." "Thirdly, on the level of technique, there is the method of *quaestio* and *disputatio* which is used throughout, not only for purposes of exposition, but also for those of research."[47]

It is chiefly against this last characteristic of scholastic thought that humanists generally, and Calvin in particular, reacted so vehemently, especially in its use by the later nominalists. While Peter Lombard and Thomas Aquinas, among other "high" medievals, used the technique of Abelard, the sapiential nature of their work is not identical with the apparatus of *sic et non*. This distinction is part of the explanation of how Calvin could be debtor to, as well as critic of, the medieval inheritance. Even though he rejected the Abelardian technique and its later excesses, he did not thereby reject the sapiential conceptuality as a means of ordering and developing his theology.

Just as the sapiential approach cannot be identified with the dialectical technique, neither can it be identified with rationalism as such. Although the quest for intelligibility is founded upon the capacity of the intellect to propose principles for disclosing the structure of meaning in creation and salvation history, the role of reason is not thereby given warrant for free speculation. The danger of Abelard's use of dialectic lay in his assumption of its "absolute metaphysical value" (Knowles), namely, in reason's presumed ability to adjudicate divine truth. On the contrary, for Aquinas, human reason in its theological exercise is animated by the supernatural gift of faith and acknowledges the radical difference between truths accessible to reason and those beyond reason's grasp. The motto of sapiential theology is Anselm's *fides quaerens intellectum*, a quest for intelligibility which constitutes a movement within, not beyond, the sphere of grace.

There is irony in the fact that Augustine, that purest of Latin doctors for Calvin, was author of the very synthesis of which high scholasticism became the pre-eminent expression. Augustine had assimilated to his own anti-Pelagian doctrine of grace the neo-platonic philosophy of his age.[48] He thus produced a synthesis of faith and reason, grace and nature, gospel and intelligibility, that persisted as the enduring framework of Christian theology throughout the middle ages. The theology of Thomas Aquinas, therefore, is as thoroughly related to Augustine, in its way, as is Calvin's. It is Augustinian in the sense that it expresses a synthesis between philosophical wisdom and revealed truth which is at the same time subject to the primacy of grace.

It is in the light of these two major qualifications that Calvin's theology may be regarded as possessing sapiential tendencies as well as fundamental evangelical intent. Calvin clearly repudiates the Abelardian dialectic and any suggested subordination of revelation to the human capacity for theologizing. He does demonstrate, nonetheless, a sensibility for the way in which the divine work narrated in Scripture can be understood according to patterns which express the overall purpose of God and which appeal to, and satisfy, intellectual hunger for God. Evidence for this can be found nowhere more obviously than in his own synthetic statement of theology, the *Institutio christianae religionis* and, specifically, in his concept of the *duplex cognitio domini creatoris et redemptoris*.

THE ORDER OF THE *INSTITUTES*

Whatever else the *Institutes* became over the course of time and through Calvin's major revisions, its unvarying aim was to be for its readers a trustworthy guide in the understanding of Scripture. It is clear that the *Institutio* exists to serve Christian instruction and piety as these are given warrant in the Bible. But it is equally clear that it does give direction to the reader, setting forth what it is that the varied content of Scripture intends to say. In other words, the *Institutio* aims at disclosing the meaning of the Scriptural narrative as expressive of the eternal purposes of God. With this task came the challenge of providing for sacred doctrine an organization appropriate to such intelligibility.

A number of proposals have been made about the way in which Calvin ordered the *Institutes*. Denying that the division of the 1559 edition into books, chapters and sections thereby makes it theological or systematic, John Dillenberger argues that it simply "received Calvin's organizational push."[49] Dillenberger's suggestion that Calvin never had a sustained period of time sufficient for theological rumination seems to underrate Calvin's intellectual power. In what might be for most of us time only for an "organizational push," is it not possible, and even likely, that Calvin was capable of acute theological insight as well?

Another approach is that of J. I. Packer who maintains that the *Institutio* reflects the structure of the Epistle to the Romans, with the doctrine of justification at the spatial and theological centre.[50] It is arguable, however, that the structural correspondence observed by Packer between the *Institutes* and Romans arises from their common reflection of the historical order of Biblical revelation: creation, sin, the appearance of the Mediator, justification and sanctification, the church. It is this order which is also reflected in the medieval *summae*, a legacy of Augustine via Peter Lombard.

Ostensibly, the ordering of the 1559 *Institutio* follows the pattern of the Apostles' Creed as Calvin, following Bucer, conceived it to embrace four major articles: God the Creator, God the Redeemer, God the Holy Spirit and the life of the Church. These moments are reflected in the four books into which the 1559 edition is divided. T. H. L. Parker is one author who takes the *prima facie* influence of the Creedal pattern at full value; Basil Hall and J.-D. Benoit are others.[51] Evidence that Calvin intended a primarily creedal organization may appear at *Inst*. II.16.18, where Calvin says: "Thus far I have followed the order of the Apostles' Creed." However, this sentence, coming as it does near the end of its chapter, could as easily refer to the content of this chapter only, in which Calvin is discussing Christ's saving work according to the successive phrases of the second article of the Creed.[52] The assertion that the Creed is the single structuring principle of the *Institutes* is therefore as much a matter of inference as any other.

François Wendel acknowledges that "the four chapters of 1543 upon the Credo were to serve as the more or less rigid framework for the whole of the work when it came to be recast in 1559."[53] But he finds this arrangement "rather external and formal," holding that Calvin's actual exposition consists of two major divisions:

> The first is constituted by Book I, and is concerned with the doctrine of God (Trinity, Creator, Providence), the scriptural revelation and man (independently of sin and the need for salvation). The second part extends over the other three books, and deals with the historic revelation and the plan of salvation. This in its turn is subdivided into two parts: first, preparation for the work of salvation under the old covenant, and its accomplishment in the incarnation of the Son of God (Book II), and secondly, the attribution and application of salvation by the Holy Spirit, (a) by the intimate operation of the Holy Spirit within the believer, even to its completion in the future life (Book III), and (b) by the external means that the Holy Spirit employs to complete this operation and bring it to its right end (Book IV).[54]

E. A. Dowey credits Julius Kostlin with first perceiving the basic structure of the *Institutes* as twofold according to the twofold knowledge of God the Creator and Redeemer. He argues that the distinction of the *duplex cognitio* explicit in the 1559 edition was implicit from the 1539 edition onward, since Chapter One of each edition always contained his discussion on the knowledge of God the Creator from nature and from Scripture.

In the revised edition of *Calvin's Doctrine of the Knowledge of God,* T. H. L. Parker offers a rebuttal of Dowey's thesis. He states that there is a twofold knowledge which is in fact the theme of the *Institutio,* but it is that knowledge of which the opening sentence speaks: "Nearly all the wisdom we possess, that is to say, true and sound wisdom, consists of two parts: the knowledge of God and of ourselves." Parker goes on to note of Calvin: "As soon as he has established this *duplex cognitio*, he says, 'But though the knowledge of God and the knowledge of ourselves be intimately connected, the proper order of teaching requires us first to treat of the former and then to proceed to the discussion of the latter.' "[55] Parker maintains that the *duplex cognitio domini* of which Dowey makes so much is actually a distinction constituting subheadings under the knowledge of God, and is therefore subordinate to the fundamental distinction, *dei cognitio et nostri*. From this perspective, he sees Dowey forcing an arbitrary scheme on Calvin's theology as he "takes one methodological distinction made in the work and magnifies it into the leading principle to interpret the whole."[56]

In assessing the respective significance of these two instances of a "twofold knowledge" in the *Institutes*, it is crucial to note that "the twofold knowledge of God the Creator and the Redeemer" is a methodological distinction. While "the knowledge of God and of ourselves" has minor methodological significance for Calvin's discussion in Book I (first he treats of God and then of human nature), it is primarily an epistemological principle. The purpose of the opening statement is to assert the irrefragable correlation of knowledge of God and of oneself: true theological knowledge is "existential apprehension."[57] True knowledge of God is consequential: it is a matter not of speculation but of lived experience. (*Inst.* I.10.2) "What help is it, in short, to know a God with whom we have nothing to do?" (*Inst.* I.2.2) The *dei cognitio et nostri* is an overture whose air will be given full expression in Book III, Chapter Two, where Calvin insists that knowledge of God must arise out of faith and generate a piety that is evangelical, existential, and experiential.

Examination of the organization of the final edition of the *Institutes* shows that the creedal pattern is no mere formality, but helps Calvin organize his extensive materials under appropriate headings with an ensuing effect of some elegance. But it is equally true, and ultimately more significant, that Books II, III and IV form a unity as distinct from Book I. These three Books together portray "the historical revelation and activity of God for the salvation of the sinner."[58] The continuity linking the three Books as a sustained exposition of the action of God the Redeemer is evident in their titles. It is pertinent to observe that they are not titled "Jesus Christ," "The Holy Spirit" and "The Church" (emphasizing the creedal structure), but rather "The Knowledge of God the Redeemer in Christ...," "The Way in Which We Receive the Grace of Christ...," "The External Means or Aids by Which God Invites Us into the Society of Christ...," focusing successively on the crucial moments of the one redeeming activity of God in Christ.

Book I of the 1559 edition is comprised of three major sources of material from the 1550 edition, as expanded, together with the former Chapter One, "The Knowledge of God." These sources are those precisely which deal with the reality of the triune God, and of human nature as created, without sustained reference to the Mediator, Jesus Christ. Dowey provides a helpful summary:

> The doctrine of the Trinity was brought forward from its place as prologue to the Apostles' Creed analysis where it had been classified under the general category of "faith." The doctrine of the general creation was taken from the analysis of the first article of the Creed, and that of the creation of man in a state of perfection was separated from the material on the fallen state with which it had stood in the chapter *De cognitione hominis et liberi arbitrio.* The doctrine of

> providence was detached from the chapter *De praedestinatione et providentia Dei*, which had stood in the series of chapters on justification. [59]

With respect to the new location of the doctrine of the Trinity, it is to be noted that for the first time Calvin's treatment of it precedes his discussion of Christ as the proper scopus of faith. This arrangement implies that Calvin conceives of the triune nature of God as logically prior to, and ontologically independent of, the Incarnation of the Word. With respect to the separation of the doctrines of providence and predestination from each other in the final edition, commentators tend to note the relocation of predestination in its proper evangelical context as the reason for the change. However, a comparison of editions shows that, in the flow of chapters, the place of predestination has changed very little; it is the doctrine of providence which has actually been given a new situation, located for the first time since 1536 in its proper context, the knowledge of God the Creator.[60]

The distinction of the knowledge of God into two contents is a fundamental methodological principle reflected in Calvin's *ordo docendi*. References to the *duplex cognitio* in the text of the *Institutes* relate specifically to the proper arrangement of sacred doctrine for the purpose of teaching and show that the proper order which Calvin has in mind is not necessarily related to the tituli of the Apostles' Creed:

> It is one thing to feel that God as our Maker supports us by his power, governs us by his providence, nourishes us by his goodness, and attends us with all sorts of blessings—and another thing to embrace the grace of reconciliation offered to us in Christ. First, in the fashioning of the universe and in the general teaching of Scripture the Lord shows himself to be the Creator. Then in the face of Christ he shows himself to be the Redeemer. Of the resulting twofold knowledge of God we shall now discuss the first aspect; the second will be dealt with in its proper place. (*Inst*. I.2.1)

Again, he notes of the Old Testament patriarchs that with the aid of Scripture they "penetrated to the intimate knowledge of him that in a way distinguished them from unbelievers," namely the knowledge of how "God, the Creator of the universe, can by sure marks be distinguished from all the throng of feigned gods." But he advises his readers that he is not yet speaking of "the proper doctrine of faith whereby they had been illumined unto the hope of eternal life":

> First in order came that kind of knowledge by which one is permitted to grasp who that God is who founded and governs the universe. Then that other inner knowledge was added, which alone quickens dead

> souls, whereby God is known not only as the Founder of the universe and sole Author and Ruler of all that is made, but also in the person of the Mediator as the Redeemer. But because we have not yet come to the fall of the world and the corruption of nature, I shall now forego discussion of the remedy. (*Inst.* I.6.1)

While not limited to Book I of the *Institutes*, Calvin's use of the *duplex cognitio* there is consistent. He observes that although the display of the works of creation "is not the chief evidence for faith, yet it is the first evidence in the order of nature."[61] While saving knowledge of God is possible only on the basis of faith in Christ, (as attested by the apostolic witness of Scripture and by the illumination of the Spirit), Calvin points out that there is a general teaching in Scripture concerning God the Creator which is identical to, and corroborative of, the knowledge of God "clearly set forth in the system of the universe and in all creatures." Accordingly, he cautions his readers:

> We, however, are still concerned with that knowledge which stops at the creation of the world, and does not mount up to Christ the Mediator. But even if it shall be worthwhile a little later to cite certain passages from the New Testament, in which the power of God the Creator and of his providence in the preservation of the primal nature are proved, yet I wish to warn my readers what I now intend to do, lest they overleap the limits set for them. (*Inst.* I.10.1)

Turning to the doctrine of creation, Calvin provides new material constituting Chapter 15 of Book I, where, for the first time, he includes a "Discussion of Human Nature as Created." He treats of those "pre-eminent endowments" by which humanity "mounted up even to God and eternal bliss . . . In this integrity man by free will had the power, if he so willed, to attain eternal life." Immediately after saying this, he rules out discussion of predestination "because our present subject is not what can happen or not, but what man's nature was like." (*Inst.* I.15.8) The scope of Book I is not the actual condition of humanity as fallen and the mystery of divine election, but those conditions originating with the creation which underlie and are presupposed by the history of salvation. The description of humanity's original, created condition -- given out of the Creator's incalculable goodness—is the necessary correlate and presupposition of our need for redemption, just as *Deus* is the necessary correlate and presupposition of *Deus manifestatus in carne*.

Calvin views the proper ordering of doctrine according to the *duplex cognitio* as important enough to split his christological discussion into two parts, assigning them to two different contexts in the *Institutio*. The question of Christ's deity strictly considered is situated in Book I under the knowledge of God the Creator, while consideration of the incarnation and of Christ's mediatorial work is situated in Book II under the knowledge of God the Redeemer. At several points in his account of the divine nature of the Word, Calvin feels constrained to remind us that he has not yet begun to speak of Christ as Mediator and does not intend to do so until Book II. Thus, at *Inst.* I.13.9, he says: "I do not touch upon the person of the Mediator, but postpone it until we reach the treatment of redemption."[62] Calvin does, in fact, refer to the mediatorial office of Christ in Book I but not substantively.[63] It is nearly impossible, of course, for Calvin to speak of Christ's deity without some reference to his humanity and mediatorial role. Yet he makes it clear that all such references in Book I are methodologically premature.

The conclusion is reached that there are two major organizing principles at work in the *Institutes,* the fourfold creedal pattern and the *duplex cognitio domini*, though the latter is of greater moment than the former. Viewed from the perspective of simply organizing sacred doctrine, the *tituli* of the Apostles' Creed present convenient and appropriate divisions. Because the pattern of the Apostles' Creed reflects the broad outline of the revelation in Scripture, this pattern may be called "historical."[64] On the other hand, viewed from the perspective of what it is that we actually know of God in revelation, doctrine is seen to consolidate around two poles—God's activity, respectively, in creation and in redemption.

This "double-barrelled" organization of the *Institutes* is not as remarkable as might at first be conceived. As observed above, the *Summa Theologiae* of Thomas Aquinas is ordered both historically and theologically. On the one hand it follows the Scriptural narrative of salvation as this is thought to include, and begin with, the pre-history of Gen. 1-3: God, creation, human nature, created activity, human destiny and moral choice, and then the incarnate Christ and the sacraments of the Church. On the other hand, the *exitus-reditus* schema represents a scientific or theological interpretation of the events of salvation history as they evidence a primordial, creative grace.

According to the Kostlin-Dowey thesis, the function of the twofold knowledge of God the Creator and the Redeemer is essentially a matter of "mutual presupposition" between the two orders of knowledge. However, the *duplex cognitio* has two other functions in the *Institutes*. The first is to underscore the double blessing of God's goodness. According to "the order of faith" God is known to piety first and preeminently as the One who brings about reconciliation in Jesus Christ. But believers should also come to know God as *beneficent* in the creation as well as *benevolent* in redemption:

> Meanwhile let us not be ashamed to take pious delight in the works of God open and manifest in this beautiful theatre. For as I have elsewhere said, although it is not the chief evidence for faith, yet is the

> first evidence in the order of nature, to be mindful that wherever we cast our eyes, all things they meet are works of God, and at the same time to ponder with pious meditation to what end God created them.[65]

Again he writes:

> We, however, are still concerned with that knowledge which stops at the creation of the world and does not mount up to Christ the Mediator . . . At present, let it be enough to grasp how God, the Maker of heaven and earth, governs the universe founded by him. Indeed, both his fatherly goodness and his beneficently inclined will are repeatedly extolled. (*Inst.* I.10.1)

Belief in the providence of God, in the continuance of God's power in sustaining human existence, is the deepest penetration of faith as respects knowledge of God the Creator for it is this "special care by which alone his fatherly favour is known." (*Inst.* I.16.1) While it is virtually impossible for the Christian to think of the fatherhood of God without reference to Jesus Christ, in Book I Calvin is concerned to attest God's parental goodness in the work of creation and providence. Although it is integral to his theology that God's providential care over the whole earth is chiefly directed to the preservation of the Church, those humans incorporate in Jesus Christ, he says this virtually in passing in the *Institutes*.[66]

The third function of the *duplex cognitio* distinction constitutes a counter-movement to the second; it serves to identify as humanity's pre-eminent need the knowledge of God not as our Creator but as our Redeemer. This is the role it assumes in the crucial sections of transition in Book II.6.1, 2, new to the 1559 edition. The incursion of sin has so vitiated the power of the intellect that humans can no longer perceive what the universe has to tell them about a heavenly father; instead, "our eyes—wherever they turn—encounter God's curse." This use is also evident in those comments in which Calvin interprets ambiguous New Testament statements about creation as referring to the new creation in Christ.[67] Related to this third function of the *duplex cognitio* is Calvin's fundamental emphasis on *Christus verus*, namely, that our need is to know Christ not in his "naked essence" but "clothed with his gospel."

CONCLUSION

On the basis of the foregoing analysis, it is possible to recognize a remarkable parallel between the structure of the 1559 edition of the *Institutes* and that of the high scholastic *summae*, particularly with respect to the use by Calvin of the *duplex cognitio* distinction and by Aquinas of the *exitus-reditus* schema. In both cases, discussion of the doctrines of the knowledge of God, of the tri-unity of God, of creation, of human nature, and of providence goes on without integral reference to the incarnation and mediatorial ministry of Christ. This structural correspondence between the two is scarcely a matter of dependence, as if Calvin read off his method from the *Summa*. Rather it derives, as we have argued, from a sapiential dimension common to both. This dimension of thought arises in part from an intellectual hunger for God (*fides quaerens intellectum*) and in part from the recognition that the life given by God is larger than the event and category of redemption.

Both Aquinas and Calvin were humanists enough to resist the theological impulse to engage culture by denying its impact or coopting its dynamic. In the typology of H. Richard Niebuhr, neither of them could embrace a "Christ against culture" or a "Christ of culture." Standing in the main stream of Augustinian tradition,

> both wish to distinguish supernatural revelation from philosophical and scientific inquiry, faith from reason, but both refuse to break the connection between them. They do not wish to surrender the uniqueness and exclusiveness of grace, but neither do they wish to surrender the universality and commonness of nature and culture. Both want to preserve both creation and redemption, nature and grace, culture and Christ.[68]

There are differences, of course.

For Aquinas, while the person and work of Christ constitute the actual way in which we know and go to God, the pattern of grace intelligible therein is ontologically independent of its historical expression and theologically prior to it. In Calvin's case, one can speak of interdependence and "mutual presupposition" but not independence. There is nothing in his Book I corresponding to Aquinas' discussion of the moral life in *Secunda secundae*, nor does he attempt to discuss grace as abstracted from its historical expression in the incarnate ministry of the Mediator. If Jesus Christ is the *proprius fidei scopus*, then the Christian life and grace itself must be referred invariably to the revelation in Christ and to his headship of his members. If the theology of Aquinas pivots on the dual theme of nature and grace, Calvin's pivots on the triadic theme of nature, sin and grace. Calvin's understanding of the radical consequence of sin entails a radical estimation of the redemptive solution. Grace is the response of divine mercy to sin and brokenness and cannot be understood apart from the actual condition which occasions it. Nor can the One who bears God's forgiveness and reconciliation to the world be separated from the gift he brings.

One of the results of the radical incursion of sin is that the positive significance of the revelation in creation has been "negatived." Sinful humanity is noetically blind and cannot see the revelation still objectively present there; without the illumination of faith and the spectacles of Scripture, its only function is to render our unbelief inexcusable. In Calvin's ordering of the *Institutes* it is not until Book III, chapter two, that there appears a full discussion of the epistemology which is crucial to his theology—the doctrine of illumination by the Holy Spirit through faith. Had there not been a fall, one could legitimately begin with the revelation in creation and the general doctrine of Scripture as cardinal theological principles and altogether without the qualifying brackets and minus signs which the reader must now apply to them as they stand in Book I.

What complicates matters is that the way of coming to know God through Christ, the *ordo cognoscendi* of faith, is quite other than the order of teaching (*ordo docendi*) in the *Institutes*. The ordo cognoscendi begins with encounter with the incarnate Mediator as the remedy for sin; in other words, with knowledge of God the Redeemer. Calvin's *ordo docendi*, however, begins with the knowledge of God the Creator and of the creation in its originally constituted integrity. If a sufficient distinction is not made between the two orders, and if the teaching and preaching of the church are undertaken on the basis of the *ordo docendi*, it might turn out that it is this order which becomes for succeeding generations the very *ordo cognoscendi*, so that Calvin's teaching on *Christus verus* is obscured. The Reformed scholasticism of the late sixteenth and seventeenth centuries, as well as the deism of the eighteenth, are arguably examples of this very process.

Part of the complexity of the relationship between the order of teaching and that of the knowing which is also conversion is occasioned by the very order of the contents of Scripture: the narrative begins with creation and with humanity in its integrity. Although the Bible opens with the account of creation and the pre-history, the origin of Yahwistic faith is to be found in the Exodus, an event in which Israel first experienced the lordship of God as its Redeemer. It was subsequent to this formative salvation event and the recollected history of election beginning in Genesis 12 that Israel had time and occasion to reflect upon the Mystery attested by the natural order and to incorporate myths of the world's origin into its credo of salvation.

Gerhard von Rad asserts that it is through regarding creation as a part of God's saving and electing work that this incorporation was possible. "Presumptuous as it may sound, creation is a part of the aetiology of Israel."[69] The Scriptural accounts of the creation thus serve an ancillary function to the main narrative of salvation and election, and the creation account is more properly described as "primeval history."[70] In the actual development of the faith of Israel, belief in a universal act of creation and in God the Creator is a reflexive movement, based on the events of redemption and belief in a redeeming God. Interestingly enough, later developments in Israel's history generated a reflexive movement back the other way: belief in God's power as Creator becomes the basis of hope that God is able to redeem the exiled nation. As Bernhard Anderson notes of Deutero-Isaiah, the prophet's expectation of deliverance rests upon the conviction that Israel's God is a sovereign and universal Lord:

> It is clear, then, that Yahweh's power as Creator is the basis of the proclamation that he is the Redeemer. The prophet's thought reaches beyond Israel's sacred history, which had proved to be a history of failure, and grounds hope for the future in the sovereignty of the God who is "the first," even as he is "the last," whose purpose moves between the ultimate horizons of beginning and end.[71]

If von Rad and Anderson are right, then the double presupposition identified by Dowey in Calvin's theology is integral to the Biblical story itself. And in this instance, we have the "sapiential" dimension of faith coming to the aid of the "existential."

Whatever ambiguity arises from the order of teaching of the *Institutes* and the methodological distinction (*duplex cognitio domini*) on which it is based, they were intended by Calvin to be more than an arrangement of convenience. Calvin employs the distinction not simply because it is useful but because he believes it to be true to what can be known faithfully of God. Thus it provides more than an order of teaching; it also implies an *ordo disciplinae* since Calvin regards it as deriving from, and being a theological expression of, God's self-revelation and the divine order informing creation. Thus Book I does have the function of "setting the context and proposing the categories within which the latter [part of the *Institutes*] is to be grasped."[72] It provides an overall background and conceptuality by means of which the events of historical salvation may be recognized as part of a divine plan to restore to its integrity a disfigured world.

NOTES

1. T. H. L. Parker, *Calvin's Doctrine of the Knowledge of God*, 72.

2. *Comm. Jn.* 1.49.

3. In *Grace and Gratitude: the Eucharistic Theology of John Calvin*, Brian Gerrish says at one point, "I want to ask the good Calvinistic question not how, but to what end Christ is our Saviour." 56.

4. *Comm. Jn.* 15.9. See also *Comm. Jn.* 17.21.

5. *Comm. Heb.* 1.3.

6. *Comm. Jn.* 14.28, 8.28, 8.58, 14.10, 16.15, 16.28, 20.31; *Comm. I Jn.* 2.22; *Comm. Heb.* 13.8; *Comm. II Cor.* 4.4.

7. *Comm. I Jn.* 2.22. The phrase, *totus Christus,* is used by Calvin in other contexts to refer to: the *unio personalis* of Christ (*Comm. Phil.* 2.7); the way in which the entire Christ is present at the Supper, though not in bodily form (*Inst.* IV.17.30); and the completeness of Jesus Christ when the members of which he is head are included with him (*Comm. Eph.* 1.23; *Comm. Jn.* 14.2, 14.19, 17.21; *Comm. Col.* 1.24.)

8. *Comm. Gal.* 1.6.

9. *Comm. Jn.* 1.45.

10. *Comm. Col.* 297.

11. Ibid., 298. For more on "the fictitious Christ," see *Comm. 1 Jn.* 2.22.

12. *Comm. Col.* 1.12

13. *Calvin's Theological Treatises,* ed. J.K.S. Reid, 194, 247.

14. *Comm. I Cor.* 1.13.

15. *Comm. Isa.* 53.5.

16. *Comm. Phil.* 2.9.

17. *Comm. Jn.* 15.5.

18. *Comm. Jn.* 15.1.

19. *Comm. Col.* 1.19.

20. Dietrich Bonhoeffer, *Christology*, 48.

21. *Comm. 1 Tim.* 3.16.

22. "Sermon on I Tim. 3.16," CO 53, 324f.

23. *Comm. Col.* 1.12.

24. *Comm. Jn.* 15.15.

25. Paul van Buren, *Christ in Our Place*, 8.

26. *Inst.* III.2.1; *Comm. I Pet.* 1.20.

27. *Comm. Acts* 16.31, 32.

28. *Comm. Jn.* 14.1. Other references to Christ as the *proprius fidei scopus* include *Comm. I Cor.* 1.30; *Comm. Eph.* 4.13; *Comm. Col.* 1.14; *Comm. I Pet.* 2.6; *Comm. I Jn.* 4.2.

29. *Comm. Gal.* 3.6.

30. "Preface to Olivétan's New Testament," in *Calvin: Commentaries*, trans. and ed. by Joseph Haroutunian, 70.

31. *Comm. Jn.* 5.39.

32. *Comm. Jn.* 14.6. See also *Comm. Jn.* 2.25; *Comm. Eph.* 4.13; and *Inst.* III.20.21.

33. *Comm. Col.* 2.9.

34. *Comm. Col.* 2.10.

35. *Comm. Col.* 2.4. See also *Comm. Gal.* 1.4; *Comm. Col.* 1.27. Brian Gerrish observes that "Calvin's disgust at human ingratitude, not disgust with humanity, lies behind his rhetoric of sin and depravity." Op. cit., 47.

36. Etienne Gilson, *The Spirit of Medieval Philosophy*, 104.

37. David Knowles, *The Evolution of Medieval Thought*, 180.

38. H. O. Taylor, *The Mediaeval Mind*, II, 354.

39. Ibid., 354-9 and 441, respectively.

40. M.-D. Chenu, *Toward Understanding St. Thomas*, 304, 7.

41. *ST. Prol. Ia.2.*

42. *ST. Prol. IIa* Pars.

43. M.-D. Chenu, *The Scope of the Summa of St. Thomas*, 30.

44. M.-D. Chenu, *Toward Understanding St. Thomas*, 315.

45. Ibid., 307, 314f.

46. Henri de Lubac, *The Mystery of the Supernatural*, 308, quoting both Maximus and Maurice Blondel.

47. Knowles, op. cit., 88-90.

48. "St. Augustine, in his search for truth, had found what he believed to be a true presentation of reality in what he had read of Plato, Plotinus, and Porphyry...In consequence, on almost all points where Scripture gave no lead, Augustine accepted from the Timaeus and Meno of Plato and the Enneads of Plotinus the explanations they gave of the intellectual problems that engaged his attention, and if a reader of Augustine is in doubt as to the origin of a particular philosophical idea, he will usually find the answer in Plotinus." David E. Knowles, op. cit., 35f.

49. John Dillenberger, ed., *John Calvin: Selections from His Writings*, 12.

50. J. I. Packer, "Calvin the Theologian," in G. E. Duffield, ed., *John Calvin,* 157.

51. Basil Hall, "Calvin against the Calvinists," in G. E. Duffield, ed., *John Calvin,* 23. J.-D. Benoit, "The History and Development of the *Institutio*," in G. E. Duffield, ed., *John Calvin*, 109f.

52. Calvin's other references in the *Institutes* to the Creed are equally inconsequential for the issue at hand. At IV.1.2, his mention of the Creed is in passing only, and at IV.1.20, he is opposing perfectionist adversaries with the argument that belief in the forgiveness of sins follows immediately after the Church in the Creed because it is the office of the Church to minister to us through forgiveness "while as yet we are in the earthly race."

53. François Wendel, *Calvin: the Origins and Development of His Religious Thought*, p. 117.

54. Ibid., 121.

55. Parker, op. cit., 119, quoting *Inst*. I.1.3.

56. Ibid., 121.

57. Editor's comment at *Inst*. I.l.lnl.

58. Kostlin, quoted by Dowey, *The Knowledge of God in Calvin's Theology*, 42.

59. Ibid., 127.

60. Alister McGrath regards the "emancipation" of the doctrine of providence from that of predestination as occasioned by Calvin's wish "to affirm that God's providence is an extension of his creation." *A Life of John Calvin*, 156.

61. *Inst*., I.14.20. In the commentaries Calvin also uses the distinction, as at, *Comm. Jn.* 17.3: "That he puts the Father first does not refer to the order of faith." Commenting on a text at I Cor. 1.21, he reflects that "the right order of things was surely this, that man, contemplating the wisdom of God in His works, by the aid of the innate light of his natural ability, might come to a knowledge of Him." Calvin also recognizes a proper order of teaching in the missionary activity chronicled in Acts: "We know that in teaching the right order requires a beginning to be made from things that are better known. Since Paul and Barnabas were preaching to Gentiles, it would have been useless for them to attempt to bring them to Christ at once. Therefore they had to begin from some other point, not so remote from common understanding, so that, when assent was given to that, they could then pass over to Christ." (*Comm.*

Acts 14.15.)

62. See also *Inst.* I.13.10, 11, 23.

63. At I.15.4, he observes that the image of God in humanity can nowhere be better recognized than in its restoration, now visible in the humanity of Christ to which the elect finally will be conformed. In Book I he also expounds the deity of Christ as it manifests its power in his redemptive work as the Mediator—in the forgiveness of sin (I.13.12), in his miracles (I.13.13), in his appearance under the figure of an angel in the Old Testament (I.13.9, 10), and as the one mediator whose saving work the angels serve (I.14.12.)

64. Although Dowey acknowledges "the excellence and even beauty of Calvin's final arrangement in terms of the creed" (op. cit., 42n4), and elsewhere observes: "The final arrangement of the *Institutes* proceeds in a more or less historical and logical order: from God, to creation, to the Fall of man and the need for Christ, to Christ himself, and then to the appropriation of Christ." (Op. cit., 152.) However he does not appear to link between this historical pattern with the organizing influence of the Creed.

65. *Inst.* I.14.20. See also I.2.1; I.14.21, 22; I.16.1.

66. *Inst.*, I.17.1. Calvin provides more sustained reference to the primary aim of providence at *Comm. Gen.*, "Argument," 64; at *Comm. Ps.* 115.3; and in *Concerning the Eternal Predestination of God,* J.K.S. Reid, trans., 164. See Chapter 3 for a fuller discussion.

67. See, e.g., *Comm. II Cor.* 5.18 and *Comm. Eph.* 4.24.

68. Henry Stob, "Calvin and Aquinas," in *Reformed Journal*, xxiv, 19. Stob concludes that Aquinas adopts the "Christ above culture" model while Calvin adopts the model of "Christ transforming culture."

69. Gerhard von Rad, *Old Testament Theology*, I, 139.

70. Gerhard von Rad, *Genesis; A Commentary*, 43f.

71. Bernhard W. Anderson, *Understanding the Old Testament*, 451.

72. Asserted by Dowey, op. cit., 41, and denied by Parker, op. cit., 118.

2

JESUS CHRIST AND THE DIVINE MAJESTY

THE DIVINE MAJESTY

Without making an exclusive claim on behalf of one tradition, it is nonetheless characteristic of Reformed theology and its confessions, of its hymnody and formularies of prayer, that a constant juxtaposition may be observed of the majesty and grace of God; or, from the point of view of the worshipper, of aweful reverence and confident assurance of the divine mercy. The root of this proclivity is in Calvin. Commenting on Col. 1.11, he observes: "As the name of 'God' expresses majesty more strongly, so the name 'Father' conveys clemency and benevolence. It becomes us to contemplate both in God, that his majesty may inspire us with fear and reverence and that his fatherly love may win our confidence." Of the relation of Scripture to the revelation in the works of creation, Calvin says: "Indeed, the knowledge of God set forth for us in Scripture is destined for the very same goal as the knowledge whose imprint shines in his creatures, in that it invites us first to fear God, then to trust in him." (*Inst.* I.11.2) In this same vein, he offers definitions only a section apart in the *Institutes*: "I call 'piety' that reverence joined with the love of God which the knowledge of his benefits induces."(*Inst.* I.2.1) "Here indeed is pure and real religion: faith so joined with an earnest fear of God that this fear also embraces willingly reverence, and carries with it such legitimate worship as is prescribed in the law."[1]

The fitting conjunction of trust and fear arises from the fact that, while the mercy of God is the proper object of faith, the majesty of God is everywhere its presupposition. In the first place, the concept of divine majesty denotes the "Godness" of God: when humans worship, the object of our reverence is said to be God's majesty. "Majesty" invokes the essence of deity, especially as that essence is understood to be incommunicable. One cannot be said to know, but rather to fear and adore, God's majesty, since it entails God's numinous power, holy otherness, and transcendence over all that is creaturely and comprehensible.[2] For this reason, any attempt to know God according to the divine nature, or essence, is both impossible and impious. Hence arises Calvin's proscription of speculative theology and his prescription of a positive theology based on God's self-accommodation to humanity in revelation. "For God himself is the sole and proper witness to himself." (*Inst.* I.11.1)

Two other concepts in Calvin's theology are closely related to the concept of the divine majesty, namely, the glory of God and the honour of God. Generally, though not exclusively, the "glory of God" refers to the divine nature as communicable through reflection to the created order, especially in and to humans. T. H. L. Parker observes that *essentia* and *gloria* tend to be opposed in Calvin's thought.[3] In the *Institutes*, at I.5.1, Calvin says: "[God's] essence, indeed, is incomprehensible, so that his majesty is not to be perceived by the human senses; but on all his works he has inscribed his glory." Yet this is a reflected glory for the "fulness of constituent nature" must be tempered to human capacity.[4]

The "honour of God" is a phrase occurring with frequency in Books III and IV of the *Institutes* and generally refers to the ethical dimension, where the observance of the divine commandments in the personal life of the believer and in the corporate life of the Church serves as an acknowledgement of God's deity and rightful rule. Although, strictly speaking, it is the divine majesty which denotes the sheer deity of God, all three concepts function to underscore human dependence upon, and accountability before, the transcendent power of God. One closely packed sentence sums up their common reference: "Because it acknowledges him as Lord and Father, the pious mind also deems it right and meet to observe his authority in all things, reverence his majesty, take care to advance his glory, and obey his commandments." (*Inst.* I.2.2)

The promise of mercy presupposes the divine majesty in a second sense also, namely that the believer's hope in the promise of salvation depends on the capacity of its author to effect it. Only God has such power. To invoke awareness of God's majesty is to call to mind the sovereign and universal power of God the Creator. Thus he comments at *Comm. Ps.* 115.15 that "the prophet, in designating him the maker of heaven and earth, reminds us that there is no ground to fear that he is unable to defend us; for, having created the heaven and the earth, he does not now remain unconcerned in heaven, but all creation is under his control." Again, he remarks on Isaiah of the exile:

> It often seems that, when he begins to speak concerning the hope of pardon and reconciliation, he turns to something else and wanders through long superfluous mazes, recalling how wonderfully God governs the frame of heaven and earth together with the whole order of nature. Yet there is nothing here that does not serve the present circumstance. For unless the power of God, by which he can do all things, confronts our

> eyes, our ears will barely receive the Word or not esteem it at its true value.[5]

In a sermon on the gospels, Calvin says, "Let us learn, therefore . . . that God must be known to us as the Almighty so that we will not doubt that he has our salvation in hand."[6] Only One in whose hand is universal rule can defend believers to the uttermost; only One who has "effectual might" can make us esteem at its true value the word of pardon and reconciliation.

This schema by which the mercy of God as Redeemer presupposes the power of God as Creator is extended by Calvin to the divine being and power of Christ, such that Christ's divine power is seen as the guarantee of the efficacy of his mediatorial interposition between God and humanity. "It is impossible for us to trust rightly in Jesus Christ unless we understand his humanity; we must also know his majesty before we can place our trust in him for salvation."[7] "The same person, therefore, who was constituted the only and eternal priest, in order that he might reconcile us to God, and who, having made expiation, might intercede for us, is also a king of infinite power to secure our salvation, and to protect us by his guardian care."[8] "For his death and resurrection, the two pillars of faith, would help us little if heavenly power were not joined with them."[9]

As a trinitarian theologian, Calvin has a concept of the divine majesty that necessarily includes Jesus Christ as he is the eternal Son of the Father. It is in this respect that he says: "For Christ, as far as his secret divinity is concerned, is no better known to us than the Father."[10] So far is this true that Christ's flesh must mediate our knowledge of his divinity:

> Thus some have said justly that by Christ-man we are led to Christ-God, because our faith progresses gradually; apprehending Christ on earth, born in a stable and hanging on a cross, it goes on to the glory of his resurrection and then at length to his eternal life and power, in which shines the divine majesty.[11]

Calvin emphasizes that Christ's majesty is so veiled by the flesh that only the Father can reveal him to us as divine.[12] Indeed, the deity of Christ, because it is the deity of the triune God, evokes both faith and fear:

> And hence we feel unspeakable joy, when we hear that Christ, who so far excels all creatures, is nevertheless joined with us. The majesty, indeed, of God, which here presents itself conspicuously to view, ought to inspire terror: so that every knee should bow to Christ, that all creatures should look up to him and adore him, and that all flesh should keep silence in

> his presence. But his friendly and lovely image is at the same time depicted.[13]

As Calvin reads Rom. 8.34, Paul is constrained to make the explicit addition, " 'Who maketh intercession for us,' to prevent the divine majesty of Christ from terrifying us."[14] There is some dissonance generated in this concept of the "naked divinity" of Christ; it raises a question about the ultimacy of the revelation in Christ. Is it ultimate because at last the very heart of God has been revealed to us, or because in him God has made the greatest accommodation that is possible to our finite capacity, an accommodation which by its very nature must leave the full reality of God still lying undisclosed behind the revelation? On the one hand, God is "entirely" revealed in Christ as a loving father who is the author of reconciliation and whose love has embraced us from the foundation of the world.[15] On the other hand, the unsearchable nature of deity transcends the very categories of revelation by which God is known at all.

The tension thus indicated between Christ's majestic power and loving mercy is also a point of dissonance in Calvin's attempt to balance both sapiential and evangelical dimensions in his theology. On the one hand, God's deity seems to consist in the divine transcendence as Creator over the creation. On the other hand, in view of the amazing mercy shown in Jesus Christ, God's deity seems no better acknowledged than in the recognition, "God is love." In the former case, the sheer relation of creature to Creator is primary and the quality of that relationship is secondary. This interest in the creature-Creator relationship as such is evidence of Calvin's sapiential trajectory in which the categories of creation appear as background and balance for those of redemption. Human awareness of God's aseity and omnipotence belongs to the human condition as created, and obtains with or without reference to the adventitious state following upon human rebellion. Thus, while the actuality of sin distances us still further from the divine majesty, it is our finitude and frailty as creatures which defines humanity in relation to God's deity.[16]

Knowledge of the eternal deity of Christ is also ascribed to the order of the creature-Creator relationship since we know from Psalm 110 "that he is God everlasting, Creator of heaven and earth, that his being is eternal, free from all change, by which his majesty is exalted to the highest and he is removed from the order of all created things."[17] All that is known of the triune God in the knowledge of God from creation is true of Christ: "As then God is known by his powers, and his works are witnesses of his eternal divinity, so Christ's divine essence is rightly proved from Christ's majesty, which he possessed equally with the Father before he humbled himself."[18] Thus, in the final ordering of the *Institutio*, the doctrine of Christ's eternal deity properly arises under the knowledge of God the Creator and in terms that convey a sense of abstraction from Christ's mediatorial ministry.

In choosing to identify Christ not only with God's loving heart but also with the divine majesty conceived as sheer transcendence, Calvin is attempting to give a full account of the reality of Christ. In so doing he sets up a tension which can be either constructive or destructive, and which qualifies his emphatic teaching on "the true Christ."[19] Further analysis of this phenomenon entails consideration of four crucial concepts—the so-called *extra-calvinisticum*; the mediatorship of Christ *etiam extra carnem;* the temporal duration of Christ's mediatorial office; and Christ's authorship of the full decree of predestination. These concepts illustrate the consistent distinction which Calvin makes between Christ's power as the eternal Word in creation and as the incarnate Mediator in redemption, and also the manner in which Christ's majesty serves as a continuing presupposition and limit of his fleshly ministry.

THE "EXTRA-CALVINISTICUM"

At two famous places in the *Institutes* Calvin refers to the way in which Christ's reality as eternal Word transcends the limits of his incarnate ministry. Lutheran opponents of this teaching dubbed it the "*extra-calvinisticum.*" In his bench-mark study, *Calvin's Catholic Christology*, David Willis defines it as Calvin's assertion of "the identity but not the absolute congruence of Christ in the flesh and the Eternal Word."[20] He adduces evidence that the so-called *extra-calvinisticum* is to be found in varying forms throughout the history of Christian theology, beginning with Origen and continuing through the middle ages. Contrary to the allegations of its opponents, this concept does not imply a Nestorian separation of Christ's deity from his humanity:

> In the "*extra-calvinisticum,*" Calvin is asserting that Christ is able to be God for us because he does not cease to be God over us in the Incarnation and because the humanity of Christ never ceases to be our humanity in the movement of God towards us.... The "*extra-calvinisticum*" is not a sign of the discontinuity between creation and redemption, but of the fact that by assuming our condition the Eternal Son did not relinquish part of his empire but extended that empire over lost ground.[21]

This means that "the *extra-calvinisticum* functions in Calvin's doctrine of the knowledge of God to bind closely together the two aspects of the *duplex cognitio Dei* (*cognitio Dei creatoris et redemptoris*), to emphasize the basic unity of the act of knowing in this twofold fashion, and above all to emphasize the unity of God thus known."[22] Furthermore, it clarifies the fact that it never entered into Calvin's mind to propose two *logoi*, one *asarkos* (the essential Word) and the other *en-*

sarkos (the incarnate Word.) "There is one eternal Logos who is *ensarkos* as *Deus manifestatus in carne* and is *asarkos* only in the sense that after the Incarnation the Word was joined to the flesh, but not restricted to it."[23]

Viewed from the perspective of the dynamic unity expressed in the phrase, "God manifest in the flesh," the function of the *extra-calvinisticum* may be conceived along the lines proposed by Willis.[24] But it is another question as to whether this is the only or even the primary use to which Calvin puts the concept. A close reading of the relevant texts will show that the most evident function of the *extra-calvinisticum* is to distinguish between the two natures of Christ and the distinctive powers associated with them and so to assert the transcendence of the divine majesty of Christ over the limiting conditions of his flesh. In this teaching, Calvin is insisting that the foundation of our hope in the *Logos ensarkos* is the reality and power of the *Logos*, just as our hope in "God manifest in the flesh" is founded on the logical presupposition of the prior reality of "God."

The classical reference for the *extra-calvinisticum* deriving from the very first edition of the *Institutes* is found at *Inst.* IV.17, where Calvin expounds his understanding of the Lord's Supper, taking account of papal, Zwinglian and Lutheran objections to his teaching. It is the Lutheran objections particularly which he has in mind in Sections 16 through 31, including the critical Section 30. In developing his position, he undertakes to refute the argument of Eutyches, and of Servetus also, which proceeds by "removing the distinction between the natures urging the unity of the person."[25] Immediately preceding the crucial sentences expressing the *extra-calvinisticum*, he emphasizes the impassibility of Christ's divine nature so as to exclude any inference that his divine properties could be transferred to the human nature. What certain passages of Scripture attest is not a *communicatio idiomatum* (a real transference of properties) but an accommodation of speech accenting the unity of Christ's person:

> Surely when the Lord of glory is said to be crucified [I Cor. 2.8], Paul does not mean that he suffered anything in his divinity, but he says this because the same Christ, who was cast down and despised, and suffered in the flesh, was God and Lord of glory. In this way, he was also Son of man in heaven [Jn. 3.13], for the very same Christ, who according to the flesh, dwelt as Son of man on earth, was God in heaven.[26]

He then goes on to say:

> In this manner, he is said to have descended to that place according to his divinity, not because divinity left heaven to hide itself in the prison house of the

> body, but because even though it filled all things, still in Christ's very humanity it dwelt bodily, that is, by nature, and in a certain ineffable way. There is a commonplace distinction of the schools to which I am not ashamed to refer: although the whole Christ is everywhere, still the whole of that which is in him is not everywhere.

Calvin credits Augustine with the insight giving rise to the *totus-totum* distinction earlier in Chapter 17.27 According to this medieval schema, reference to Christ's person as a whole (masculine, *totus*) is distinguished from reference to his human nature (neuter, *totum*), thereby making it logically possible to assert that, while Christ is truly present at the Supper, he is not wholly present. What is missing is the flesh of his human nature, confined in heaven (whither Christ ascended) by its property as spatially finite. It thus belongs to the reality of the risen and ascended Christ that he is everywhere present as the human Jesus Christ, although his body is not. Calvin's teaching is in conformity with Aquinas who observes that, while it is false to say "*Christus secundum quod homo est ubique*," it is true to say "*Iste homo est ubique*."[28] According to the *totus-totum* distinction it would seem to be the case that, while Christ's humanity is everywhere present because of the *unio personalis*, it is not so with respect to every aspect, that is, his physical body.[29] Here Calvin proves himself capable of the dialectical virtuosity for which he excoriates the scholastics and leaves us wondering whether we have really understood the matter, or if, indeed, it is understandable.

However, Luther's concept of the ubiquity of Christ's human nature (including the body) gives rise to its own problems as Calvin was acutely aware. Nonetheless it does have the advantage of avoiding the mind-splitting logic of the *totus-totum* schema and of pressing the evangelical dimension of christology to complete expression. It was not hyperbole alone when Luther averred that "no God will avail for you except the God of him who sucked the virgin's breasts."[30] According to Luther, the exaltation of the human Christ began with the moment of the Incarnation through the communication of divine attributes to his human nature in a real, not merely figurative sense. After discussing the eternal generation of the Son, Luther says:

> According to the second, the temporal birth, Christ was also given the eternal dominion of God, yet temporally and not from eternity. For the human nature of Christ was not from eternity as his divine nature was. It is computed that Jesus, Mary's Son, is 1543 years old this year. But from the moment when deity and humanity were united in one person, the man, Mary's son, is and is called almighty, eternal God, who has eternal dominion, who has created all things

> and preserves them "through the communication of attributes" because he is one person with the Godhead and is also very God.[31]

Luther will go so far as to assert the communication not only of divine properties to the human nature (*genus maiestaticum*) but also of human properties to the divine nature (*genus tapeinoticon*): "The sufferings of Christ are attributed to God because they are one."[32] In sharp contrast to Luther, Calvin rejected the idea of a real communication of attributes. In the case of the *genus maiestaticum*, he took his position to guard the true humanity of Christ, and in the case of the *genus tapeinoticon*, the possibility of which he would not even consider, he acted to guard Christ's divine majesty. The *extra-calvinisticum* was called into service in this defence.

The other *locus classicus* for the *extra-calvinisticum* in the *Institutes* is found in a short chapter entitled, "Christ Assumed the True Substance of Our Flesh." (*Inst.* II.13) Calvin's concern is to guard against the docetism of "the new Marcionites."[33] In the final section of the chapter, Calvin is engaged in qualifying what he means by Christ's true humanity so that his position is not susceptible of a *reductio ad absurdum*. Against the objection that a true humanity would necessarily include original sin, Calvin points out that Christ is "true man but without fault or corruption." (*Inst.* II.13.4) Then against the further objection that "if the Word became flesh, then he was confined within the narrow prison of an earthly body," Calvin says:

> This is mere impudence! For if the Word in his immeasurable essence united with the nature of man into one person, we do not imagine that he was confined therein. Here is something marvellous: the Son of God descended from heaven in such a way that, without leaving heaven, he willed to be born in a virgin's womb, to go about the earth, and to hang on the cross; yet he continuously filled the world even as he had done from the beginning!

While Calvin's overall argument is mounted in defence of the *verus homo*, the immediate context of discussion shows him at this moment defending the *verus deus*. In order to present a credible concept of the *verus homo* to its detractors, he carefully delineates its limits. He does this by asserting Christ's transcendence as the eternal Word beyond any earthly confinement.

This limiting function of the *extra-calvinisticum* is evident in allusions to it in other writings than the *Institutes*. Commenting on Christ's forgiveness of the thief on the cross, Calvin speaks of the "extra" dimension of Christ's divine resources: "Even if, under God's mighty hand he might give the appearance of a man almost beyond relief, yet as he did not cease to be the world's Preserver, he ever kept the reserves of heavenly power to fulfil his task."[34] In a sermon, he observes of Christ's miracles that they constitute an "incontrovertible testimony that in abasing himself he never left off his heavenly majesty."[35] Again, at *Comm. Gen.* 28.12, he remarks:

> For although all power is committed even to his human nature by the Father, he still would not truly sustain our faith, unless he were God manifest in the flesh. And the fact that the body of Christ is finite, does not prevent him from filling heaven and earth because his grace and power are everywhere diffused.

The theological stance adopted in the extra-calvinisticum derives, in part, at least, from Calvin's conviction that the doctrine of the Incarnation should not imply change or diminution in the deity. For example at *Comm. Jn.* 1.14, he says:

> Again, since he distinctly attributes the name of Word to the man Christ, it follows that when he became man Christ did not cease to be what he was before and that nothing was changed in that eternal essence of God which assumed flesh. In short, the Son of God began to be man in such a way that he is still that eternal Word who had no temporal beginning.

Is this denial of change in the deity a Scriptural or an extra Scriptural axiom? That it is an axiom and that Calvin regarded it as a Scriptural axiom is clear, and an indication of the degree to which sapiential perspective is important in his thought.

It is in the light of a theological dilemma arising from the Lutheran conception of the hypostatic union that the need for Calvin's sapiential balance is most evident. William Temple put it this way:

> What was happening to the rest of the universe during the period of our Lord's earthly life? To say that the infant Jesus was from his cradle exercising providential care over it all is certainly monstrous; but to deny this, and yet to say that the Creative Word was so self-emptied as to have no being except in the infant Jesus, is to assert that for a certain period the history of the world was let loose from the control of the Creative Word.[36]

Taking the lead of the sounder schoolmen, Calvin chooses to go through the horns of the dilemma, and in so doing eschews the unequivocally evangelical though extreme position of Luther. Instead, in the *extra-calvinisticum*, he asserts the transcendence of Christ's deity beyond the conditions of his mediatorial ministry to provide appropriate balance for his evangelical conception of *Christus verus*. Christ's majesty and power as the eternal Word remain the presupposition of his incarnate ministry and the *conditio sine qua non* of its efficacy. This balance, of course, is not meant to put in question the ultimacy of the revelation of a God's fatherly love in the flesh of Jesus Christ, but is intended to guard the majesty and transcendence without which God would cease to be God.

CHRIST AS MEDIATOR ALSO BEYOND THE FLESH

Closely related to the transcendence expressed in the *extra-calvinisticum* is Calvin's concept of a mediatorial function carried out by Christ beyond the flesh. In one sense, Christ's transcendence as the eternal Word beyond the flesh simply refers to the divine majesty which he shares in common with the Father and the Spirit in the undifferentiated unity of the Godhead. In another sense, however, it refers to his differentiated *persona* as the *Logos* to whom belong peculiarly "wisdom, counsel, and the ordered disposition of all things." (*Inst.* I.13.8) As characteristic of Calvin's theology as the extra-calvinisticum is his forthright exposition of Christ's instrumental authorship of creation, a concept which will receive fuller exposition in Chapter Three but is implicit in Calvin's conviction that there are two distinct powers which belong to the person of Christ.

Calvin repeatedly reminds us that the office of the eternal Son is not redemptive only. "For there are two distinct powers of the Son of God. The first appears in the architecture of the world and in the order of nature. By the second he renews and restores fallen nature."[37] At *Comm. I Jn.* 1.1, he observes that the expression "Word of life" has two possible referents: "The title belongs to the Son of God on two counts: he has poured out life on all creatures; and he now restores life in us who had perished, dead through Adam's sin." In interpreting a Pauline text, he invites us to attend to specific aspects of the two powers:

> First, in so far as he is God's eternal Word, he is the "first-born of all creation" . . . Secondly in so far as he was made man, he was the "first-born from the dead." The Apostle in one short passage sets forth two things to be considered: 1) "through the Son all things have been created," that he might rule over the angels; 2) he was made man that he might begin to be our Redeemer. (*Inst.* II.12.7)

"That he might rule over the angels." Calvin's reference to the headship of Christ over the angels, an apparently inconsequential notion, is actually of major significance for his theology of creation because the angels collectively constitute the one dimension of created existence still to be found in its integrity. Thus, Christ's relationship to them can serve as illustrative of the relationship which obtained between him and the entire creation as it was once unfallen.

In the Colossians commentary, Calvin discourses at some length upon Christ's lordship over the angels. Rescuing the phrase, "first-born of every creature" from Arian misconstruction, he refers it to the eternal generation of the Son and to his subsequent instrumentality in the divine authorship of creatures. "Hence he is not called the 'first-born' because he preceded all creatures in time, but because he was begotten by the Father, that they might be created through him, and that he might be, as it were, the substance or foundation of all things."[38] The reference to "things invisible" he assigns to the angels: "Thus he [Paul] places the Son of God in the highest seat of honour that he may preside over angels as well as men, and may bring into order all creatures in heaven and earth."[39]

Thus far Calvin's interest in Christ's headship of the angels may be characterized as a specific case of Christ's power in creating and sustaining the world. However, he goes on to describe this ordering and sustaining activity as an act of mediation between the intact creation and God. Calvin's conviction is that a mediator is required even in the case of the intact creation because of the creature's mutable nature:

> For what is the analogy between the creature and the Creator, without the interposition of the Mediator? So far as they are creatures, they would have been liable to change and to falling, and not blessed eternally, had they not been exempted by the benefit of Christ. Who then will deny that angels as well as men have been restored to a steadfast order by the grace of Christ? Men had been lost, but angels were not out of danger.[40]

Again, he writes:

> Between God and the angels the relationship is very different, for there was no revolt, no sin, and consequently no separation. It was, however, necessary for two reasons for angels also to be set at peace with God; for, being creatures, they were not beyond the risk of falling, had they not been confirmed by the grace of Christ...Further, in that very obedience which they render to God, there is not such absolute perfection as to satisfy God in every respect and without pardon . . . We must therefore lay it down that there is not in the angels so much righteousness as would suffice for full union with God. They have therefore, need of a peace-maker, through whose grace they may wholly cleave to God.[41]

These last two sentences indicate that Calvin has in mind not merely the angels' perseverance in obedience, but also their fitness for participation in the consummation when God will be "everything to all." In other words, Calvin is calling our attention to the need of the creature for what the medievals called *gratia elevans*, and what might be called, in his case, sustaining and perfecting grace.

Medieval theology observed a distinction between grace as healing (*gratia sanans*) and as perfecting (*gratia elevans*). This distinction arises from humanity's twofold need of grace, expressed as follows by Aquinas:

> Thus in the state of intact nature, man needs a gratuitous capacity supplementing the capacity of his nature in one respect, namely to perform and will the supernatural good. But in the state of spoiled nature he needs it in two respects, namely, in order to be healed, and further that he may perform the good proper to supernatural capacity, which is meritorious.[42]
> Now eternal life is an end which lies beyond the proportionate scope of human nature . . . And so by his natural endowments man cannot produce meritorious works proportionate to eternal life, but a higher power is needed for this, which is the power of grace.[43]

Gratia elevans enables humans to attain the end for which we were created, the glory of the *visio dei*, and as such brings about our perfection.[44]

Calvin does not employ the typical scholastic terminology, nor would he endorse the concept of meritorious human works, but he does acknowledge the human need for grace in the condition of rectitude (because of creaturely finitude and fallibility), as well as in the state of corruption. "Even if man had remained free from all stain, his condition would have been too lowly for him to reach God without a Mediator." (*Inst.* II.12.1) In assessing the depth of the divine condescension in the Incarnation as recorded by John, he says:

> How great is the distance between the spiritual glory of the Word of God and the stinking filth of our flesh! Yet the Son of God stooped so low as to take to himself that flesh addicted to so many wretchednesses. "Flesh" is here not used for corrupt nature (as in Paul) but for mortal man. It denotes derogatorily his frail and almost transient nature.[45]

At *Comm. I Peter* 1.20, he makes his point in a parallel manner to Aquinas:

> There are two reasons why faith cannot be in God unless Christ intervenes as a Mediator. First, the greatness of the divine glory must be taken into account, and at the same time the littleness of our capacity . . . The second reason is that, as faith ought to unite us to God, we shun and dread every access to him, unless a Mediator comes who can deliver us from fear, for sin, which reigns in us, renders us hateful to God and him in turn to us.

It is clear that as respects humans as well as angels, Christ has a mediatorial role arising from his right and power as the creative Word: "In the original order of creation and the unfallen state of nature Christ was set over angels and men as their head." (*Inst.* II.12.4) Characteristically, Cal vin puts the matter in terms of relation rather than ontology, and he speaks of our need for a mediator rather than for (abstract) grace.

This is a mediatorship "*etiam extra carnem,*" and the very notion of mediation is extrapolated from the redemptive ministry of Christ. However, in opposing Andreas Osiander, Calvin goes so far as to entertain the notion of a mediatorship solely beyond the flesh:

> But Osiander is always deceived—or tricks himself—in the false principle that the church would have been without a head if Christ had not appeared in the flesh. As the angels rejoiced in his headship, why could not Christ rule over men also by his divine power, quicken and nourish them like his own body by the secret power of his Spirit until, gathered up into heaven, they might enjoy the same life as the angels! (*Inst.* II.12.7)

Again in refutation of Osiander, Calvin avers that Adam bore God's image in his integrity not by any infusion of the divine essence but by creaturely endowments of excellence. He goes on to relate these endowments to Christ:

> All men unanimously admit that Christ was even then the image of God. Hence whatever excellence was engraved upon Adam derived from the fact that he approached the glory of his Creator through the only-begotten Son. "So man was created in the image of God"; in him the Creator willed that his own glory be seen as in a mirror. Adam was advanced to this degree of honour, thanks to the only-begotten Son. (*Inst.* II.12.6)

As the creative Word, and with regard to the potential for defection in a finite nature, Christ is already and eternally the Mediator between creatures and their Creator.

Generally, Calvin avoids and condemns a speculative attitude concerning the cause of the Incarnation. Thus, he says that "since all Scripture proclaims that to become our Redeemer he was clothed with flesh, it is presumptuous to imagine another reason or another end." (*Inst.* II.12.4) Again, he insists that since the Spirit declares the inseparable connection of our redemption with the Incarnation, "it is not lawful to inquire further how Christ became our Redeemer and the partaker of our nature." (*Inst.* II.12.5) Calvin emphatically rejects the speculative inquiry as to whether the eternal Word would have become incarnate if no means of human redemption were needed. However, he does allow that it is both legitimate and vital to ascribe to humans the need for a mediator even in their created integrity, and to Christ the added glory of the power to sustain and perfect all creatures. "We must note in these words what we have touched on elsewhere; the office of Redeemer was laid upon him that he might be our Saviour. Still, our redemption would be imperfect if he did not lead us ever onward to the final goal of salvation." (*Inst.* II.16.1)

Given the event of the fall, the perfecting of human nature can occur in no other way than as the completion of Christ's redemptive work, but this perfecting work would be necessary even without the fall. The final goal of salvation includes the resurrection of transformed bodies as well as the gift of immortality to the soul. Furthermore, eternal blessedness consists in seeing God "as God is." In this manner the elect will become "partakers of the divine nature" and "one with God." (*Inst.*III.25.10) This condition of perfection is manifestly something for which humans have no capacity even in the rectitude of created nature. Although in our created rectitude we could have passed into heaven without passing the portal of death, this passage would still have been accomplished only by benefit of Christ's grace.[46] The transformations of perfection which render superfluous the necessities, for example, of food and procreation, present a sharp contrast to the order of nature. (*Inst.* III.25.11)

What is the effect of Calvin's concept of Christ's mediatorial role *extra hanc carnem*? From one point of view the centrality of *Christus verus* is affirmed, since Christ's power as the creative Word is expressed through extrapolation from his redemptive work as the Mediator incarnate.[47] A term deriving from the knowledge of God the Redeemer is extended to use in the knowledge of God the Creator. Christ's mediatorial power in the creation and preservation of the unfallen creation is a work *etiam extra carnem*. The "*etiam*" is crucial because it indicates an extension of Christ's ministry rather than a departure from it.[48]

However, from another point of view, Calvin's assertion of a mediatorial ministry *etiam extra hanc carnem* also announces the freedom of the *Logos* for a ministry of mediation from all eternity and irrespective of the adventitious[49] event of the fall. As fallen, humanity's pre-eminent need is for redemptive grace; but creatures will always have the need for the sustaining and perfecting grace of the creative Word. Clearly, Calvin is not minimizing the redemptive mediatorial role of Christ but he is grounding this role in the being and power of the eternal *Logos* who is the instrumental author of the creation ("first-born of creatures") and its continuing Mediator.

THE TEMPORAL DURATION OF CHRIST'S FLESHLY MEDIATORSHIP

As a strict matter of temporal sequence, Christ's pre-existence as the eternal Word is clearly prior to the event of the Incarnation, and to the Old Testament expectation of it. But it is another matter to ascribe theological significance to this sequence. The basis of Christ's ministry in the flesh lies in an eternal appointment of the Son to be the Redeemer. "In addition to the fact that novelty is always dangerous, what foundation would our faith have if we believed that a remedy for mankind had suddenly occurred to God at last after some thousands of years?"[50] The complicated matter of time-sequence actually turns out to attest the goodness of God's initiative in grace. Foreseeing the fall, God "anticipated our disease by the remedy of his grace, and provided a restoration before the first man had fallen into death." [51]

In his earliest theological treatise, "Psychopannychia," Calvin underlines the indissoluble connection between the eternal appointment of Christ to be the Mediator and his human nature. Against the spiritualist argument that the significance of Jesus Christ is to be restricted to the dispensation of the New Testament, he exclaims, "Where then will be Jesus, the eternal God, in respect of his humanity, even the first-born of every creature, and the Lamb slain from the foundation of the world?"[52] By these words, Calvin does not imply the consubstantiality of the flesh of Jesus with the Godhead. What he does imply is that though the appearance of Christ in the flesh occurs late in time, it is this appearance which defines for all time humanity's *raison d'être* in the purpose of God. Of a prophetic oracle, Calvin remarks: "Micah speaks of God without specific mention of Christ because Christ had not yet been manifested in the flesh. But we know God's rule of the world and the submission of the peoples of the whole earth to him had its fulfilment in Christ."[53] From eternity, therefore, God's disposition toward us is determined by the *assumptio carnis* occurring in time.

There is, nonetheless, a curious ambivalence in Calvin's attitude to "the flesh of Christ." The specific phrase is used by Calvin as a short-hand way of referring to the incarnate, mediatorial aspect of the person of Christ and has an unequivocally positive connotation. As well, since faith is not only believing in Christ but communion with him, [54] Calvin speaks of Christ's flesh as "life-giving," the medium of our spiritual union with him. "You will only find life in Christ when you seek the substance of life in his flesh."[55] "For none will ever come to Christ-God who neglects the man."[56] While "feeding on Christ" remains a purely spiritual event in the life of faith generally and in the particular case of the Lord's Supper, Calvin's insistence on this "fleshly" dimension and on the importance of Christ's humanity is almost winsome. In his discussion of the relationship of "the flesh of Christ" to the Lord's Supper he even concedes the appropriateness of some form of the *communicatio idiomatum*.[57]

But what Calvin gives with one hand he takes away with the other. This essential flesh is in reality only a channel for what belongs properly and essentially to Christ's divinity: "For as the eternal Word of God is the fountain of life, so his flesh is a channel to pour out to us the life which resides intrinsically, as they say, in his divinity."[58] So far, one might say, so good: Calvin is balancing his statements so that he honours *homo verus* and *deus verus* alike. But there is a discomfiting attitude of disdain for human flesh that surfaces in Calvin's writing and it spills over into his consideration of the flesh of Christ: "The divine majesty of Christ was not so concealed under the contemptible and lowly appearance of the flesh that it did not send forth beams of his manifold brightness."[59] One has the unhappy impression that Calvin might actually be uncomfortable in the presence of One who was a "wine-bibber and a glutton."

These considerations are not irrelevant to the fact that Calvin conceives of an end to Christ's mediatorial ministry. Although Christ's appointment to be Mediator has an eternal origin, he regards its duration as temporal. Commenting on I Cor. 15.24ff., where Christ is said to deliver the Kingdom to the Father, Calvin offers this remarkable interpretation. After the rule through Christ is fully realized,

> Christ will then hand back the Kingdom which he has received, so that we may cleave completely to God. This does not mean that he will abdicate from the Kingdom in this way, but will transfer it in some way or other from his humanity to his glorious divinity, because then there will open up for us a way of approach, from which we are now kept back by our weakness. In this way, Christ will be subjected to the Father because, when the veil has been removed, we will see God plainly, reigning in his majesty, and the humanity of Christ will no longer be in between us to hold us back from a nearer vision of God.[60]

When the elect are perfected in glory, the veil of our creaturely and once corrupted nature, and the veil of Christ's humanity will be lifted simultaneously, and God's majesty seen, though not fully comprehended.[61] Like the ministry of John the Baptist at the appearance of the Lamb, the humanity of Christ must now decrease; the function of mediation is superfluous. "When as partakers in heavenly glory we shall see God as he is, Christ, having discharged the office of Mediator, will cease to be the Ambassador of his Father, and will be satisfied with that glory which he enjoyed before the creation of the world." (*Inst.* II.14.3) As Calvin observes at *Inst.* II.15.5, "In these words [Phil. 2.9-11] Paul rightly infers [that] God will then of himself become the sole Head of the church, since the duties of Christ in defending the church have been accomplished."

When God is everything to all, Christ will not cease to rule in concert with the Father and the Spirit, but he will no longer do so according to his human nature. Then "God shall cease to be the head of Christ, for Christ's own deity will shine of itself, although it is as yet covered by a veil."[62] In continuity with the tradition before him, Calvin teaches a doctrine of the *visio dei* as the final term of believers' election through grace to glory.[63] The divine essence of Christ, which was no more accessible to humans during the course of his earthly ministry than that of the Creator, will, in the unity of the triune Godhead, be part of that vision. The human countenance of Christ, which was at once the revelation of God's redeeming purpose and also a concealment of the divine majesty, will then "rest" or "withdraw" from Christ's exercise of power.[64]

Does all of this mean that Christ will finally divest himself of his human nature and thus effectively sever the hypostatic union? Calvin never says or suggests this and according to his own principle of Scriptural positivity he could not, since Scripture nowhere proposes such an eventuality. Nor is it conceivable that there could be a human Jesus in heaven, apart from the eternal Word, since, on the principle of en-hypostasis, the humanity of Christ has no existence save through the *unio personalis*. In the consummation, the human nature of Christ will continue to exist in union with the divine nature of the eternal Son, but it will no longer exercise the functions of veiling, reconciling, or even ruling. The power and the glory which the human Christ once shared in the mediatorial ministry will revert to the divine nature alone. It will still be the case that Christ is Jesus Christ but the action of Christ will not now be predicated of his human nature, but rather of the divine nature shared by the *personae* of the triune Godhead.

A subtlety on the order of the *totus-totum* schema faces us here. In so far as the identity of Christ is concerned, he is still "whole" according to the hypostatic union, but in the exercise of sovereign power, his human nature is not engaged. The transcendence of Christ's divine majesty beyond the flesh is hereby asserted in a conclusive and unsettling way. In his account of the temporal duration of Christ's mediatorial role, Calvin takes us to the very brink with respect to the integrity of the *unio personalis* and sets a temporal limit to the significance of his own fundamental insight concerning *Christus verus*.

CHRIST AS MIRROR AND AUTHOR OF ELECTION

Calvin's doctrine of election also is informed by his basic distinction between the two powers of the Son of God. Not only is the concept of Christ's divine transcendence an evident factor in the doctrine of predestination, but it serves to explain a specific complexity, namely that the decrees of election do not seem to be integrally related to Jesus Christ. As Karl Barth puts it, in such a circumstance, we would have to do with an electing God who "is not Christ but God the Father, or the triune God, in a decision which precedes the being and will and word of Christ."[65] Christ would then serve the decrees in an essentially instrumental capacity.

The problematic derives from Calvin's understanding of predestination as constituted by a double decree:

> We call predestination God's eternal decree, by which he determined with himself what he willed to become of each man. For all are not created in equal condition; rather, eternal life is fore-ordained for some, eternal damnation for others. Therefore, as any man has been created to one or the other of these ends, we speak of him as predestined to life or to death. (*Inst.* III.21.5)

"The decree is dreadful, I confess. Yet no one can deny that God foreknew what end man was to have before he created him and consequently foreknew because he so ordained by his decree." (*Inst.* III.23.7) The implication of these formulae, abstracted as they are from the actual revelation and work of God in the Incarnation, is that the fundamental determination of our destiny seems to arise from a divine decision made independently of Jesus Christ.

It is sobering to realize that Calvin does not treat the appointment of Christ to be Mediator as an integral part of his doctrine of election. When he speaks of predestination (*praedestinatio*), the reference of the word is always to human creatures and never to Christ.[66] Christ's place in the doctrine of election is confined to his role as either electing God or elected humanity. This omission of the appointment of Christ is evident when Calvin gives expression to an "order of decrees":

> First the eternal predestination of God, by which before the fall of Adam he decreed what should take place concerning the whole human race and every individual, was fixed and determined. Secondly, Adam himself, on account of his defection, is appointed to death. Lastly, in his person now fallen and lost, all his offspring is condemned in such a way that God deems worthy of the honour of adoption those whom he gratuitously elects out of it.[67]

Calvin's understanding of the role of Christ in the decree of election is based on the distinction between the two powers of Christ according to his dual nature. By virtue of his human nature and as engaged in the mediatorial office, Christ is the pre-eminent elect creature, the mirror image in which Scripture encourages humans to behold their own election. Without Jesus Christ, the "predestination of God is hidden"[68] and the attempt to know more than is given in Christ will cause the curious to "enter a labyrinth from which there is no exit." (*Inst.* III.21.1) "To each one, his faith is a sufficient witness of the eternal predestination of God, so that it would be a horrible sacrilege to seek higher assurance."[69] Calvin reminds us that Christ "did not seek or receive anything for himself, but everything for us."[70] In the face of the momentous divide entailed by predestination, confidence rather than terror arises from this evangelical conviction:

> Christ, then, is the mirror wherein we must, and without self-deception, may, contemplate our own election. For since it is into his body the Father has destined those to be engrafted whom he has willed from eternity to be his own, that he may hold as sons all whom he acknowledges to be among his members, we have a sufficient and firm testimony that we have been inscribed in the book of life if we are in communion with Christ.[71]

Those in union with Christ, "the visible image of the invisible God" will find in him the only trustworthy knowledge of election.

It is with respect to Christ's nature and power as the eternal Word that Calvin regards him as the author of election and reprobation, sharing in the *consilium* of the Godhead concerning each individual human. While he conceives of the decree of election and reprobation as occurring beyond Christ's role as the incarnate Mediator, Christ does participate in the decree according to his power as the eternal *Logos*. Signs of this are seen to break through even in his incarnate ministry. At *Comm. Jn.* 13.18, Calvin says:

> Moreover, Christ here gives a clear witness to his divinity: first by declaring that he does not judge in a human way; and secondly, by making himself the author of election. For when he says "I know," the knowledge of which he speaks is peculiar to God. But the second proof is the more powerful, for he testifies that those who were chosen before the creation of the world were chosen by himself. Such a remarkable demonstration of his divine power should affect us more deeply than if Scripture had called him God a hundred times.

Again, observing his distinction between the two powers, he remarks that "although Christ interposes himself as Mediator, he claims for himself, in common with the Father, the right to choose." (*Inst.* III.22.7) The double decree, therefore, while not made *extra Christum*, is made *extra carnem Christi*. As Mediator, Christ plays a positive, saving role as "the material cause of election"[72] and as head of the body of the elect. As eternal Word he exercises the power of the Creator (in concert with the Father and the Spirit) and is author of election and of reprobation alike.

The importance Calvin assigns to the doctrine of election has to do with its unequivocal witness to the initiative and sovereignty of grace:

> We shall never be clearly persuaded, as we ought to be, that our salvation flows from the wellspring of God's free mercy until we come to know his eternal election, which illumines God's grace by this contrast: that he does not indiscriminately adopt all men into the hope of salvation but gives to some what he denies to others. (*Inst.* III.21.1)

As Brian Gerrish observes, "Free adoption is the citadel of Calvin's faith; double predestination is a defensive outwork," adding wryly, "and it has not proved a very effective one."[73] Calvin's evangelical intent is clear; why then does he insist on the second decree so that what might have appeared only as a boundary notion—like the shadow cast behind an object on whose face the sun is shining—becomes the concept of a deliberate reprobation?

As might be expected, Calvin supports his argument for the double decree with Scriptural warrants, adducing, for example, Romans 9-11 and the choice of Jacob over Esau. (*Inst.* III.22.4,5) But these are buttresses, not the foundation, of the edifice. The sovereignty of grace is paramount and Calvin thinks the double decree is its unavoidable complement. However, there are other considerations to which Calvin assigns considerable weight. The first is his conviction that the overruling power operative in divine providence extends to God's work in predestination. If God had ordained only to treat humans according to their deserts, "where will that omnipotence of God be whereby he regulates all things according to his secret plan?" The attribution of mere foreknowledge to God concerning future contingent response to the Gospel is conceived to impugn "his might to rule and control everything by his hand." (*Inst.* III.23.7)

The second derives from a logical consideration, namely, that the decree of reprobation is a necessary inference, "since election could not stand except as set over against reprobation":

> God is said to set apart those whom he adopts into salvation; it will be highly absurd to say that others

> acquire by chance or obtain by their own effort what election alone confers on a few, Therefore, those whom God passes over, he condemns and this he does for no other reason than that he wills to exclude them from the inheritance which he predestines for his own children. Therefore, those whom God passes over, he condemns ....[74]

To ask for a cause of the determination of God's will is equally absurd since "you are seeking something greater and higher than God's will, which cannot be found." (*Inst.* III.23.2)

Third, according to his conception of "God's ceaseless, inexhaustible activity" in governing the world, Calvin takes the perceived fact of diversity in the human spiritual condition as evidence of a positive act of reprobation.[75] Experience thus becomes an occasion for pondering the divine ordination to either bliss or damnation and a corroboration of his doctrine. "We teach nothing not borne out by experience." (*Inst.* III.21.1) With a certain petulance he notes that "If the same sermon is preached, say to a hundred people, twenty receive it with the ready obedience of faith, while the rest hold it valueless, or laugh or hiss or loathe it." (*Inst.* III.24.12) "Experience teaches that God wills the repentance of those whom he invites to himself, in such a way that he does not touch the hearts of all." (*Inst.* III.24.15)

Calvin properly situates the doctrine of election in the context of faith in Book III of the *Institutes*, since it is for him both a corollary and a bulwark of free adoption. However, it is clear that his conception of divine omnipotence and sovereignty, articulated under the knowledge of God the Creator, is crucial to his insistence on the double dimension of predestination.[76] It is in reference to the power of the Creator that Calvin refers to Christ as the author of election, a power which he exercises in distinction from his mirroring power as the incarnate Mediator and elect creature.

As Alister McGrath notes,[77] a doctrine of double predestination is not a novelty in the curriculum of Christian theology; it belongs to the Augustinian mainstream and was part of the teaching of the *schola Augustiniana moderna*. However, in Calvin's theology it constitutes a particular problem because of the relation it bears to his crucial concept of accommodation. Nowhere is the problem more acute than in his teaching on the atonement, which is set forth as follows.

At *Inst.* II.16.1-3, Calvin discusses the way in which God is said to be our enemy before reconciliation in Christ, and avers that "No one can descend into himself and seriously consider what he is without feeling God's wrath against him." Only so can humans be moved to repentance and to embrace "God's fatherly love in Christ." Then he comments, "Although this statement [of divine wrath and hostility] is tempered to our feeble comprehension, it is not said falsely." Perhaps Calvin is saying only that God is like a good human parent whose heart never wavers in its love but who must be strict in order to keep beloved children from harm. However, the ambiguity is compounded by the fact that Calvin's account of the atonement is an "objective" one and implies real change, and not merely an adjustment of perspective, in the relationship between God and humanity, and in God's attitude toward us.

While the whole of Christ's obedience is essential to the work of redemption, on the cross Christ offers an expiatory sacrifice to appease God's wrath. If so great a sacrifice as that of the incarnate Son is required for human salvation, a transaction so momentous is indicated as can scarcely be attributed to attempered images. In Calvin's thought, God is both the author and the object of the work of reconciliation. One might attempt to argue that God is only the author of the work of reconciliation and that the language of wrath is therefore only an "accommodation."[78] But this does not take into account the fact that only the elect actually receive the benefit of the atonement; the reprobate continue under the condemnation of God's wrath. Only a doctrine of universal salvation could sustain the coherence of this interpretation, and, manifestly, this is not possible with Calvin.

In his teaching on the *accommodatio dei*, Calvin is wrestling with the central epistemological question addressed by terminism, namely, the relationship between the mental conception of an object and the object itself. How can human (accommodated) conceptions of God be related to God's own being and character?[79] On the one hand, the notion of divine accommodation is but the expression of God's gracious condescension to human finitude and need, "the presence of his grace to our capacity,"[80] the paradigmatic instance of which is the incarnation of Christ. On the other hand, it can also connote mere appearance, as in this definition of Calvin's: "the mode of accommodation is for [God] to represent himself to us not as he is in himself but as he seems to be." (*Inst.* I.17.13) Is the revelation of divine love in fact a revelation of God *in se*, a self-disclosure of the divine character so that it can be said without reserve that God is love? If so, then it is not an accommodation at all; only the expression of wrath is an accommodation. But if we take into account the damned, can it be said that God's wrath is only an accommodation? It seems difficult to avoid the conclusion that for Calvin the amazing counterpoint of love and wrath revealed in the work of redemption is rooted in God's own being. His account of the sacrifice of Christ and of the destiny of the damned both seem to require it.

CONCLUSION

Calvin's reforming intent is characterized by an evangelical focus on the mediatorial role of Jesus Christ, who alone, through the hypostatic union of the divine and human natures in his single person, is able to perform the work of reconciliation. "In short, since neither as God alone could he feel death, nor as man alone could he overcome it, he coupled human nature with divine that to atone for sin he might submit the weakness of the one to death; and that, wrestling with death by the power of the other nature, he might win victory for us." (*Inst.* II.12.3) Nonetheless, his sapiential interest pushes him to explore the work of Christ *etiam extra carnem.* To emphasize the incarnate, redemptive ministry of Christ as essential to faith is one thing; it would be another to restrict our understanding of Christ's reality to this "usward" redemptive role. The reality and majesty of God is to be valued for more than the provision of our human need for salvation, albeit no greater commendation of the divine goodness may be found. The mystery of God's own being and the divine power sustaining the creation also ought to be extolled. As *Deus*, then, is the presupposition and foundation of *Deus manifestatus in carne*, *Logos* is the presupposition and foundation of *Logos ensarkos.* Without some understanding of the being and work of the eternal Word in creation we are impoverished in our knowledge of, and trust in, the One incarnate in Jesus.

In the four concepts given exposition in this chapter, the common factor of Christ's transcendence as the eternal Word beyond the condition of his enfleshed existence is clearly discerned. One might be tempted even to observe the "Nestorian tendency" in Calvin's christology, but he is no more Nestorian, strictly speaking, than Luther is Monophysite.[81] Calvin never intended that his teaching concerning the transcendence of Christ should imply a split in the identity of Christ, as if somehow there could be an incarnate *Logos* and a discarnate *Logos.* The distinction which he makes has to do not with two identities but with two powers exercised by the one Christ. There is one kind of power that is appropriate to Christ as eternal Word and author of creation; there is another that is appropriate to Christ as incarnate Mediator. To confuse these powers or to collapse the one into the other would be to dishonour the wisdom of God in the work of both creation and redemption. In particular, Calvin guards the transcendent deity of Christ, since, as Word of creation and eternal Son, Christ shares a divine nature which cannot be communicated to a creature, and exercises a power which makes efficacious and fully intelligible his work as incarnate Redeemer.

Calvin's adoption of sapiential perspective is generally constructive as he takes care to relate what he has to say about the reality and will of God as majestic Creator to the only trustworthy point of access, faith in God's self-revelation in Jesus Christ. Though there is nothing more vital for faith than to know that God has graciously met our human need for redemption, he knows that there is more to say about God and the life God wills for the creation than a purely redemptive focus will allow. There is a pleasing coherence when Calvin's sapiential interest provides background and balance for understanding the economy of redemption, and when his discussion is dependent on terms extrapolated from Christ's mediatorial ministry. While *Logos* is the ontological presupposition of *Logos ensarkos*, *Logos ensarkos* interprets, and is the epistemological presupposition of, *Logos*. However, there are moments, particularly in his accounts of election and of the temporal duration of Christ's mediatorial ministry, when Calvin's sapiential interest verges on speculative indulgence and becomes destructive of coherence. This occurs when discussion of Christ's reality as eternal Word is abstracted from what we have been given to know of *Christus verus*.

As we follow the interplay of evangelical and sapiential dimensions in Calvin's theology, the next stage of inquiry concerns his doctrine of the creation, especially with respect to human nature. How does Calvin relate the creation and the destiny of humankind to the creative Word who may be distinguished from his incarnate mediatorial office but not separated from it?

NOTES

1. *Inst.* I.2.2. See also *Inst.* III.2.23; 20.11.
2. E. g., *Inst.* I. 3.1.
3. *Calvin's Doctrine of the Knowledge of God*, 52.
4. *Comm. Acts* 7. 55,6.
5. *Inst.* III.2.31. While for Dowey the "mutual presupposition" of the two orders of knowledge (of God the Creator and of God the Redeemer) is a purely logical inference, Calvin may be seen to adduce this "logical or conceptual" presupposition repeatedly from Biblical warrant, as in this citation and the following ones.
6. "Eighth Sermon on the Harmony of the Gospels," *CO* 46, 92.
7. "Sermon on I Tim. 3.16," *CO*, 53, 324f.
8. *Comm. Gen.* 14.18.
9. *Comm. Jn.* 16.28. See also *Comm. Jn.* 1.1; *Comm. Matt.*, 22.42; *Comm. Phil.*, 3.21.
10. *Comm. Jn.* 14.10.
11. *Comm. Jn.* 20.28.
12. *Comm. Matt.* 11.27.
13. *Comm. Gen.* 28.12.
14. *Comm. Rom.* 8.34.
15. *Inst.* II.16.4; 17.2; *Comm. Eph.* 1.4.
16. *Inst.* I.1.3: "Hence that dread and wonder with which Scripture commonly represents the saints as stricken and overcome whenever they felt the presence of God . . . As a consequence we must infer that man is never sufficiently touched and affected by the awareness of his lowly estate until he has compared himself with God's majesty." At *Inst.* I.1.1, he says: "Thus from the feeling of our own ignorance, vanity, poverty, infirmity and—what is more—depravity and corruption, we recognize that the true light of wisdom, sound virtue, full abundance, and purity of righteousness rest in the Lord alone."
17. *Comm. Heb.* 1.10.

18. *Comm. Phil.* 2.6.

19. "Calvin's understanding of the divine nature of Christ is constantly threatened . . . by a concept of God as impassable Being which he inherited from the whole history of theology." Paul van Buren, *Christ in Our Place*, 141.

20. Op. cit., 125.

21. Ibid., 7. See also Marvin Hoogland, *Calvin's Perspective on the Exaltation of Christ: in Comparison with the Post-Reformation Doctrine of the Two States*, 217. He argues that "there exists a fundamental unity not only between the Christological thought of Luther and Calvin but also between that of the Reformers and the later Reformation orthodoxies, and further between the Christology of orthodoxy broadly understood and the Christology of Karl Barth." Irenic perhaps to a fault, Hoogland's thesis is that the union of the Logos with the flesh of Christ is not menaced by the "*extra-calvinisticum*" of either Calvin or the later Reformed.

22. Ibid., 104.

23. Ibid., 109

24. Willis acknowledges that Calvin's christology is more complex than a straightforward insistence on the unity implied in *Deus manifestatus in carne* will allow. He observes: "The reality of the divine efficacy beyond the flesh is a pronounced feature of Calvin's treatment of the ministry of Jesus. In some passages, Calvin employs this teaching even in such a way as to dwindle [thus] the necessity of Christ's bodily presence during his earthly ministry. Here the *extra-calvinisticum* provides unsteady and soft terrain for theological movement" (op. cit., 89f.). He cites in this regard the passage at Comm. Matt. 8.23 where, while Christ slept, "his divinity watched over him," and several other passages in the commentaries where Christ's efficacy in his earthly ministry is affirmed as independent of his bodily presence. See *Comm. Matt.* 8.3, 10, 23,25; 9.18; *Comm. Mark* 1.29, 7.32; *Comm. Jn.* 11.32.

25. *Inst.* IV.17.30. H. A. Oberman, "The 'Extra' Dimension in Calvin's Theology," *The Journal of Ecclesiastical History*, 21 (1970), 56, argues that "the scopus of the *extra-calvinisticum* is not a rejection of Cyril with possible Nestorian results. Indeed it is not at all to be placed in the dimension of the alternatives Cyril-Nestorius, but in an earlier age in the history of Christian thought, the period when adoptionism and docetism were the decisive alternatives." Oberman maintains that at *Inst.* IV.17.30 Calvin is writing against Marcionite docetism, defending the *verus homo*. However, the scopus of IV.17 is actually very broad; in this chapter, Calvin deals not only with the integrity of the *verus homo*, but also, among other things, with the manner in which we are fed in the sacrament by Christ's body, the secret power of the Holy Spirit to unite things separated in space (Christ's body at the right hand of the Father and his members on earth) and the integrity of Christ's divine nature. Oberman isolates one aspect of Calvin's wide-ranging discussion on the Supper and elevates it to pre-eminence, while apparently overlooking Calvin's explicit reference to the monophysite position of Eutyches.

26. Ibid. Calvin's point in the rather obscure second sentence is that a (Lutheran) misuse of texts like John 3.13, in ascribing divine properties to the human nature *realiter*, is excluded once the proper purpose of the *communicatio* is understood. It actually serves as an interpretive device to explain how an otherwise contradictory phrase such as "Son of man in heaven" attests the indissoluble reality of the hypostatic union. So he writes at *Inst.* II.14.2: "But since Christ, who was true God and also true man, was crucified and shed his

blood for us, the things that he carried out in his human nature are transferred improperly, although not without reason, to his divinity."

27. *Inst.* IV.17.28. David Willis locates other references to the distinction in Calvin's writings at op. cit., 31-3.

28. *Commentum in Quattuor Libros Sententiarum Magistri Petri Lombardi.* Vol. 7 of *Opera Omnia*, D. 22.1.2.

29. Thus Calvin can write at *Comm. Eph.* 4.10: "When we hear of the ascension of Christ, it instantly comes to our minds that he is removed from us, and so indeed he is, with respect to his body and human presence. But Paul tells us that he is removed from us in bodily presence in such a way that he nevertheless fills all things, and that by the power of his Spirit."

30. *LW*, 16, 55.

31. *LW*, 15, 293f.

32. *Martin Luthers Werke*, 39.2, 121.

33. Identified at *Inst.* II.13.ln2 and 3n5 as, among others, the followers of Menno Simons and Menno himself.

34. *Comm. Luke* 23.43.

35. "Sermon on I Tim. 3.16," *CO* 53, 328.

36. From *Christus Veritas*, 142f., quoted by Donald Baillie, *God Was in Christ*, 96.

37. *Comm. Jn.* 1.5.

38. *Comm. Col.* 1.15.

39. *Comm. Col.* 1.17.

40. *Comm. Eph.* 1.8-10.

41. *Comm. Col.* 1.20.

42. *ST, Ia IIae*, 109.2.

43. *ST, Ia IIae*, 109.3.

44. As Karl Rahner observes, the very distinguishing mark of a Catholic theology of grace is that "grace is not only pardon for the poor sinner, but 'sharing in the divine nature'." *Nature and Grace*, 117.

45. *Comm. Jn.* 1.14.

46. *Comm. Gen.* 2.7; 3.19.

47. David Willis reminds us that although Christ's power as the eternal Logos in sustaining the created order is more comprehensive than his redemptive power, "It is the same Person who orders unfallen creation and who reconciles rebellious creation." *Calvin's Catholic Christology*, 71.

48. With reference to the *extra-calvinisticum*, Oberman notes: "The *extra-calvinisticum* is not an isolated phenomenon but rather, like the top of an iceberg, only the most controversial aspect of a whole 'extra' dimension in Calvin's theology: *extra ecclesiam, extra coenam, extra legem, extra praedicationem.* The word '*etiam*' is important because it underscores the fact that the primary and basic concern is the very *ecclesia, coena, caro, lex, and praedicatio* itself. To these means of revelation and redemption God has committed himself, since he has attached his *promissio* to them." "The 'Extra' Dimension in the Theology of Calvin," in *The Journal of Ecclesiastical History*, Vol. 21.1, 62.

49. From the point of view of an eternal election, which includes the divine decree and foreknowledge of the fall, there is nothing adventitious about the fall; it is a necessary event. However, this is the perspective from eternity. From an earthly perspective the fall is something that cannot be foreseen. This Calvin makes clear in refuting the argument that Satan contrived the destruc-

tion of humanity out of jealousy, foreseeing "that the Son of God was to be clothed in human flesh." "Since the Son of God was made man in order to restore us, who were already lost, from our miserable overthrow, how could that be foreseen which would never have happened unless man had sinned?" *Comm. Gen.* 3.1-3.

50. *Comm. I Pet.* 1.20.

51. Ibid.

52. "Psychopannychia," in T.F. Torrance, ed., *Tracts and Treatises*, III, 447.

53. *Comm. Micah* 4. 3

54. Brian Gerrish makes this point, referring to *Comm. Eph.* 3.17. Op. cit., 72.

55. *Comm. Jn.* 6.55.

56. *Comm. Jn.* 6.56.

57. *Comm. Jn.* 6.62.

58. *Comm. Jn.* 6.51.

59. *Comm. Jn.* 6.41.

60. *Comm. I Cor.* 15.27.

61. *Comm. I Jn.* 3.2.

62. Ibid.

63. *Comm. I Cor.* 13.12; *Comm. I Jn.* 3.2.

64. *Comm. Jn.* 14.28.

65. *Church Dogmatics*, II/2, 64.

66. Calvin speaks rather of Christ being "appointed" to be Mediator. For example, at *Inst.* II.17.1, the verb is statuit (*CO* 2, 386) and at *Comm. I Peter* 1.20, the participle *destinatus* is used (*CO* 55, 225). Calvin reserves the technical terms *praeordino* and *praedestino* and their cognates for reference to humans -- as indicated, for example, at *Inst.* III.21.5 (*CO* 2, 683).

67. *Concerning the Eternal Predestination of God*, trans. and ed. by J.K.S. Reid, 121.

68. *Comm. Jn.* 17.6.

69. *Comm. Jn.* 6.40.

70. *Comm. Phil.* 2.9.

71. *Inst.* III.24.5. The mirror image is vital for Calvin. In *Concerning the Eternal Predestination of God*, 127, he says: "Christ therefore is for us the bright mirror of the eternal and hidden election of God and also the earnest and pledge...Therefore Christ, when commending the eternal election of his own in the counsel of his Father, at the same time shows where their faith may rest secure." See also *Inst.* III.21.1; 24.5.

72. *Comm. Eph.* 1.5.

73. Op. cit., 170.

74. *Inst.* III.23.1.

75. *Inst.* III.21.1, 7. See also III.24.1.

76. Alister McGrath observes that Calvin's appeal to experience is evidence that his "analysis of predestination begins from observable facts." "Calvin's predestinarianism is to be regarded as *a posteriori* reflection upon the data of human experience, interpreted in the light of scripture, rather than something which is deduced *a priori* on the basis of preconceived ideas concerning divine omnipotence." Our argument is that it is a case of both/and rather than either/or. Op. cit., 167f.

77. Op. cit., 168.

78. Paul van Buren maintains this to be the case. *Christ in Our Place*, 8.

79. Alister McGrath, op. cit., 42.

80. *Inst.* I.14.11. In this passage, Calvin is referring to the use of angelic guardians to mediate the divine presence and encouragement to humans. In other references to the *accommodatio dei*, Calvin says that as nurses do with infants, "God is wont in a measure to 'lisp' in speaking to us" (*Inst.* I.13.1), and that in the sacraments God uses material means to strengthen faith, "shut up as we are in this prison house of our flesh" (*Inst.* IV.1.1). See also *Inst.* II.6.4.

81. In contrast to Calvin, Martin Luther conceived of the person of Christ as the result rather than the presupposition of the union of the two natures, thus allowing divine attributes to be predicated of the human nature, as in the case of miracle-working power. In Calvin's case the person of Christ is essentially and properly the eternal Son who also assumed our humanity, manifesting himself in time and space. The dynamic of the Incarnation is interpreted by Calvin to assert not only the identity of Christ as the eternal Word and as incarnate Redeemer but also the transcendent majesty and power which belong to the *Logos* even in the course of the radical self-limitation entailed by the *assumptio carnis*. In regarding the person of Christ as a presupposition of the *unio personalis*, therefore, Calvin understands the *assumptio carnis* to be as much a self-limitation of the Son of God (where "deity" connotes transcendence) as a self-manifestation of the heart of God (where "deity" connotes divine *agape*). See Marvin Hoogland, *Calvin's Perspective on the Exaltation of Christ in Comparison with the Post-Reformation Doctrine of the Two States*, 15.

3

JESUS CHRIST AND CREATION

If only the evangelical dimension is regarded as integral to his thought, then there might be grounds for the allegation that Calvin sets grace against nature or sees grace supplanting nature. If, on the other hand, the sapiential dimension is also discerned and valued, then a more mutual relationship may be seen to exist between nature and grace in his thought. Clearly Calvin does reject the position that the grace of Jesus Christ only fulfills nature's potential, though we have seen that the grace of Christ also accomplishes this perfecting role of "*gratia elevans*." With Calvin, grace is primarily redemptive and meets the need of sinful creatures for regeneration. However, it does not do so by overturning the natural order or subverting the gifts of the divine Spirit operating in human community. Calvin's target is not nature but pride in the flesh, that is, a confidence in the existing human condition that would preclude recognition of our need for thorough-going repentance and transformation.

Far from overturning or supplanting nature, grace restores it to its intended integrity. According to Calvin, redemption is nothing less than a second creation, an act of God in which "he promises under the reign of Christ the complete restoration of a sound and well-constituted nature."[1] In the cross of Christ, "the whole world was renewed and all things restored to order."[2] "In the resurrection there is the restoration of all things, and thus it is the beginning of the second and new creation, for the former had fallen in the ruin of the first man."[3]

Here is introduced a major theme in Calvin's work, namely, that regeneration is essentially the restoration of the original order of human nature in creation.[4] New creation is re-creation:

> Adam was at first created in the image of God, so that he might reflect, as in a mirror, the righteousness of God. But that image, having been wiped out by sin, must now be restored in Christ. The regeneration of the godly is indeed, as it is said in II Cor. 3.18, nothing else than the reformation of the image of God in them . . . Therefore he teaches that the design in regeneration is to lead us back from error to that end for which we were created.[5]

Even though there is a "richer measure of grace in regeneration" this fact "does not remove that other principal point, that the end of regeneration is that Christ should reform us to God's image." "This principle cannot be overthrown, that what was primary in the renewing of God's image also held the highest place in creation itself." (*Inst.* I.15.4)

Look at the grain of the wood one way and the evangelical import of this doctrine is clear: "the reduction of the world to order"[6] is the unique work of the redemptive mediator. Look at the grain from the other direction and the sapiential quality appears: the work of the mediator is to restore the creation to its original integrity. Our only access to knowledge and experience of the original integrity of creation comes through Jesus Christ. But because Jesus Christ is none other than the Logos incarnate, his redemptive work is necessarily an affirmation of the original goodness instilled in creation. Life in its brokenness and alienation from God needs healing and a new beginning. Yet because life ever remains in the hands of a provident God, it is also greater and more resilient than the distortion that mars it. The sapiential eye sees that at the heart of things is a divinely intended order and goodness which revolutionary spiritual change will not sweep away but rather recover and claim.

CHRIST AS INSTRUMENTAL AUTHOR OF CREATION

As alluded to in Chapter Two, Calvin's teaching on the role of the eternal Word in creation constitutes a singular aspect of his theology. In describing the relationship between Jesus Christ and creation, Calvin boldly ascribes a creative and sustaining agency to the eternal Word who is also the reconciling Mediator. It was Augustine who laid down the rubric for Latin theology that all divine action external to the Godhead is to be ascribed to all three Persons without distinction: *opera trinitatis ad extra sunt indivisa.* The spectre of Arianism still haunted the Church in Augustine's day and this formula removed the possibility of any hint of subordination of the Son to the Father as a mere instrument of divine activity. Calvin also knew this spectre as a contemporary phenomenon in the person of Servetus. Yet we find him subscribing to what is historically the Greek principle of differentiation, "From the Father, through the Son, in the Holy Spirit."[7] Thus Calvin writes of the Trinity: "To the Father is attributed the beginning of activity, and the fountain and wellspring of all things; to the Son, wisdom, counsel, and the ordered disposition of all things; but to the Spirit is assigned the power and efficacy of that activity."[8] In short, rather than avoiding those formulations which might invite Arian speculation and which led to accusations against his own orthodoxy,[9] Calvin meets the challenge of Servetus head-on, insisting that proper consideration of the power which Christ exercises as *Logos*, or instrumental Author of creation, actually proves "his eternity, his true essence and his divinity."

(*Inst.* I.13.7, 8)

The role of "intermediary" which Christ assumes in the act of creation functions ultimately not to qualify either his eternal essence or glory, but rather to establish them, because of the common divine nature implied in the intimate relationship obtaining between Christ as Son and God the Father. In an important summary statement, he writes of Christ:

> The world was created by him as being the eternal Wisdom of God which was the director of all his works from the beginning . . . It is the usual manner of speaking to call the Father the Creator: and what is added in some passages—by Wisdom (Prov. 8.27) or by the Word (Jn. 1.3) or by the Son (Col. 1.16)—has the same force as if Wisdom were named as Creator. It must be noted that there is distinction of persons, not only in respect of men, but also in God himself, between the Father and the Son. Unity of essence requires that what is of the essence of God is as much of the Son as of the Father: and therefore whatever belongs to God alone is common to both. This does not prevent each from having the property of his own person.[10]

Calvin believes that differentiated reference to Christ as the instrumental author of creation simply reflects the economy of divine activity attested in Scripture, and it is this attested economy which underlies, and drives us to articulate, the Christian doctrine of the Trinity. It is according to the nature of God that the objective manifestation of the divine being and will *ad extra* is attributed to God's Wisdom, or Word. Because the *personae* of the Godhead represent real hypostases in God, it is legitimate and even desirable to refer to God's relations with the world according to the differentiated *personae*.

To assert the distinctive role which the *Logos* plays *ad extra* in creation is to affirm the divinity according to which alone such power can be attributed. Accordingly, it is vitally important for Calvin to distinguish between Christ's eternal office and power as (instrumental) Creator and Sustainer of the universe and his office and power as incarnate Mediator. In the latter case, there is an evident subordination of the Son to the Father in the sense that the Son willingly adopts the form of a servant and interposes himself as the reconciler between God and humanity. Such apparently difficult words as those spoken at John 14.28, "For the Father is greater than I," Calvin understands to be attributed to Christ in virtue of this mediatorial interposition.[11]

No distinction of identity is implied by Calvin in this teaching. His repeated description of the Incarnation as the manifestation, or appearing, of the eternal Son obviates any suggestion that we have to do with anyone other than the one person of Christ. "For God was not manifested in the flesh from the beginning; but he who always was life and the eternal Word of God, appeared in the fulness of time as man."[12] "The Scriptures often teach in other places, that the world was created by that Eternal Word, who, being the only begotten Son of God, appeared afterwards in the flesh."[13] The distinction is drawn primarily between the two powers which Christ exercises in accordance with his divine and human natures, but it presupposes the distinction between the two natures themselves.

Even with respect to his language concerning Christ's appearing or manifestation, it is evident that Calvin regards it as equally important to affirm Christ's power and transcendence as the eternal Word beyond the flesh as to affirm the *unio personalis* and the *verus homo*. In this respect, he understands Christ's power and majesty to be the source of the efficacy and authority of his mediatorial office. Christ's mighty works, including his miracles, declare him to be a divine saviour. "What he claims for himself now pertains to his divinity—in the words of the apostle, 'He upholds all things by his powerful will' (Heb. 1.3). And the reason why he declares he is God is that he, manifested in the flesh, might execute the office of the Christ."[14] Again, the power to raise the dead Calvin assigns to Christ in virtue of his divinity:

> The right and power of raising the dead, in fact, of doing everything according to his own pleasure, is assigned to the person of Christ, a panegyric by which his divine majesty is lucently set forth. More, we gather from this that the world was created by him, for to subject all things to himself belongs to the Creator alone.[15]

While the purview of Book I of the *Institutes* is as broad as the creation and deals, among other things, with the role of angels and devils, it is chiefly devoted to exposition of the doctrines of the knowledge of the triune God in creation and Scripture, human nature as created, and providence. As the knowledge of God is the major focus of Chapter Four, consideration turns now to Calvin's doctrines of providence and human nature as crucial instances of the relationship of Jesus Christ to creation and the natural order.

PROVIDENCE AND THE PURPOSE OF CREATION

Calvin offers an account of providence in several places;[16] from a comparison of the various sources, an essentially common pattern can be recognized, with three major aspects named. First, there is God's general government of the world; then follows the heavenly control of particulars, especially of the private and public life of humans; and finally is noted "the truly paternal protection with which he guards his church."[17] The three successive moments of providence—as universal, particular, and special (the preservation of the church)—are like concentric circles whose innermost core is the preservation of the elect. While God's widest direction of the creation extends to every creature, the focus of divine providential care is the inner circle of the elect in Jesus Christ.

Special Providence

"Special Providence" denotes the manner in which the divine government of creation focuses upon the fulfillment of a single primary aim, the provision and preservation of a holy people. Of the account of creation traditionally ascribed to Moses, Calvin observes: "The end to which the whole scope of the history tends is to this point, that the human race has been preserved by God in such a manner as to manifest his special care for his church."[18] The preservation of the race as a whole is crucial, but it is for the sake of God's elect. In the scope of providence there are, accordingly, "degrees of direction."

> For though God shows himself father and judge of the whole human race, yet since the Church is the sanctuary in which he resides, he there displays his presence with clearer evidence . . . For the church is God's own workshop in which he exercises his providence—the chief theatre of the same providence.[19]

This focus upon the preservation of the elect as the principal aim of providence raises for us the question of God's overall purpose in creation. If the aim of providence is the preservation of the elect, then must not God's purpose in the act of creation be the provision of an elect people? Although Calvin does not pose the question in so explicit a manner, his affirmative answer to it may be inferred from his writings in two steps.

First, Calvin regards the creation as existing to serve humankind and its knowledge of God's goodness:

> For if it is asked, why the world was created, why we have been put in it to have dominion over the earth, why we are preserved in this life to enjoy innumerable blessings and are endowed with light and understanding, no reason can be given but the free love of God towards us.[20]

The very work of creation was completed not in a moment but in a succession of days in order that we might learn from the order and fulness of this distribution "God's fatherly love to mankind" (*Inst.* I.14.2) and "that he created all things for man's sake." (*Inst.* I.14.22) "As [God] does not stand in need of anything himself, he has destined all the riches, both of heaven and earth, for their use . . . The whole order of the world is arranged for the purpose of conducing to the comfort and happiness of men."[21]

The world, then, was made for the sake of humanity. The second step follows when we ask for what purpose humanity was made. Calvin's repeated answer is this, that there might be intelligent creatures capable of knowing and praising God. Let one famous statement represent the many which could be cited: "To know God is man's chief end, and justifies his existence. Even if a hundred lives were ours, this one aim would be sufficient for them all."[22]

Intelligent creatures are central to God's creative purpose not as ends in themselves, but as, ennobled by the gifts distinguishing them from the beasts, they are capable of a profound appreciation of the goodness of creation and of spiritual communion with their Maker. This is why it is not so much humanity in general for whom the world is made, as that body of people who are the elect.

> The Holy Spirit declares that all things were created principally for the use of men, that they might thereby recognize God as their Father. In fine, the prophet concludes that the whole course of nature would be subverted, unless God saved his Church. The creation of the world would serve no good purpose, if there were no people to call upon God.[23]

The Church constitutes that minority amongst humans which, in spite of the continued defection of the majority, God gathers by grace into the household of faith, thereby providing the fulfillment of the divine creative purpose. Creation exists ultimately for the sake of the human praise of God in Jesus Christ.

When the question of the divine purpose in creation is raised, several answers are possible. It is unlikely that the existence of creation could be regarded as an end in itself. Certainly this would be an impossible position for Calvin since he does not regard creation as an "intrinsic good"; it is good in virtue of the goodness of its Giver and in light of the purposes of the Giver. At least possible in Calvin's thought would be the position that creation exists for the sake of redemption, as Irenaeus taught.[24] Because of the fall, Calvin can and does speak as if this were the case, as at *Comm. Gal.* 4.19: "For we were born that we might be new creatures in [Christ]." However, this isolated statement may be construed as an instance of hyperbole in which the complex relationship among an eternal election, an originally intact creation, and the adventitious need of humans for redemption is compressed and simplified for rhetorical advantage.

Creation might also be for the purpose of the assumption of our humanity by Christ, as Duns Scotus maintained. On occasion, Calvin can give the impression that this also might be his position: "When we have been gathered to God and incorporated in one body with our Lord Jesus Christ, we shall apprehend the end for which we were created, namely, that we might know that God is conjoined and one with us in the person of his Son."[25] For Scotus, the Incarnation would have taken place irrespective of the fall since its cause is to be sought not in human rebellion but in the nature of God, whose essence is love.[26] All divine action *ad extra* is therefore aimed at the communication of this love to the fullest extent possible, and this communication includes the enabling of a creaturely response to the fullest extent possible.[27] Such a love could only be manifested by the union of divine and human natures in the eternal Word incarnate, so that Christ is predestined to assume our humanity not primarily as the Redeemer, but rather as "*supremus inter viatores*."[28] In point of fact, because of sin, Christ appeared as Redeemer, but his eternal predestination was to be the head and fulness of creation. Thus the world exists for Christ and because of him: Christ is its final cause.

We know from passages in which Calvin opposes Osiander that he did not hold the Scotist position, since Osiander's argument is a variant of that of Duns Scotus. Calvin's position is actually in harmony with Aquinas, who saw that a reverent agnosticism is appropriate to the question of what might have transpired with respect to the Incarnation of the Word if there had been no fall.[29] All that we can know with the certainty and humility appropriate to piety is the Scripturally warranted fact that Christ was predestined to be human as the remedy for sin. (*Inst.* II.12.4, 5)

Calvin's account of a special providence implies a preeminence for the category of election in his thought, with the corollary that creation, redemption, and even the predestination of Christ to be incarnate are all subordinate moments to it. The goal of creation is not the election of Christ (to be incarnate) but the election in Christ of a holy people. Yet God's eternal plan for the provision of this holy people is premised on the mediatorial role of the eternal Word. Thus it is also correct to say that creation is ordered through and to Christ who as Logos is Creator of all creatures and, as incarnate is the Redeemer of the elect community of praise.

The importance of election is worthy of note in the theology of Aquinas also, since for him the goal of creation is humanity engraced and glorified. The return of creatures to God expounded in the *Secunda Pars* of the *Summa Theologiae* focuses upon humanity and its attainment, through grace, of its final end, the *visio Dei*. While God is the final end for all creatures without exception, rational creatures lay hold of it in knowing and loving God.[30] The goal of eternal beatitude does not mean, however, that God is displaced by humanity at the centre of theology. In the schema of Aquinas, humans exist and are enabled intelligently and freely to glorify God only because of God's original willingness to share the divine being and goodness with creatures. On this theocentric quality of Aquinas' theology, Otto Pesch has finely observed:

> It is always necessary for us, who through anxiety and inner turmoil have quite easily become self-centred men of little courage, to learn anew from a tradition concerned with a totally different type of God question that faith in God reaches its ultimate maturity only when the believer is in a position to say, as the Gloria of the Mass puts it: *Gratias agimus tibi propter magnam gloriam tuam*—"We give thanks to you," not primarily and finally because you save us, but "because of your great glory."[31]

Does Calvin also place God and the divine glory at the center, as the older interpreters, like Doumergue, were wont to say? Calvin speaks as if this were the case. Thus, while conceding the nobility of the Christian's hope of an eternal life, he also declares: "It is not very sound theology to confine man's thoughts so much to himself, and not to set before him as the prime motive of his existence zeal to show forth the glory of God."[32] In the same vein, he addresses the King of Navarre:

> You will, I am sure, Sire, pardon the necessity which causes us to speak thus, that however much we have at heart your salvation, there is something still more worthy and precious which we seek, namely the glory of God and the spread of the kingdom of Jesus Christ, wherein lies the salvation of the whole world.[33]

Commenting on a text at Eph. 1.4, Calvin makes clear that, in the aim of election, the holiness of believers is "the immediate, but not the chief design." "The glory of God is the highest end, to which our sanctification is subordinate."[34]

In assessing the import of these statements, we need to keep in view the interplay of the dimensions of evangelical intent and sapiential perspective in Calvin's thought. What he is subordinating to God's glory is concern for the individual believer's salvation, not the revelation of God's benevolent purpose in Jesus Christ. In Calvin's teaching, God's glory and praiseworthiness are particularly defined by the supreme act of benevolence in the incarnation of Christ. God's glory is not only the reflection of the divine majesty and power, but also of the gift of God's love for humanity in creation and redemption. The purpose of creation is God's praise—by a people who are gathered by grace and whose gratitude is shaped not only by who God is but also by what God has done.

The Role of Christ in Universal Providence

Calvin's concepts of providence and of creation are intimately related since he regards the former as the extension of the latter, and the latter as lacking significance for faith without the former. "To make God a momentary Creator, who once for all finished his work, would be cold and barren and we must differ from profane men especially in that we see the presence of divine power shining as much in the continuing state of the universe as in its inception." (*Inst.* I.16.1) God is not, therefore, a spectator of the unfolding life of the world but its divine governor, ceaselessly active in superintendence of it. (*Inst.* I.16.3) So far is this true that were the sustaining hand of God withdrawn, the world would "immediately perish and dissolve into nothing."[35] In a phrase of concise brilliance, Calvin avers that "providence is lodged in the act." (*Inst.* I.16.4)

According to his understanding of Christ as instrumental Author of creation, and in virtue of the continuity of creation and providence, Calvin attributes the power of God which sustains the creation in being to the eternal Word:

> The Word of God was not only the fount of life to all creatures, so that those which had not yet existed began to be, but...his life-giving power makes them remain in state. For did not his continued inspiration quicken the world, whatsoever flourishes would without doubt decay or be reduced to nothing. In short, what Paul ascribes to God, that in him we have our being and move and live, John declares to be accomplished by the blessing of the Word. It is God, therefore, who gives us life; but he does so by the eternal Word.[36]

The distinction between the two powers of the Son of God is assumed in the case of the preservation of creation also, since it is one thing to consider the power of the Word diffused through the creation, which "quickens all things," and another to consider his power to free these things from "the exigency of corruption." (*Inst.* II.10.7) Commenting on the feeding of the five thousand, Calvin draws attention to the continuing work of the eternal Christ and the way in which the supernatural miracles of Christ's earthly ministry attest God's provision of "natural" miracles each day:

> And though he does not now satiate five thousand men with five loaves, he nevertheless does not cease to feed the whole world wonderfully. It seems contradictory to us that man does not live by bread only, but by the Word that proceeds out of the mouth of God (Deut. 8.3.). For we are so attached to outward

> means that nothing is harder than to depend on God's providence. This is why there is such agitation as soon as we run short of food. If we consider everything aright, we shall be forced to see God's blessing in all food. But custom and familiarity make us undervalue the miracles of nature.[37]

There is an interesting parallel to the distinction of the two powers of the Son of God with respect to the Holy Spirit. The objective manifestation of God's providential power in the Word is matched by the subjective work of the Spirit in all creatures. Thus, the Holy Spirit has a twofold power and is called "the Spirit of sanctification" in a twofold sense: "because he not only quickens and nourishes us by a general power that is visible both in the human race and in the rest of the living creatures, but he is also the root and seed of heavenly life in us." Calvin relates this twofold understanding of the work of the Spirit specifically to the Scriptural identification of the Holy Spirit as the Spirit of Christ. "Also one ought to know that he is called the 'Spirit of Christ' not only because Christ, as the eternal Word of God, is joined in the same Spirit with the Father, but also from his character as the Mediator." (*Inst.* III.1.2) While Calvin's emphasis here falls on the recognition of the empowerment of Christ's mediatorial ministry by the Holy Spirit, we are informed, in passing, of the relation of the Spirit to Christ's power as the eternal and creative Word.

The one instance in which Christ's human nature is seen to be engaged unambiguously in providential government is in the royal office of the exalted and glorified Mediator. As a result of the resurrection, ascension, and session at the right hand of Power, dominion and glory are ascribed to the human Christ, though not in abstraction from his divinity, since this exaltation is affirmed of the entire person of the Mediator. Calvin makes it clear that it is a fresh accession to power that is visible in the appearance of the risen Christ to the apostles at Matt. 28.16ff.:

> Let us recall, that what Christ always had by right, at the Father's side, was also allowed him in our flesh; that is (to speak clearly) in his Person as Mediator. He does not boast of the eternal power he enjoyed before the foundation of the world, but the power he now took, when appointed Judge of the world. We must note, his authority was not openly displayed until He rose from the dead.[38]

Again he writes: "Now the Son of God, after he had been manifested in the flesh, received from the Father lordship and power over all things, so that he alone reigns in heaven and earth; and the Father exercises power through him."[39] Here, in the ascription of authority and power over the entire creation to the person of the Mediator, Calvin affirms the integrity of the hypostatic union in thorough-going consistency with his evangelical aim.

However, the question arises as to whether there is any sense in which Calvin conceives Christ as human to possess dominion over the creation not only in his exalted state, but also during his earthly ministry.[40] By and large, Calvin was wary of the idea of a *communicatio idiomatum*, but there are instances in which he seems to allow some exercise of divine power by the human Christ even during his earthly ministry. "Christ, inasmuch as he is man, was appointed by the Father to be the Author of life, that we should not have to seek it afar off. What had been hidden in God is revealed in Christ the man, and life, formerly inaccessible, is now close at hand."[41] A further reference to Christ as the visible image of God implies that dominion and power belonged to him in his earthly ministry:

> The Kingdom was delivered to the Son by the Father, that he might govern heaven and earth according to his will. But it might seem very absurd that the Father should surrender his right to govern, and be idle in heaven like a private person. The answer is easy . . . No change took place in the Father when he appointed Christ supreme King and Lord of heaven and earth, for he himself is in the Son and works in him. But since all our senses fail as soon as we wish to rise to God, Christ is set before our eyes as the visible image of the invisible God.[42]

Finally, at *Comm. Phil.* 2.10, both the exaltation and abasement of Christ are attributed to "Christ's entire person, as he was God manifested in the flesh."

It would appear possible from such references as the above to conclude that Calvin does think of the power of the creative Word to rule over and sustain the world as communicated to the human nature of Christ during the course of his earthly ministry.[43] But this runs against the strong current of Calvin's distinction between the two powers of Christ and it is not clear that this indeed is what Calvin is saying. Each reference is ambiguous enough to admit of a different interpretation, namely, that even while engaged in his mediatorial ministry, Christ continued to exercise the universal power belonging to his divine nature and that even under the limitations of the flesh he possessed this power, occasionally manifesting it in his miracles and mighty works.

More characteristic of Calvin's teaching, as well as that of the Reformed after him, is the conception that the successive states of Christ's abasement and exaltation do not properly and essentially have reference to the divine nature. Commenting on the ascription of the title, "Governor of the world," to the risen Christ, Calvin observes:

> As the eternal Word of God, Christ, it is true, has always had in his hands, by right, sovereign authority and majesty, and as such can receive no accessions thereto; but still he is exalted in human nature, in which he took upon him the form of a servant. This title, therefore, is not applied to him only as God, but is extended to the whole person of the Mediator.[44]

The attribution of dominion and power to the human Christ can only be affirmed enhypostatically, that is, as a result of the fact that the humanity of Jesus exists only in union with the divine nature.

Calvin's references to "the entire person of the Mediator" do not constitute, therefore, a reference to a *communicatio idiomatum* during the earthly ministry but rather the basis on which an attribution of universal power to human nature could be made at all. Thus, at *Comm. Eph.* 4.10, Calvin notes that the ascension was for the purpose, "that he, who was formerly contained in a little space, might fill heaven and earth." He then raises a question: "But did not he fill them before? In his divinity, I own, he did; but he did not exert the power of his spirit, nor manifest his presence as after he had entered into the possession of his kingdom." Only after the exaltation and session at the right hand of power is it possible to attribute divine amplitude to Christ as human, and then only as his humanity is united to the divine nature, that is, only as there is reference to the entire person of Christ.

The accession to universal power ascribed to the human Christ is therefore an extension of the power belonging properly and essentially to the eternal Word. This accession has a beginning in time according to the exaltation of Christ's humanity and, as noted in Chapter II, an end also. The power of world government now vested in the glorified Mediator will finally be transferred back to his divinity alone. Thus, while the kingdom is said to be delivered by the Father to the Son, it will then be delivered up again to the Father.

Particular Providence in the Discernment of the Elect

Characteristic of Calvin's teaching on providence is an emphasis on God's paternal care. He aims at much more than do the scholastics in attributing to God the origin of universal movement according to natural law. God is everlasting Governor and Preserver "not only in that he drives the celestial frame as well as its parts by a universal motion, but also that he sustains, nourishes and cares for, everything he has made, even to the last sparrow." (*Inst.* I.16.1) This is the scope of "particular providence" and only as the divine care for individuals is taken into account can God's rule be known as it really is, namely, on the basis of a fatherly favour. (*Inst.* I.16.1; 17.6)

One aspect of particular providence may be called retributive since it concerns the fact that in God's government of the world there operates a moral law as potent and unremitting as physical law. "For in administering human society [God] so tempers his providence, that, although kindly and beneficent toward all in numberless ways, he still by open and daily indications declares his clemency to the godly and his severity to the wicked and criminal." (*Inst.* I.5.7) Calvin includes in this definition the effect of apparently "natural" causes: "As if the fruitfulness of one year were not a singular blessing of God, and scarcity and famine were not his curse and vengeance . . . It is certain that not one drop of rain falls without God's sure command." (*Inst.* I.16.5)

Calvin is not so fondly pious, however, as to fail to recognize that this neat (Deuteronomic) formula of blessing and curse often seems contradicted by experience. Confronted by the prosperity of the wicked and the suffering of the innocent, the believer must cast her eyes to the eschatological horizon, for "the present condition of men is to be estimated by the state in which it will terminate."[45] Not until the final judgment will the righteous be clearly vindicated. Until then, it will take a supple interpretive skill to assess rightly the various negativities of existence:

> And indeed the unfailing rule of his righteousness ought not to be obscured by the fact that he frequently allows the wicked and malefactors to exult unpunished for some time, while he permits the upright and deserving to be tossed about by many adversities and even to be oppressed by the malice and iniquity of the impious. But a far different consideration ought, rather, to enter our minds: that, when with a manifest show of his anger he punishes one sin, he hates all sins; that, when he leaves many sins unpunished, there will be another judgment to which have been deferred the sins yet to be punished. Similarly, what great occasion he gives us to contemplate his mercy when he often pursues miserable sinners with unwearied kindness, until he shatters their wickedness by imparting benefits and by recalling them to him with more than fatherly kindness. (*Inst.* I.5.7)

Seemingly arbitrary and unfair events must be scrutinized in the light of the fact that although God's specific purposes in these events may not be perfectly known, nonetheless "God always has the best reason for his plan," a reason that will culminate in the sanctification of believers and the destruction of the obstinately rebellious. Accordingly, "God's providence must be considered with regard to the future as well as the past." (*Inst.* I.17.1) While it is commonplace for believers to see God's hand at work chiefly through retrospective reflection, Calvin urges his readers to regard providence prospectively -- as the ground of hope and of expectation of unfailing guidance by God. Belief in the retributive justice of providence is essential for faith: "For unless we are persuaded that the world is governed by him in righteousness and truth, our minds would soon stagger, and at length entirely fail us."[46]

Manifestly, "the upright and deserving" are the elect in Jesus Christ. It is the elect only who are in a position to comprehend the complex nature of a providence in which tragic experience is to be recognized now as a punishment of the wicked and now as a fatherly chastisement of the godly, for they alone know the benevolence of God the Redeemer and the secret heart of providence. To know God's loving, parental care is the result not of natural birth but of the second birth of regeneration, and of adoption into Christ. Thus, knowledge of particular providence implies knowledge of the incarnate Son who is elder brother to the elect. Calvin's discussion of particular providence in Book I does not develop this implication and, according to the methodological distinction, *duplex cognitio*, it ought not to do so. The focus of Book I is the nature of divine providence, not the conditions under which we come to know and enjoy its benefits. Moreover, from a sapiential perspective, while true knowledge of God's providential government is accessible only to believers, it is an objective reality obtaining in the world irrespective of the specific character of humans as regenerate or unregenerate.

Omnipotence and Divine Justice

As in the case of Luther, Calvin has a conception of God as the One whose omnipotence "works all in all" (*qua omnia operatur in omnibus*).[47] For Luther, God is said to be hidden (*absconditus*) because the divine government and preservation of the universe unfolds by instrumentality; God works concealed behind the masks (*larvae*) which are the manifold ordinances of creation.[48] For Calvin, God remains hidden in the work of providence because the divine ordination of all events takes place according to a Will which by its nature remains inaccessible to us. While we must confess that every occurrence has been knowingly and willingly decreed, we cannot know God's reasons. "His wonderful method of governing the universe is rightly called an abyss because, while it is hidden from us, we ought reverently to adore it." (*Inst.* I.17.2)

God's "hidden will" or "secret plan" is worked by the power of omnipotence which is the common factor in Calvin's doctrines of predestination and providence; this accounts for their treatment in the same chapter of the *Institutes* through all the editions from 1539 to 1554. The ordination of events in both categories derives from this all-controlling power in God the Creator. The inclusion of a discussion of providence in the treatise, *Concerning the Eternal Predestination of God*, indicates this link also; significantly, the full title runs, "Concerning the Eternal Predestination of God by Which He Has Chosen Some to Salvation While Consigning Others to Their Own Destruction; and also concerning the Providence by Which He Governs Human Affairs."[49] Thus, the logic of a mutual presupposition is invoked again: while the predestination and preservation of the elect is the heart of Calvin's doctrine of providence (and its point of noetic access), the efficacy and certainty of such an eternal election depends on the omnipotence of the provident God.

It needs to be said, however, that Calvin's concept of *Deus absconditus* is distinct from a concept of *Deus nudus*. While God's providential will is hidden, this fact ought not to be a source of terror to the believer for God's power can never be separated from God's justice.[50] Calvin emphatically rejects the nominalist conception that as well as possessing an "ordinary" power of omnipotence (*potentia ordinata*), God has an absolute power (*potentia absoluta*), that is, one that is unlimited by considerations of justice and covenant-keeping. This would mean that God might possess two wills, so that lying behind the revealed will of God there could be an utterly unknown, capricious, even malevolent will. Though there is nothing higher to which the will of God might be bound, God's own justice is integral to the divine being and will. God is faithful and acts in an integrity of will which, although hidden from us, is utterly trustworthy.[51]

Thus, from knowledge of divine providence "appears the immeasurable felicity of the godly mind" (*Inst.* I.17.10) and "the highest blessedness lies in the knowledge of it." (*Inst.* I.17.1). Inviting us to ponder how different was the sixteenth-century ethos from our own, John Dillenberger offers an instructive observation on this effect of belief in providence:

> The notion that God controls all things, as Calvin delineated it in his concept of Providence under the knowledge of God the Creator and in Predestination under the knowledge of God the Redeemer, was the positive rock of consolation to the believer. That it should be an oppressive idea had hardly entered the level of consciousness, certainly not for Luther and Calvin, believing as they did that powers, not man's freedom, controlled the world. [52]

Providence and Secondary Causality

Integral to Calvin's definition of providence is its character as chance-excluding. "For if every success is God's blessing, and calamity and adversity his curse, no place now remains in human affairs for fortune or chance."[53] Thus, although it is permissible to speak of contingency as respects future events (in common speech), these events do not fall out fortuitously but according to "the secret stirring of God's hand." (*Inst.* I.16.9)

Calvin's definition of providence as excluding chance and authentic contingency would seem to render a notion of secondary causality unlikely in his theology. However, he does allow it a restricted place, since providence "is the determinative principle of all things in such a way that sometimes it works through an intermediary, sometimes without an intermediary, sometimes contrary to every intermediary." (*Inst.* I.17.1) Thus, "God's providence does not always meet us in its naked form, but God in a sense clothes it with the means employed." (*Inst.* I.17.4) What Calvin refuses to countenance is any concept of secondary causation implying an autonomous cause-and-effect series or casting the slightest shadow on the ceaseless primary causality of God.[54]

A theological account of secondary causality is important on at least two counts for Calvin. First, common human experience is aware of laws immanent in the order of nature according to which events evidently take place, and this can scarcely be denied. Calvin's response is to claim secondary causation as an instrumentality under divine direction. Thus he attributes the fecundity of the earth to natural factors like the shining of the sun, while maintaining the primary causality of God: "The First Cause is self-sufficient and intermediate and secondary causes have only what they borrow from the First Cause . . . God acts through creatures, not as if he needed external help, but because it was his pleasure."[55] Commenting on the function of the creaturely elements employed in the Lord's Supper, he observes: "God uses means and instruments which he himself sees to be expedient...yet neither bread, nor sun, nor fire, is anything save in so far as he distributes his blessings to us by these instruments." (*Inst.* IV.14.12) With regard to pastoral leadership in the church also, God presumably could bring about conversion directly; yet employs the instruments of preaching and teaching to do so. (*Inst.* II.5.4, 5) Faith itself is something real and indispensable in the ordering of our life by God and as such possesses essential instrumentality, "For who is such a fool as to assert that God moves man just as we throw a stone?" (*Inst.* II.5.14) On the other hand, in faith "believers act passively," since it is God who is at work in them and who supplies their capacity for faith. (*Inst.* II.5.11)

The significance of Calvin's teaching on secondary causation extends also to human attitudes about future events. Belief in providence does not excuse us from taking counsel or from the responsibility of securing our own safety, and a godly mind will take advantage of every instrument offered by God.

> Since God manifests his power through means and inferior causes, it is not to be separated from them. It would be foolish to think that, because God has decreed what is future, all care and endeavour on our part is rendered superfluous. If there was anything

> that we must do, he prescribed it, and wills us to be the instruments of his power.[56]

The concept of secondary causality is important enough for Calvin to ascribe to Christ the providence directing inferior causes. Predictably enough, this ascription is made with respect to his power as the creative Word:

> It must always be remembered that the world does not properly stand by any other power than that of the Word of God, that secondary causes derive their power from him, and that they have different effects as they are directed. Thus the world was established on the waters, but they had no power of themselves, but were rather subject to the Word of God as an inferior element. [57]

A conception of secondary causality is also required for a second reason—lest humans seek to excuse their sin and guilt on account of God's ordination of all events. "Man while he is acted upon by God, yet at the same time himself acts." (*Inst.* I.18.2) A paradox emerges in which evil deeds done by human rebellion and obstinacy are at the same time righteous works of God.[58] In so far as humans willingly choose to do what God has ordained, we sin necessarily but without compulsion. Without such an implied distinction and the assertion of human volition as the "inferior cause" of human acts, responsibility for wrongdoing could not be attributed to human agents.

Calvin's qualified use of secondary causality is nowhere of more interest than in the christological discussion with which he ends Book II of the 1559 edition of the *Institutes*. Here, according to the chapter title, he defends the proposition that "Christ rightly and properly [is] said to have merited God's grace and salvation for us." But how can Christ be said to have merited our salvation when its cause is God's good pleasure? In order to take into account both the free mercy of God and the obedience offered voluntarily by Christ, Calvin employs the conceptuality of secondary causation.

So that God's sovereign grace is not obscured, Calvin avers: "In discussing Christ's merit, we do not consider the beginning of merit to be in him, but we go back to God's ordinance, the first cause. God solely of his own good pleasure appointed him Mediator to obtain salvation for us."(*Inst.* II.17.1) He goes on to say: "By his obedience, however, Christ truly acquired and merited grace for us with the Father."

> I take it to be a commonplace that if Christ made satisfaction for our sins, if he paid the penalty owed by us, if he appeased God by his obedience—in short, if as a righteous man he suffered for unrighteous men—

> then he acquired salvation for us by his righteousness, which is tantamount to deserving it. (*Inst.* II.17.3)

Thus with respect to human salvation "we see how God's love holds first place, as the highest cause or origin; how faith in Christ follows this as the second and proximate cause."[59]

Might this mean that Calvin derives his understanding of secondary causality on a christological basis? Christ's voluntary obedience would then represent a revelatory point from which Calvin developed his conception of human instrumentality under divine ordination. This is scarcely likely, for in his other discussions of secondary causality he does not adduce what would be the paradigmatic case of the merit of Christ. On the contrary, there is much more to be said for the case that Calvin is simply applying to christology a general principle identified in the course of his discussion of providence. He draws on the intelligibility inhering in the creative and providential work of God to sort out the complexity of the question of Christ's merit.

HUMAN NATURE AS CREATED: THE *"IMAGO DEI"*

In expounding the concept of the *imago Dei* in humanity, Calvin employs a favourite image: "Man represents as in a mirror the wisdom, righteousness and goodness of God."[60] "Adam was at first created in the image of God so that he might reflect, as in a mirror, the righteousness of God."[61] By their marvellous lineaments all God's works point to the glory of their Maker. Humans, however, are the most sharply focussed instance of this reflecting capacity and Calvin agrees that a human being "is deservedly called by the ancients, microcosmos, 'a world in miniature'."[62] "Above all other creatures he is a proof of the glory of God, full of countless miracles as he is."[63]

As straightforward as the above sentences seem, a significant question arises as to the manner in which humanity is said to reflect the glory of God. Is it by virtue of endowments which belong to humankind by nature or by virtue of a relationship with God which depends upon God's continuing gracious initiative and the quality of our response to that initiative? The former approach results in an ontological definition of human nature in which the categories of creation predominate. The latter results in a relational definition in which Jesus Christ is central as the One who restores and perfects the creation. Both appear in Calvin's thought and represent respectively the sapiential and evangelical dimensions of his doctrine of humanity.

The Dynamic-Relational Definition

T. F. Torrance's study, *Calvin's Doctrine of Man*, is notable for its insistence that the *imago Dei* in Calvin's thought denotes a dynamic relationship rather than an ontological state. Apprehending Calvin's metaphor of the mirror on a literal basis, Torrance argues that the attribution of the *imago* to humanity is dependent on God's continued willingness to behold the divine glory in humans, and, in a subordinate sense, upon humanity's "active response to the Will of God and to the Word of God."[64] Thus, for example, Calvin says, "God's children are pleasing and lovable to him, since he sees in them the marks and features of his own countenance." (*Inst.* III.17.5) The *imago Dei* therefore does not denote "a static quiddity but a dynamic relation."[65]

The character of the *imago* is dynamic in the further sense that the disfigurement of human nature by sin prevents us from perceiving the *imago* directly in anything but a refracted sense. "Even though we grant that God's image was not totally annihilated and destroyed in him, yet it was so corrupted that whatever remains is frightful deformity." This means that the image of God "can be nowhere better recognized than from the restoration of [humanity's] corrupted nature." Thus, the *imago* can only be understood aright when its eschatological and teleological character is taken into account. "In some part it [the *imago*] is now manifest in the elect, in so far as they have been reborn in the Spirit; but it will attain to its full splendour in heaven." (*Inst.* I.15.4)

The *imago* understood eschatologically is also the *imago* understood christologically, since, until the eschaton, there is only one instance in which its content is visible as unrefracted and that is in the humanity of Jesus Christ. "Now we see how Christ is the most perfect image of God; if we are conformed to it, we are so restored that with true piety, righteousness, purity and intelligence we bear God's image." (*Inst.* I.15.4) In the perfect obedience of his humanity, Christ provides us with the only example of the intact *imago* and also, through his redemptive power, the means by which we may be restored to that image.

This transformation into the image of Christ is the actual means of the recovery of the image of God. "For we now begin to bear the image of Christ and we are daily being transformed into it more and more, but that image depends upon spiritual regeneration."[66] "Therefore, the only way we can enter into the Kingdom of Christ is by Christ's renewing us according to his own image."[67] The transformation into the image of Christ induces not only gratitude for God's benevolence in redemption but also the renewed capacity to enjoy God's beneficence in creation. The elect are restored not only for the sake of sanctification but also "so that we may enjoy the whole world with God's blessing."[68]

Does the achievement of the *imago Dei* through conformity to the image of Christ imply that humans were created in the image of the humanity of Christ? To adopt such an interpretation would be to ignore Calvin's own explicit statements to the contrary.[69] Moreover, at least two problems would arise if it were held that humanity was created in the image of Christ. First, the meaning of regeneration as conformity to Christ would be obscured: manifestly, only the elect are in the process of being conformed to Christ; accordingly, to maintain that the "image of God" is equivalent to the "image of Christ" would imply a universal salvation, since all humans are created in God's image. Second, to adopt this position would be to ascribe to Adam certain properties which belong only to the humanity of Christ, including possession of the life-giving Spirit and an "inspired" body.[70] Therefore, while Calvin denies that humans are created in the image of Christ's humanity, he is still able to affirm that they are created in the image of God whose true content and *raison d'être* becomes manifest only in Christ.

Calvin's fundamental insight is that regeneration is the restoration of the *imago Dei*. At times, Calvin assays the original condition of Adam as so favourable that he "would have passed into heaven without death and without injury"[71] and "there would have been no separation of the soul from the body, no corruption, no kind of destruction, and, in short, no violent change."[72] However, the fact that the recovery of the image comes through Christ's redemptive work and incarnate image means that the resultant state is in an improvement on the original condition of rectitude. "There is a richer measure of grace in regeneration." (*Inst.* I.15.4) "For his [God's] grace is more abundantly poured forth, through Christ, upon the world, than it was imparted to Adam in the beginning."[73] In what does this richer measure of grace consist?

Calvin's view seems to be that in the transformation into Christ's image, humans are not only restored but "perfected" through a constancy integral to a celestial existence:

> Man became a living soul....Paul makes an antithesis between this living soul and the quickening spirit which Christ confers upon the faithful (I Cor. 15.45), for no other purpose than to teach us that the state of man was not perfected in Adam; but it is a peculiar benefit conferred by Christ, that we may be renewed to a life which is celestial, whereas before the fall of Adam, man's life was only earthly, seeing it had no firm and settled constancy.[74]

This lack of constancy in human nature as created appears to be the vulnerability to an alteration of faith arising from creaturely limitation: "When Adam was not yet perverted and he persisted in the state and condition in which he had been created, it happened that he was both hot and cold, and that he had to endure anxieties and fears and like things."[75] Only the perfection of human nature through Christ will finally put humans beyond the risk of defection from God.

Even Adam's original immortality was qualified. This immortality, being a supernatural rather than a natural gift, remained conditional upon the actual bestowing of the gift according to God's good pleasure; Adam did not possess it either by nature or by right. Hence, his life, blessed though it was through the harmony of natural powers and the expectation of immortality, still awaited a perfecting power. In Christ alone can humans possess the gift of eternal life, and, therefore truly be immortal: "Believers are said never to die because their souls, in that they are born of incorruptible seed, have Christ dwelling in them, by whom they are continually quickened . . . "[76] It is the perpetual power of Christ indwelling believers that chiefly distinguishes them from Adam. "The condition which we acquire through Christ is far better than the situation of the first man, because a living soul was given to Adam for himself and for his posterity, but Christ, on the other hand, has brought us the Spirit who is Life."[77]

Commenting on the "more" in regeneration as "consciousness of the continuous energy of the Spirit," Ralph C. Hancock offers a summary statement of the dynamic-relational interpretation of Calvin's doctrine of the *imago*:

> Order is not a perfected condition of intelligible being but a consciousness of perpetual becoming. The active and fluid energy of the Spirit is not merely the agent of the process of the restoration of order; it is the basis of order itself, for order is a process. That is why the process of regeneration is not only the restoration of order but an enrichment of order: it is an enhancement of consciousness of the power of the Spirit through the Spirit's confrontation with the flesh—that is, with human self-assertion.[78]

The Static-Ontological Conception

Calvin clearly does maintain that we are in the image of God in so far as we are in a relationship of continued dependence upon divine grace. But he also asserts, especially in the context of his doctrine of the creation, that humans bear the image of God as possessing characteristics distinguishing us from all other creatures and belonging to our nature as such. The *imago Dei* thus pertains not only to the category of relation but also to that of being.

Calvin repeatedly refers to God engraving the divine image upon the human soul:

> Three gradations, indeed, are to be noted in the creation of man; that his dead body was formed out of the dust of the earth; that it was endued with a soul, whence it should receive vital motion; and that on this soul God engraved (*insculpsit*) his own image, to which immortality is annexed.[79]

At *Comm. Gen.* 9.6, Calvin explains the heinous nature of murder as owing to the fact that humans "bear the image of God engraven (*insculptam*) upon them." Again he writes that "the many pre-eminent gifts with which the human mind is endowed proclaim that something divine has been engraved (*insculptum*) upon it." (*Inst.* I.15.2) "The image of God is impressed on us to the degree that we have intelligence and reason, that we distinguish between good and evil, and that humans are born to a certain order, a certain society among them."[80]

The crucial distinguishing mark of the human soul is that it is "joined with the light of understanding." (*Inst.* I.15.4) Differentiating the soul from the life-principle common to all creatures is "the light of understanding and reason."[81] It is with regard to our reason that humans are actually like God: "All mortal men, without distinction, are called 'sons' because they resemble God in mind and intelligence."[82] Referring to the unseemly attempt to make visual representations of the deity, Calvin asserts that "the mind of man is the true image of him."[83]

With respect to his ontological definition, Calvin's concept of the *imago* bears strong affinity to medieval teaching. Aquinas refers the *imago Dei* in humanity to the fact that "he is intelligent and free to judge and master of himself."[84] According to Aquinas, human nature as intact is characterized by a harmony of subordination in which reason is the indispensable intermediate moment: "The rightness of the original state was such that the reason was submissive to God and the lower powers to reason. Now all that the virtues are is a set of perfections by which the reason is directed to God and the lower powers are managed to the standard of reason."[85] Again, he describes the condition of integrity as existing when "what is highest in man is subject to God and the lower parts of his soul are subject to what is highest in him."[86] In the harmony resulting from this proper subordination of inferior to superior, even the body and its appetites are included; original justice "not only kept the lower powers of the soul in subjection to reason, without any disorder, but kept the whole body in subjection to the soul without any defect."[87]

Although Calvin's estimate of the damage inflicted by sin upon the *imago* is more radical, his definition of the original rectitude in humanity is scarcely inimical to that of Aquinas:

> Therefore by this word the perfection of our whole nature is designated, as it appeared when Adam was endued with a right judgment, had affections in harmony with reason, had all his senses sound and well-regulated, and truly excelled in everything good . . . In the mind perfect intelligence flourished and reigned, uprightness attended as its companion, and all the senses were prepared and moulded for due obedience to reason; and in the body there was a suit-

> able correspondence with this internal order. (*Inst.* I.15.4)

Again, at *Inst.* I.15.3, he says:

> The integrity with which Adam was endowed is expressed by this word, when he had full possession of right understanding, when he had his affections kept within the bounds of reason, all his senses tempered in right order, and he truly referred his excellence to exceptional gifts bestowed upon him by his Maker.

"When God created man, he implanted emotions in him, but emotions which were obedient and submissive to reason."[88]

Moreover, Calvin can define the perfection of Christ's humanity in just such terms. What impresses him at *Comm. Jn.* 11.33 is not the strong and positive obedience by which Christ enters fully into our humanity, but an essentially negative quality, namely, the avoidance of sin and immoderation. "...No passion of his ever went beyond its proper bounds. He had none that was not right and founded on reason and sound judgment."

Reformed definitions more consonant with the spirit of Aquinas would be difficult to imagine. At their heart is the fitting subjection of all parts of the soul, of the senses, and of the body, to the rule of reason. Order, far from being synonymous with process, is an expression of hierarchical placement and a bulwark against deviation from divine standards. In a pertinent discourse at *Comm. Eph.* 1.8, Calvin interprets the "recapitulation" accomplished by Christ as a reduction of the chaotic to divinely mandated stability:

> To my mind, Paul wants to teach that outside Christ all things were upset, but that through him they have been reduced to order.... The proper state of creatures is to cleave to God. Such an *anakephalaiosis* as would bring us back to the regular order, the apostle tells us, has been made in Christ.

Nonetheless, one clause in the quotation from *Inst.* I.15.3 is worthy of closer attention: "he truly referred his excellence to exceptional gifts bestowed upon him by his Maker." This clause has resonance with the dynamic conception of the image of God in that a response on the part of believing humanity is integral to it. Indeed, Calvin on occasion speaks of the capacity for worship as the distinguishing characteristic of human nature. "It is worship alone that renders men higher than the brutes, and through it alone they aspire to immortality." (*Inst.* I.3.3)

However, Calvin is not contradicting himself in these statements since he regards divine worship as the principal and proper use of reason. "Why are men endowed with reason and intellect," he asks, "except for the purpose of recognizing their Creator?"[89] Humanity is endowed with reason precisely in order that we, among all creatures, might recognize God's glory in the world and thus be led to praise God. "And there is certainly nothing more absurd than for men to be ignorant of their Creator, when they have been endowed with intelligence to be exercised most of all in this way."[90] "Hence the more anyone endeavours to approach to God, the more he proves himself endowed with reason." (*Inst.* I.15.6) In brief, human intelligence is ordered to the knowledge of God.[91]

By the endowment of understanding, humanity not only is raised above the level of animation common to living creatures, but also is able to recognize (at least in the unfallen state) that it is the eternal Son who is the author of so unrivalled a blessing. The self-conscious reflection of reason should lead it to attribute its origin to the instrumental author of creation: "Since this light streamed forth to us from the Word its source, it should be a mirror in which we may see clearly the divine power of the Word."[92]

In Calvin's recognition of the theonomous nature of *intelligentia*, the relational and ontological aspects of the image of God coincide. While one might choose to regard these aspects as essentially oppositional, Calvin does not seem to: for him they represent the complementarity existing between being and relation, intellect and piety.[93] That which belongs to human nature as created has been distorted by sin; nonetheless, what was once engraved by God's hand is still graciously preserved amid the ruin by God. The full recovery of the *imago* can come about only through the progress of sanctification into the image of Christ; yet that recovery will include the restoration to integrity of humanity's original nature.

The Incursion of Sin and the Preserving Influence of Common Grace

A sense of equivocation attaches to theological description of human nature after the fall. On the one hand, the desperate condition of humanity as alienated from God cannot be understated, and in this respect Calvin speaks of the *imago Dei* as obliterated (*obliterata*) in Adam.[94] He approves "the common opinion of the schools," deriving from Augustine, that through the fall, our natural gifts were corrupted and the supernatural ones stripped away. (*Inst.* II.2.12) He complains, however, that scarcely one person in a hundred has an inkling of the ruinous condition in which this leaves humans. (*Inst.* II.2.4) The corruption of our natural powers means that human nature as such has been vitiated in the fall, including the essential faculties of mind and heart. On the other hand, the account of our fallen condition cannot imply the abolition of our humanity and so Calvin speaks of the *imago* as corrupted (*corruptam*) but not destroyed. [95] Although Calvin speaks of the destruction of the *imago*, he means, more accurately, the destruction of its integrity.

> Since reason, therefore, by which man distinguishes between good and evil, and by which he understands and judges is a natural gift, it could not be completely wiped out; but it was partly weakened and partly corrupted, so that its misshapen ruins appear.[96]

Inalienable to the human condition, therefore, are certain "distinguished endowments which clearly manifest that men were formed after the image of God, and created to the hope of a blessed and immortal life."[97] These natural endowments do not persist in humanity, however, any longer by nature, as they once did, but by God's grace. "For if he had not spared us, our fall would have entailed the destruction of our whole nature." (*Inst.* II.2.17) This is the threshold of Calvin's notion of a "common grace"; it is common because it extends to all generally, and it is grace because it is the gratuitous continuance of divine providence in the face of human ingratitude and rebellion. It is a grace that presupposes the event of the fall and yet focuses on the preservation of human nature (compromised by sin though it is) rather than on its redemption. God not only continues to provide, but also graciously preserves, the gifts and norms of natural life among all without distinction.

The actual phrase, *generalem dei gratiam*, occurs at *Inst.* II.2.17 as a summary statement of the preceding five sections.[98] The concept of a common grace serves to explain how notable human abilities continue to flourish despite the radical corruption predicated of the fall. Calvin's purpose is also to reclaim the apparently secular realm of human achievement as another realm of God's undeserved gifts and sovereign grace.[99] Pondering the contribution of the classical philosophers, Calvin counsels, "Let that admirable light of truth shining in them teach us that the mind of man, though fallen and perverted from its wholeness, is nevertheless clothed and ornamented with God's excellent gifts." (*Inst.* II.2.15) This endowment of excellence includes the search for truth, the innate sense of political economy by which society is preserved, and the liberal arts and manual skills by which life is ennobled and adorned.[100]

While human knowledge without illumination by the Holy Spirit is inevitably perverse and counter-productive in its attempt to know God, its exercise in pursuit of earthly knowledge is actually empowered by the Spirit. "If we regard the Spirit of God as the sole fountain of truth, we shall neither reject the truth itself, nor despise it wherever it shall appear, unless we wish to dishonour the Spirit of God." (*Inst.* II.2.15) The essential office of the Spirit is the conversion of people to Christ, a redemptive office exercised only on behalf of the elect. Nonetheless, the Spirit also quickens all things "according to the character bestowed upon each kind by the law of creation." (*Inst.* II.2.16) Rejecting alike the options of dismissing the insight of secular authors or maintaining a standard of double truth, Calvin avers that truth is one: "For since all truth is of God, if any ungodly man has said anything true, we should not reject it, for it also has come from God."[101]

As an extension of the concept of common grace, Calvin takes into account the "special graces" which distinguish individual statesmen, authors and artists who make extraordinary contributions to human culture. These specific abilities are also "common" since they are bestowed indiscriminately upon the pious and impious alike.[102] The excellence of these gifts points beyond their possessors to the Giver and the Giver's continuing grace. "Let us, accordingly, learn by their example how many gifts the Lord left to human nature even after it was despoiled ue good." (*Inst.* II.2.15)

Calvin's teaching on common grace constitutes an interesting facet of his theology since it is an explicit instance in which the spheres of creation and redemption overlap. It portrays the renewal of providence in response to the event and effect of the fall, and therefore is linked to God's work in redemption more directly than the bulk of Calvin's discussion under the knowledge of God the Creator. Nevertheless its focus is not on the redemption (full restoration) of the natural order but its preservation (in the compromised estate in which wheat and tares grow together).

Karl Barth has insisted, against Emil Brunner, that there is no special, preserving grace distinct from the one grace of God in Jesus Christ:

> We could agree that the grace of Jesus Christ includes the patience with which God again and again gives us time for repentance and for the practice of perseverance, the patience by which he upholds and preserves man and his world, not for his own sake but for the sake of Christ, for the sake of the Church, for the sake of the elect children of God. [103]

But again, one may ask whether it need be a matter of mutual exclusivity, the preservation of actual existence for the purpose either of salvation or of the continuance of "natural" gifts. While preservation for the sake of the ingathering of all the elect is Calvin's paramount consideration, this does not exclude the ancillary and complementary purpose of the expression and enjoyment of the good gifts of creation.

CONCLUSION

In his discussion at *Comm. Gen.* 2.9, Calvin establishes the significance of the tree of life as an inescapable reminder that humanity lives in constant dependence on its Creator. "Life is not (as they commonly speak) an intrinsic good, but proceeds from God." This statement might be an ensign over all that he says about the work of God in creation and providence: life is not an intrinsic good. Its value arises from its origin in God and it achieves its *raison d'être* when creatures know and praise their Maker.

In his consideration of the doctrines belonging to the knowledge of God the Creator, Calvin attempts to honour the goodness in life deriving from God by steering a middle way between two extremes. One extreme would be to embrace life and expound its purpose as if there were no ugly scar of rebellion and ingratitude across its face. The other would be to dismiss the excellence of the divine gift and the continued work of the Giver by treating the scar as a fatal blow. Life and life in its fulness are not antithetical, but complementary, concepts for Calvin.

Wise enough to embrace both sapiential and evangelical approaches in his thought, Calvin makes room in his doctrines of the creation for: the *Logos* who orders existence and its intelligibility, and the Word incarnate through whom alone life reaches its goal; the providence which preserves all life, even after the perfidy of human sin, and the providence which especially guards the community of the elect; a humanity which bears God's image as qualities of excellence engraved by a loving hand, and a humanity which can truly mirror God's excellence and goodness only as remade in the image of Christ.

On occasion Calvin's sharp distinction between Christ's powers as the creative Word and as the incarnate Mediator leads him to distinguish between the two natures on a preferential basis. Because he views the person of Christ as the presupposition rather than the result of the *unio personalis*, it is as important (if not more important) for him to guard Christ's transcendence as the eternal Word beyond the flesh (*verus Deus*) as to affirm the eternal appointment of Christ to assume our human nature (*verus homo*). While this sapiential tendency is justified as an expression of the way in which creation attests its origin and intelligibility in the *Logos*, the reserve and even reluctance with which Calvin approaches the earthly flesh of Christ—the truly human Jesus—is not.

We turn now to consideration of the epistemological significance of the created order in Calvin's thought.

NOTES

1. *Comm. Gen.* 3.14.
2. *Comm. Jn.* 13.31.
3. *Comm. Col.* 1.18.
4. In *Calvin's Doctrine of the Church*, Benjamin Milner finds the underlying unity of Calvin's theology in the continuum, original order of creation/

disorder of the fall/restoration of order in Christ. On this basis there emerges "the centrality of Calvin's doctrine of the church for his theology as a whole: since the church is the restoration of order in the world." (193f.) Milner also stresses the pneumatological dimension of Calvin's thought specifically as he sees Calvin correlating the work of the Spirit with the *ordinatio dei* objectively expressed in revelation. (44.)

5. *Comm. Eph.* 4.24.

6. *Comm. Eph.* 1.8.

7. Eugene Portalié, *A Guide to the Thought of Saint Augustine*, 132f.

8. *Inst.* I.13.18. At *Comm. I Cor.* 8.6, he writes, "For Paul wished to ascribe a common activity to the Father and the Son, yet maintaining the distinction, which is appropriate to the Persons. Therefore he says that we subsist in the Father, and we do so through the Son; for the Father is indeed the source of all existence, but as we cleave to him through the Son, so he pours out the power of being into us through him alone."

9. Shortly after the appearance of the first edition of the *Institutes*, Peter Caroli, then minister of Lausanne, accused Calvin and Farel of complicity with Arianism. The Council of Bern to whom he appealed, however, cleared the Genevan reformers and deposed Caroli.

10. *Comm. Heb.* 1.2.

11. *Comm. Jn.* 14.28.

12. *Comm. I Jn.* 1.1.

13. *Comm. Ps.* 33.6. See also *Comm. Phil.* 2.7.

14. *Comm. Jn.* 5.17.

15. *Comm. Phil* 3.21.

16. These include: *Contre la secte phantastique et furieuse des Libertines qui se nomment spirituelz* (*CO*, 7, 186; 187; 190 respectively); *Concerninq the Eternal Predestination of God*, trans. by J. K. S. Reid, 164f., and *Comm. Jn.* 5.17.

17. *Concerning the Eternal Predestination of God*, trans. by J. K. S. Reid, 164f.

18. *Comm. Gen.* "Argument," 64.

19. *Concerning the Eternal Predestination of God,* trans. by J. K. S. Reid, 164. See also *Comm. Ps.* 115.3.

20. *Comm. I Jn.* 4.9.

21. *Comm. Ps.* 8.6.

22. *Comm. Jer.* 9.24. See also, e.g., statements at *Comm. Acts* 17.26; *Inst.* I.3.3; *Comm. Ps.* 89.47; and *Comm. Deut.* 13.12.

23. *Comm. Ps.* 115.17.

24. "For inasmuch as [Christ] had pre-existence as a saving Being, it was necessary that what might be saved should also be called into existence, in order that the Being who saves should not exist in vain." "Against the Heresies," III.22.3, in Alexander Roberts and James Donaldson, eds., *The Ante-Nicene Fathers*, I, 455.

25. "Sermon Twenty-seven on the First Book of Timothy" (3.16). *CO* 53, 320.

26. *Opus Oxoniense* I, d.17, q.3, n.31.

27. *Reportata Parisiensia* III, d.7, q. 4, n.5.

28. *Rep. Paris.* I, d.41, q.1, n.1.

29. *ST*, *IIIa*.1.3.

30. *Summa Theologiae*, *Ia IIae*. 1.8.

31. *The God Question in Thomas Aquinas and Martin Luther*, 33.

32. "Reply to Sadolet," in J.K.S. Reid, trans., *Calvin: Theological Treatises*, 228.

33. Letter 3664 in *CO* 19, 201. This translation is by Jean-Daniel Benoit, "Calvin the Letter-Writer," in G. E. Duffield, ed., *John Calvin*, 87.

34. *Comm. Eph.* 1.4.

35. *Comm. Gen.* 2.2. See also *Comm. Ps.* 104.29.

36. *Comm. Jn.* 1.4.

37. *Comm. Jn.* 6.11.

38. *Comm. Matt.* 28.18.

39. *Comm. I Cor.* 8.6.

40. This question the second-generation Lutherans answered in the affirmative, maintaining that Christ as human had this power but refrained from its exercise (Chemnitz) or else concealed his exercise of it (Brenz).

41. *Comm. Jn.* 5.27.

42. *Comm. Jn.* 5.22.

43. This is an important aspect of the thesis of Marvin Hoogland in *Calvin's Perspective on the Exaltation of Christ in Comparison with the Post-Reformation Doctrine of the Two States*. Hoogland maintains that Calvin is actually closer to the teaching of the Lutherans and of Karl Barth than to the Reformed positions fully developed after Calvin. See especially 110-5, 206, 209-12.

44. *Comm. Ps.* 2.8.

45. *Comm. Ps.* 37.9.

46. *Comm. Ps.* 37.1.

47. *CO* 1, 63 (*Institutio*, 1536).

48. *LW* 26, 95.

49. *De Aeterna Dei Praedestione Qua in Salutem Alios ex Hominibus Elegit: Alios Suo Exitio Reliquit: Item de Providentia Qua Res Humanas Gubernat*. *CO* 8, 249f.

50. *Inst.* I.17.2. See also *Comm. Gen.* 18.14 and *Comm. Rom.* 3.6.

51. H. A. Oberman, *The Harvest of Medieval Theology*, 63, points out that Calvin's concept of omnipotent will differs radically from that of the nominalists: "With Calvin the *potentia absoluta* does not indicate what God could have done but what he actually does (*Inst.* I.17.2). For Calvin, the *potentia* (or *voluntas*) *absoluta* is not the realm of *Deus exlex* but of God's rule *etiam extra legem*; it is *'ius mundi regendi nobis incognitum'*...God's rule *per legem* and the rule *etiam extra legem* are both to the same extent an expression of his very being, his power, and his justice."

52. John Dillenberger, ed., *John Calvin: Selections from His Writings*, from the Introduction, 17.

53. *Inst.* I.16.8. See also, e.g., *Comm. Ps.* 115.3.

54. *Inst.* I.17.6. E. Gilson, *The Spirit of Medieval Philosophy*, 376, observes that the medievals gradually developed a concept of nature as possessing "the character of an intelligible created order" through consideration of the function of secondary causes, "until at last with St. Thomas and Duns Scotus the doctrinal development attains its term. Nature is henceforth defined as the order of second causes willed by God." T. F. Torrance, *Calvin's Doctrine of Man*, 29, overstates the degree to which the Reformer contests the medieval position when he says: "For Calvin, all secondary causation is highly suspicious, and has no real place in theology." Charles Partee, *Calvin and Classical Philos-*

ophy, 78, errs in his assertion that Calvin's exaltation of the comprehensive will of God leads him to deny secondary causation.

55. *Comm. Gen.* 1.11.

56. *Concerning the Eternal Predestination of God*, trans. by J.K.S. Reid, 170f.

57. *Comm. II Pet.* 3.5. In his commentary on Genesis, Calvin sees the tree of life in the garden as an assertion of the continual dependence of humanity on God. Calvin's agreement with Augustine that "the tree of life was a figure of Christ" is based on the premise, "inasmuch as he is the eternal Word." *Comm. Gen.* 2.9.

58. *Inst.* I.17.5. See also *Inst.* I.18.3, 4.

59. *Inst.* II.17.2. In *A Life of John Calvin*, Alister McGrath argues that Calvin aligned himself with the medieval voluntarist tradition (and against Luther) that "the merit of Christ's death depended on the value God chose to assign to it, rather than on its intrinsic merit." (163.) However, Calvin's use of the dialectic of secondary causality at II.17 suggests that he wanted to have it both ways and believed he had found the means.

60. *Comm. Col.* 3.10.

61. *Comm. Eph.* 4.24.

62. *Comm. Gen.* 1.26.

63. *Comm. Acts* 17.27.

64. T. F. Torrance, *Calvin's Doctrine of Man*, 39, 54f., 64.

65. Ronald Wallace, *Calvin's Doctrine of the Christian Life*, 105.

66. *Comm. I Cor.* 15.49.

67. *Comm. I Cor.* 15.50.

68. *Comm. Heb.* 2.5.

69. Thus Calvin writes at *Comm. Gen.* 1.26: "It is also truly said that Christ is the only image of the Father, but yet these words of Moses do not bear the interpretation that 'in the image' means 'in Christ'." See also *Inst.* II.12.6.

70. See Richard Prins, "The Image of God in Adam and the Restoration of Man in Jesus Christ," *Scottish Journal of Theology*, 27, (1972), 43f.

71. *Comm. Gen.* 2.16.

72. *Comm. Gen.* 3.19. Thomas Aquinas, *ST*, *Ia.* 97.1, asks, "Would man in the state of innocence have been immortal?" and answers affirmatively. "Not indeed that his body had some inherent sap of immortality to make it imperishable, but that his soul was equipped by God with a supernatural force capable of preserving the body from all decay, as long as it remained submissive to God himself."

73. *Comm. Gen.* 3.7.

74. *Comm. Gen.* 2.7.

75. "First Sermon on the Passion of Our Lord Jesus Christ," *CO* 46, 839.

76. *Comm. Jn.* 11.26.

77. *Comm. I Cor.* 15.45.

78. Ralph C. Hancock, *Calvin and the Foundation of Modern Politics*, 161.

79. *Comm. Gen.* 2.7.

80. In "Sermon on Job 10.7-15," *CO* 33, 489. See also *Comm. Acts* 17.27,29.

81. *Comm. I Cor.* 15.45.

82. *Comm. Acts* 17.28.

83. *Comm. Acts* 17.22.
84. *ST*, *Ia IIae.*, Prologue.
85. *ST*, *Ia.* 95.3.
86. *Ia IIae.* 113.1.
87. *ST*, *Ia IIae.* 85.5. See also *Ia.* 97.1.
88. *Comm. Jn.* 11.33.
89. *Comm. Heb.* 11.3.
90. *Comm. Acts* 17.27.
91. Edward Dowey observes that in Calvin's theology "religion, whether true or false, is co-extensive with beings who know"; accordingly, "all knowledge is theonomous." *The Knowledge of God in Calvin's Theology*, 22.
92. *Comm. Jn.* 1.4.
93. A further example of the difficulty of attributing to Calvin a purely eschatological-christological definition of the *imago* is to be found in the fact that the Reformer does not uniformly identify the process of the progressive transformation of the elect with "the image of Christ." At *Comm. II Cor.* 3.18, for example, transformation "into the same image" is interpreted by Calvin to mean transformation into the image of God.
94. *Inst.* II.1.5. See also *Comm. Gen.* 3.1.
95. E. g., at *Inst.* II. 1.9.
96. *Inst.* II.2.12. The complexity of assessing the damage of sin exists in the writing of the medievals as well as in Calvin's. Aquinas, for instance, distinguishes between "the constitutive principles" of human nature and the actual "inclination to virtue" in humanity. "The constitution of human nature is neither destroyed nor diminished by sin," but "the natural inclination to virtue, finally, is diminished by sin." (*ST*, *Ia IIae.* 85.1.) Such a distinction is necessary since "a man would not be able to sin without his rational nature." (*ST*, *Ia IIae*, 85.2.) "The natural inclination to virtue remains even in the damned, who would not otherwise feel the remorse of conscience." (*ST*, *Ia IIae.* 85.2*ad* 3.) The connatural powers which constitute humans as human remain undiminished, but our ability to direct these powers aright is affected since the adventitious inclination to sin blocks the natural inclination to virtue. For Aquinas, the effect of original sin upon human nature is a corruption in the specific sense that a derangement of the powers of human nature is the consequence of the withdrawal of the gift of supernatural harmony.
97. *Comm. Ps.* 8.5.
98. H. Kuiper, in *Calvin on Common Grace*, locates variants of the phrase four times in the commentaries, but these expressions are, at best, only tenuously related to the concept which Calvin expounds in the *locus classicus* of the *Institutes*.
99. Quirinus Breen argues that the doctrine of common grace is essentially an *apologia* for humanist learning and a defence on Calvin's part of his continued use of pagan authors. *John Calvin: A Study in French Humanism*, 108, 166. A defence of humanism is implied in Calvin's position but it is essentially a theological assertion of God's sovereign grace over all of life.
100. At, respectively, *Inst.* II.2.12; 13; 14.
101. *Comm. Titus* 1.2.
102. Peter Schaefer's *Amadeus* is an interesting commentary on this doctrine. The pious but unheralded composer Antonio Salieri observes—with anguish—the acclaim accorded the frivolous, if not impious, Mozart.
103. In Karl Barth and Emil Brunner, *Natural Theology*, 83.

4

JESUS CHRIST AND THE KNOWLEDGE OF GOD FROM CREATION

THE NATURE OF SPIRITUAL KNOWLEDGE

Calvin's doctrine of the knowledge of God is characterized by a rigorous positivity. What counts in spiritual knowing is not what might or might not be the case, given human presupposition, but what has actually been given us to know of God. "The pious mind does not dream up for itself any god it pleases, but contemplates the one and only true God. And it does not attach to him whatever it pleases but is content to behold him as he manifests himself" (I.2.2). When we attempt to deduce conclusions about the character and intentions of God from assumed first principles, or from experience, or from the perceived natural order, the results will inevitably be flawed. Though humans are "born and live to the end that they may know God" (*Inst.* I.3.3), yet the mind is "like a labyrinth" (*Inst.* I.5.12) and "in seeking God, miserable men do not rise above themselves as they should, but measure him by their own carnal stupidity" (*Inst.* I.4.1). Only one source of divine knowledge can deliver us from the morass of metaphysical conjecture: "God himself is the sole and proper witness of himself" (I.11.1).[1]

Again and again Calvin proscribes a speculative approach in theology, and in particular the bold folly of a theology which attempts to make the essence of God its object. It is axiomatic for him that God's nature is incomprehensible and beyond all human perception. How, then, is it possible to know anything of God? Calvin supplies a twofold answer, one related to the knowledge of God the Redeemer, and the other related to the knowledge of God the Creator. In the redemptive sphere, the spurious project of speculative theology is contrasted with proper knowledge of God through the Mediator, Jesus Christ. In the sphere of creation, the attempt to penetrate the "abyss" of God's deity is contrasted with knowing God through attentive and grateful contemplation of the works of the divine hand.

The emphatic positivity of Calvin's epistemology thus finds as vigorous an expression in his theology of creation as in that of redemption. "Since both the eternity of God's existence and the infinity of his glory would prove a twofold labyrinth, let us content ourselves with modestly desiring to proceed no further in our inquiries than the Lord, by the guidance and instruction of his own works, invites us."[2] While some simply neglect God, "others, overlooking the works of God, aspire with a foolish and insane curiosity to inquire into his essence."[3]

> Consequently, we know the most perfect way of seeking God, and the most suitable order, is not for us to attempt with bold curiosity to penetrate to the investigation of his essence, which we ought more to adore than meticulously to search out, but for us to contemplate him in his works whereby he renders himself near and familiar to us, and in some manner communicates himself. (*Inst.* I.5.9)

Not only does the principle of positivity find expression in Calvin's theology of creation, but, in the original order of nature, the marvellous endowments of creaturely existence were intended to be the sole and sufficient means by which God would be known by humankind.

While Calvin would never describe the world as "God's body," his use of the metaphor of clothing is significant: "In respect of his essence, God undoubtedly dwells in light inaccessible; but as he irradiates the whole world by his splendor, this is the garment in which he, who is hidden in himself, appears in a manner visible to us."[4] Again, "God...clothes himself, so to speak, with the image of the world, in which he would present himself to our contemplation."[5] Just as we must have Christ "clothed with his gospel" (*Inst.* II.2.6) to attain proper knowledge of God the Redeemer, so to attain proper knowledge of God the Creator we must have God clothed with the universe. As the incarnate Christ is the "image" of God in redemptive activity toward humanity, the creation is the image of God's activity as Creator and Sustainer.

Faith-originated Knowledge

For Calvin, a speculative approach to the knowledge of God is programmed not only for error but also for peril. What is at stake is not mere intellectual belief or assent, but spiritual knowledge—relationship with the living God. In Calvin's lexicon, spiritual knowledge and faith are virtually synonymous terms, possessing, as they do, the same authenticating qualities. "Not only faith, perfect and in every way complete, but all right knowledge of God is born of obedience." (*Inst.* I.6.2) "Knowledge of God will be sound and fruitful only if it takes root in the heart." (*Inst.* I.5.9). As engendered by the Holy Spirit, spiritual knowledge appeals to the heart as well as the mind. Thus, "the one act of Christian knowing engages two distinct but inseparable modes," the cordial and the intellective.[6] As the full title of the first edition of the *Institutes* describes the work, it is a *summa pietatis*.[7]

As well as insisting on the faith-originated character of spiritual knowledge, Calvin also takes pains to point out the reverse of the coin of convertibility, namely, that faith is a "higher knowledge" and entails definite cognitive content. It is not enough to give assent to what one does not understand nor choose to investigate, since "faith rests not on ignorance, but on knowledge" (*Inst.* III.2.2). But the priority of faith over cognition is never in doubt; an observation at *Comm. John* 6.69 nicely summarizes Calvin's insistence on both a knowledge-content for faith and faith's priority:

> The word *believe* is put first, because the obedience of faith is the beginning of true understanding; or rather, faith itself is truly the eye of the mind. But at once knowledge is added, which distinguishes faith from erroneous and false opinions. For Turks and Jews and Papists believe, but without knowing or understanding anything. Knowledge is joined to faith, because we have a sure and undoubted conviction of God's truth, not in the same way as human sciences are apprehended, but when the Spirit seals it in our hearts.

On the one hand, then, knowledge of God presupposes faith and is suffused with the qualities of trust and obedience which are intrinsic to faith; on the other, it belongs to the nature of faith to elucidate in explicit credenda, however qualified by our finite capacity, received truth about faith's Object.

The synonymous or convertible relationship between spiritual knowledge and faith is buttressed by Calvin's distinctive definition of knowledge. For Calvin, though it possesses cognitive import by definition, spiritual knowledge is not primarily intellectual. While Aquinas, for example, denies that faith is a form of knowledge (terming it "firm belief"), Calvin regards certitude, not thorough comprehension, as the essential criterion of knowledge.[8] "The knowledge of faith consists in assurance rather than comprehension." (*Inst.* III.2.14) His point is that comprehension is "usually concerned with those things which fall under human sense perception" while the reality embraced by faith is infinite. In the nature of the case, then, spiritual knowledge is persuasive rather than critical. Calvin's criterion of certitude and the virtual equivalence of spiritual knowledge and faith are both evident in the famous definition at *Inst.* III.2.7: "Now we shall possess a right definition of faith if we call it a firm and certain knowledge of God's benevolence toward us, founded upon the truth of the freely given promise in Christ, both revealed to our minds and sealed upon our hearts by the Holy

Spirit." Again, he says: "faith is a knowledge of the divine benevolence toward us and a sure persuasion of its truth." (*Inst*. III.2.12)

The "Pro Nobis" Character of Knowledge of God

The faith-full nature of authentic spiritual knowledge is underscored by its character as *pro nobis* or "us-ward." "Now the knowledge of God, as I understand it, is that by which we not only conceive that there is a God, but also grasp what befits us and is proper to his glory, in fine, what is to our advantage to know of him." (*Inst*. I.2.1) "In understanding faith it is not merely a question of knowing that God exists, but also—and this especially—of knowing what is his will toward us. For it is not so much our concern to know who he is in himself, as what he wills to be toward us." (*Inst*. III.2.6) "What help is it, in short, to know a God with whom we have nothing to do?" (*Inst*. I.2.2)

Among the "General Characteristics of the Knowledge of God" noted by E.A. Dowey in the first chapter of his study, *The Knowledge of God in Calvin's Theology*,[9] are those marking it as accommodated, correlative, and existential, all of which lend texture to a knowledge of God which is *pro nobis*. To employ Dowey's terms, then, spiritual knowledge is *pro nobis* because God is actually known not *in se* (according to the divine essence) but only according to our limited capacity, as God **accommodates** the divine being and ways to finite comprehension. It is *pro nobis* also because true knowledge of God leads to new awareness of our own condition, and this awareness leads, in turn, to increased understanding of God's will and ways (the principle of **correlation**). Finally, it is *pro nobis* because knowledge of God entails decision and commitment on the part of the knower (and is thus **existential**).

The Reformers as a whole substituted the evangelical question *Qualis sit deus*? for the medieval *Quis sit deus*? It is a notable contribution of Calvin to have shown that the question as to the nature of God's disposition toward us has an answer in the sphere of creation as well as redemption. If what God reveals in redemption is the divine **benevolence**, in creation it is the divine **beneficence**. Not only is God so kindly disposed to us as to send the Redeemer, but from the beginning God has revealed the divine loving-kindness in making the world good. At *Inst*. I.2.1, Calvin observes: "It will not suffice simply to hold that there is One whom all ought to honour and adore, unless we are also persuaded that he is the fountain of every good."[10]

The Testimony of the Creation and Its Vitiation

After all the learned treatises and interpretive firestorms of the secondary literature have been accorded their place, it remains an astonishing experience to read straight through Book I of the *Institutes*. If

Spinoza has been called "the God-intoxicated philosopher," then Calvin surely must be the creation-intoxicated theologian. In his view, to turn one's eye upon the vast and well-ordered creation is to be confronted by the boundless generosity of a heavenly Parent who will supply all our needs. More important than this supply of human need, however, is the fact that the creation, in macrocosm and microcosm, reflects the glory of its Maker. There, as in a painting, as in a mirror, as in a theater (the metaphors multiply and become a tribute to the extravagance of the Giver) God's powers and perfections are declared.

However, all that Calvin says about the revelatory significance of the creation must fall at last under the ban of "*si integer stetessit Adam*": "the primal and simple knowledge to which the order of nature would have led us" avails only "if Adam had remained upright." (*Inst.* I.2.1) The *pro nobis* character of faith is defined finally by its reach to our condition as sinners. In a chapter new to the 1559 edition of the *Institutio*, chapter six of Book II, inserted to clarify the significance of the *duplex cognitio* distinction, Calvin posts the following notice of warning:

> Therefore, since we have fallen from life into death, the whole of knowledge of God the Creator that we have discussed would be useless unless faith also followed, setting forth for us God our Father in Christ. The natural order was that the frame of the universe should be the school in which we were to learn piety, and from it to pass over to eternal life and perfect felicity. But after man's rebellion, our eyes— wherever they turn—encounter God's curse ... For even if God wills to manifest his fatherly favor to us in many ways, yet we cannot by contemplating the universe infer that he is Father. (*Inst.* II.6.1)

E. A. Dowey does well to remind us of "the magnitude of the sum thus negatived"[11]: the universe with its magnificence and message for us has not gone out of existence. What has changed is not the revelatory character of creation but the human capacity to perceive it aright.

Because of this, faith is the fulcrum of Calvin's epistemology. While an important supplementary discussion occurs in his "Argument" to the *Commentary on Genesis*, the Reformer offers his thematic account of faith in the opening chapters of Book III of the *Institutes*, where it appears as fundamental to "The Way We Receive the Grace of Christ." Because of sin, knowledge of God must begin with apprehension of the divine grace in sending the Redeemer. Calvin underscores the necessity of a correct starting point in the following comment on Paul's statement that "the world through wisdom knew not God" (I Cor. 1.21):

> For he thus intimates, that God is sought in vain under the guidance of visible things; and that nothing

> remains for us but to be take ourselves immediately to Christ; and that we must not therefore commence with the elements of this world, but with the Gospel, which sets Christ alone before us with his cross, and holds us to this one point. I answer, it is vain for any to reason as philosophers on the workmanship of the world, except those, who having been first humbled by the preaching of the Gospel, have learned to submit the whole of their intellectual wisdom (as Paul expresses it) to the foolishness of the cross (I Cor. 1.21). Nothing shall we find, I say, above or below, which can raise us up to God, until Christ shall have instructed us in his own school.[12]

Moreover, given our sin, the illuminating work of the Holy Spirit is required to bring about the regeneration of the inner person. Without this inner transformation, humans are spiritually dead and noetically blind. Faith, therefore, "is the fruit of spiritual regeneration."[13] So indispensable is this transforming ministry of the Holy Spirit that "until our minds become intent upon the Spirit, Christ, so to speak, lies idle because we coldly contemplate him as outside ourselves —indeed, far from us." (*Inst.* III.1.3) As is the case with Scripture, Christ himself is a "dead letter" without the regenerative illumination of the Holy Spirit.

Given the actual and urgent condition of humanity as sinful, we can attain knowledge of the true God only through faith in that God's saving grace. Thus, the significance of the sources of the knowledge of God the Creator—the revelation from creation and the clarification of it in Scripture—can be assessed accurately only after consideration of Calvin's doctrine of faith. However, complexity arises from the fact that in the *Institutes* the full account of faith does not occur until Book III, well after the discussion of the sources.

On the one hand, then, faith properly conceived is the subjective correlate of the revelation of God redemptively focused in Jesus Christ. On the other hand, Calvin works throughout Book I of the *Institutes* without a definition of faith so explicitly focused. There, he regards faith in more general terms as the subjective correlate of the revelation of God as Creator; at *Inst.* I.14.21 he offers such a definition of faith:

> ...Let all readers know that they have with true faith apprehended what it is for God to be the Creator of heaven and earth, if they first of all follow the universal rule, not to pass over in ungrateful thoughtfulness or forgetfulness those conspicuous powers which God shows forth in his creatures, and then learn to apply it to themselves that their very hearts are touched.

If the first part of faithful apprehension of God as Creator is grateful contemplation of the divine perfections displayed in nature, the second part is decisive response, namely "to recognize that God has destined all things for our good and salvation but at the same time to feel his power and grace in ourselves...and so bestir ourselves to trust, invoke, praise and love him." (*Inst.* I.14.22) Again, at *Comm. Heb.* 11.3, Calvin states: "Those who believe do not just think that God is the Architect of the world, but there is a firm conviction deep in their hearts and they behold the true God." Further indication of the presence of this more general conception of faith in Calvin's theology is the fact that, as noted above, he can offer accounts of the positivity and *pro nobis* character of spiritual knowledge under the rubric of knowledge of God the Creator.

Since Book I contains Calvin's doctrine of the Trinity, it is clear that God the Creator is none other than the triune God who is author of creation and redemption alike. All knowledge of God in Calvin's thought is knowledge of God in Christ through the power of the Holy Spirit; thus, the knowledge of God, whether in creation or redemption, is one knowledge. Yet, in ruling out substantive discussion of Christ's incarnation and mediatorial ministry in Book I, he invites the conjecture that, while faith properly has to do with the promise of mercy in the mediatorial Christ, its qualities of trust and obedience may be abstracted, or extrapolated, from the redemptive context to serve in describing a general attitude of believing humans to their Creator. And which is it—abstraction or extrapolation? The former term connotes a certain illegitimacy: "abstraction" suggests some contradiction of Calvin's insistence on *Christus verus* as faith's object. The latter term, on the other hand, connotes a more legitimate operation: "extrapolation" recalls the phrase, *etiam extra carnem*, according to which Calvin extends a concept initially arising in the sphere of redemption to depict Christ's perfecting work in the sphere of creation as one of mediation.

This leads us to ask, therefore, whether the discussion of the knowledge of God and faith in Book I is to be regarded as wholly hypothetical, or whether there are contexts in which one may speak appropriately about faith more generally conceived. In the latter case, this would mean that faith has as its object/correlate under the knowledge of God the Redeemer the benevolence of God in Jesus Christ, and another object/correlate under the knowledge of God the Creator, namely, the beneficence of God in the gifts and testimony of the creation.

THE SOURCES OF THE KNOWLEDGE OF GOD THE CREATOR

In an important announcement of the *duplex cognitio*, Calvin introduces us to the double source of the knowledge of God the Creator in nature and in Scripture:

> First, in the fashioning of the universe and in the general teaching of Scripture the Lord shows himself to be the Creator. Then in the face of Christ he shows himself to be the Redeemer. Of the resulting twofold knowledge of God we shall now discuss the first aspect; the second will be dealt with in its proper place. (*Inst.* I.2.1)

The reader is thus introduced to the revelatory function of creation and Scripture under the separate and prior heading of the knowledge of God the Creator. This passage might suggest that there are two, if not three, not only distinct but also equally important sources of revelation. The first is the creation, the fundamental source of the knowledge of God the Creator. The second is the revelation in Jesus Christ, treated under the knowledge of God the Redeemer. The third would be Scripture, a record of revelation comprehensive of the knowledge of God both as Creator and Redeemer. Calvin certainly means to distinguish among the sources, but not to put in question the controlling epistemological significance of faith focused on Jesus Christ. Still, the question persists: does Calvin's high regard for the revelation in creation lead him to posit a provisional and more general definition of faith, one evoked by the witness of creation and also with potential for expression outside the household of Christian belief?

Innate Knowledge of the Creator

In agreement with Cicero and in contrast to Aquinas, Calvin believes that there is a natural, instinctive awareness of divinity which is in all, implanted by God as if it were a seed.[14] He justifies this conviction on the basis of the perceived universality of religious experience: "Since from the beginning of the world there has been no region, no city, in short, no household, that could do without religion, there lies in this a tacit confession of a sense of deity inscribed in the hearts of all."[15]

Humans know innately not only that a deity exists but also that they can appeal to God as a faithful help in time of distress. Thus, the pagan sailors at sea with Jonah resorted to *invocatio*, calling upon their gods, and Jonah himself is implored by the captain to call upon his:

> For there there is no need of any law, there is no need of any Scriptures, in short, there is no need of any teaching, to enable men to know, that this life is in the hand of God, that deliverance is to be sought from him alone, and that nothing, as we have said, ought to be looked for from any other quarter: for invocation proves that men have this conviction respecting God; and invocation comes from nothing else but from some hidden instinct (*arcano instinctu*),

> and indeed from the guidance and teaching of nature (*duce ac magistra naturae*).[16]

The "notion or preconception (*prolepsis*)" that our wellbeing is in the hands of God and varies according to divine pleasure or displeasure is "imprinted, then, in the minds of all."[17]

Calvin makes explicit that this natural knowledge extends to a conception of divine providence, but it is not sufficiently focused to produce confident access to God:

> All agree to this truth, that there is some God, and also that no dead idol can do anything, but that the world is governed by the providence and power of God, and further that safety is to be sought from him. All this has been received by the common consent of all; but when we come to particulars, then everyone is in the dark; how God is to be sought they know not.[18]

The problematic that "all men have a vague general veneration for God but very few really reverence him" (*Inst.* I.2.2) stems from the lack of direction attending the innate proclivity for religion. In the absence of a properly focused faith, superstition and idolatry arise to fill the vacuum: "They seek gods which are nigh to them, and when they find none, they hesitate not to invent them."[19]

Although humans have within them a light attesting the supreme God, yet it cannot carry them beyond the first general awareness or sustain them in it; ultimately "the pure seed degenerates into corruptions."[20] Though Calvin's terminology suggests that this inevitable deterioration results more from human mutability and ignorance than from sin, he adjudges humanity culpable of disobedience. Accordingly, the seed of religion in humanity ultimately bears fruit only to its condemnation: "Since, therefore, men one and all perceive that there is a God and that he is their Maker, they are condemned by their own testimony because they have failed to honor him and to consecrate their lives to his will."[21]

Acquired Knowledge of the Creator

Acquired (*acquisita*) knowledge of God the Creator arises from observation of the work of God in the macrocosm of the universe and also in the microcosm of the human frame. Indeed, "the world was founded for this purpose, that it should be the sphere of the divine glory."[22] In an oft-repeated image, Calvin compares the universe to a "dazzling theater" in which humans are set as spectators of the divine glory.[23] In another favourite image, he speaks of the ordering of the universe as "a sort of mirror in which we contemplate God, who is the otherwise invisible."[24] Again, he regards the individual works of creation as sources of revelation in which "God's powers are actually represented as in a painting." (*Inst.* I.5.1) The world is the means by which God is rendered visible to us.

Calvin underlines the fact that humans do not have to engage in detection to find evidence for God's divinity and power: it is openly displayed in the *opera Dei*. "Upon his individual works he has engraved (*insculpsit*) unmistakable marks of his glory, so clear and so prominent that even unlettered and stupid folk cannot plead the excuse of ignorance." (Ibid.) The obstinate refusal to acknowledge the unique Creator of heaven and earth is all the more intolerable since God is not only "visible" in the opera but also "palpable." "For God has not given obscure hints of his glory in the handiwork of the world, but has engraved such plain marks everywhere, that they can be known also by the touch of the blind."[25] The human frame is itself a microcosm of the glory of God which is manifested everywhere about us. "Every man will find [God] in himself, if only he is willing to pay attention . . . Above all other creatures, he is proof of the glory of God, full of countless miracles as he is."[26]

It is noteworthy that Calvin does not attempt to use the *opera* as the basis of a proof of the existence of God, as does Aquinas, for example. One reason is that believers are "more strengthened by persuasion than instructed in rational proof." (*Inst.* III.2.14) Another reason is that the *opera* demonstrate much more than the divine existence; "the beautiful arrangement and wonderful variety which distinguish the courses and station of the heavenly bodies . . . cannot but furnish us with an evident proof of his providence."[27] God "daily discloses himself in the whole workmanship of the world" (*Inst.* I.5.1.) and "the amazing ingenuity of nature plainly points to the providence of God."[28]

More than this, Calvin believes that what is attested by the creation is the very character and perfections of God. He urges an uninterrupted contemplation of all creatures so that we may perceive in them, "as in mirrors," the divine attributes (*virtutes*)—"those immense riches of his wisdom, justice, goodness and power." (*Inst.* I.14.21)[29] Commenting on the meaning of the Biblical phrase, "the name of God," Calvin underscores the revelatory nature of the relationship obtaining between the *opera Dei* and the character of God:

> The name of God, as I explain it, is here to be understood of the knowledge of the character and perfections of God, in so far as he makes himself known to us. I do not approve of the subtle speculations of those who think the name of God means nothing else but God himself. It ought rather to be referred to the works and properties by which he is known, than to his essence.[30]

And then, in a stunning and comprehensive passage at *Comm. Rom.* 1. 21, Calvin explains the derivation of each of the divine perfections from observation of the ongoing life of creation:

> No conception of God can be found without including his eternity, power, wisdom, goodness, truth, righteousness and mercy. His eternity is evidenced by the fact that he holds all things in his hand and makes all things to consist in himself. His wisdom is seen, because he has arranged all things in perfect order; his goodness, because there is no other cause for his creation of all things, nor can any other reason than his goodness itself induce him to preserve them. His justice is evident in his governing of the world, because he punishes the guilty and defends the innocent; his mercy, because he bears the perversity of men with so much patience; and his truth, because he is unchangeable. Those, therefore, who have formed a conception of God ought to give him the praise due to his eternity, wisdom, goodness and justice.

Few of us today would entertain the notion that the divine character can so easily be discerned from contemplation of the universe, but Calvin believes the content of the knowledge of God the Creator is to be derived from that source.

Nevertheless, the knowledge of God the Creator derived from the *opera* falls prey to the same process of degeneration that undoes the efficacy of the innate awareness of God given in and with human existence. Although the revelation of God reflected there never ceases to bear its objective testimony—it is "engraved"—it is subjectively vitiated. Again Calvin finds humans culpable of sin: "The world is therefore rightly called the mirror of divinity not because there is enough clarity for men to know God by looking at the world but because he makes himself clear to unbelievers in such a way that they are without excuse for their ignorance."[31] Here as well, his descriptive language suggests that human mutability and ignorance are as much a factor as sin.

As in the case of innate knowledge, the deterioration occurs because humans do not remain constant in their first awareness of God, allowing themselves to be deflected from the course of true knowledge. Thus Calvin reflects on the Athenians to whom Paul preached:

> For they were convinced that there was some divinity; their perverted religion was merely requiring to be corrected. From that we conclude that the world wanders through ever-changing, roundabout ways, one should rather say, is involved in a labyrinth, as long as confused opinion about the nature of God holds sway.[32]

On the one hand "their perverted religion was merely requiring to be corrected." On the other hand, the failure "to set God above the world," leads to idolatry, namely, the association of God's power and glory with visible forms.[33]

Since the Law forbids the worship of false gods, idolatry and superstition may be regarded as disobedience to divine command, and as requiring not merely correction but replacement, if not eradication. These sinful distortions of the religious impulse are an indication of the human need for redemption, and the distinguishing characteristic of true religion now may be recognized as explicit faith in the Mediator:

> ...Our faith is chiefly distinguished from the superstitions of the Gentiles by these features; that it sets forth Christ as the one Mediator; that it teaches that salvation must be sought from him alone; that it bids us seek the expiation, by which we may be reconciled to God, in his death; that it teaches that men, who had previously been unclean and in the grip of sin, are restored and renewed by his Spirit, to begin to live righteous and holy lives; lastly, that, from such beginnings, which make it clear that the Kingdom of God is spiritual, it finally lifts our minds to the hope of the future resurrection.[34]

Such an account of true religion is in perfect coherence with Calvin's evangelical aim; yet he is also concerned to show that idolatry and superstition are as unnatural as they are sinful. At *Comm. Acts* 17.26, he observes that "religion is the thing which most unites men or separates them" and that the multiplicity of pagan sects serves to prove "that those who are so at variance in religion and the worship of God, have deviated from nature." He continues his discussion of Paul's argument:

> In a word, he wished to teach that the order of nature was violated when religion was torn to pieces among them, and that the dispersion, which is to be seen among themselves, is evidence of the overthrow of godliness, because they have broken loose from God, the common Father, from whom all blood-relationship is derived.

In actual fact, human disobedience to divine command has universally determined human existence so that our need for Christ as the redemptive Mediator everywhere overtakes and integrates into its own urgency our need for Christ's interposition as the sustaining and perfecting Mediator of the natural order. But Calvin continues to regard the universal instinct for religion as divine gift, and to keep in view the pathos of those who as creatures stretch after the

Ultimate with resources incommensurate to their reach. Even Karl Barth does not regard "religion" (distinguished from faith and identified as its usurping double) as sin, but rather as "misfortune," a strange no-man's-land in which the religious impulse of humanity becomes recognizable as our peril before God.[35]

"Eristics"

Concerning Calvin's theology, it is the conviction of scholars of the Barth-Niesel school that the single remaining purpose served by the revelation in creation for fallen humanity is to condemn unbelief by cutting off all excuse. This conviction coheres well with the reformer's evangelical intent, but it fails to take into account Calvin's own estimation that the revelation in creation may be used eristically, since the creation continues objectively to attest its eternal Maker. "Eristics" (so-named by Brunner) does not attempt an apologia for faith, let alone a demonstration of its truth. Rather it attempts the refutation of idolatry and superstition by using a resource that is equally accessible to believer and unbeliever—the light of nature. Especially in his Commentary on Acts, we find Calvin placing the evangelical and sapiential emphases in better balance than the Barth-Niesel interpretation would allow. The two crucial *loci* relate to Paul's preaching at Lystra (Acts 14. 5-18), and at Thessalonica and Athens (Acts 17).

Faithful to an evangelical resolve is the view that the best argument against false faith is nothing other than the proclamation of the gospel. The appearance of authentic coinage serves of itself to identify and discredit the counterfeit. Of Paul's address to the Athenians, Calvin observes: "For if they had known any god at all they would have been content with him and never been reduced to "unknown gods"; since the knowledge of the true God is indeed sufficient in itself for the destruction of all idols."[36] He goes on to remark that Paul's apologia at Athens is not fully recorded and that only further reference to Christ could explain its persuasive power:

> There is no doubt that Paul said a good deal more about Christ, so that the Athenians might know that he is the Son of God, by whom salvation had been brought to the world, and to whom all power in heaven and earth had been given. Otherwise the speech, such as we read it here, would have been powerless to persuade.[37]

Furthermore, Calvin tells us that it is the proclamation of the redemptive Word which actually makes humankind aware of its inexcusability in the face of the revelation in creation. Because of natural revelation, we are inexcusable whether we know it or not, but it is the *kerygma* which awakens us to our dire predicament. Calvin thus understands Paul to reject any attempted defence of human ignorance of God in the face of explicit gospel preaching:

> But Paul denies that when God addressed us, an excuse is to be sought from the ignorance of the fathers; because even if they are not innocent in God's sight, yet our negligence is not to be tolerated, if we are blind in the full light of day, and lie deaf or asleep while the Gospel trumpet is sounding.[38]

Neither the Athenians nor the later inhabitants of Christendom can claim exemption from condemnation since with the preaching of the gospel comes specific, aural arraignment of our culpability. "Blindness has prevailed among all peoples, but God is now giving you light."[39]

Nevertheless, Paul and Barnabas are free, in Calvin's mind, to appeal to the primal knowledge of God from creation as a preliminary in their proclamation: "They assume this principle, that in the order of nature there is a certain and clear manifestation of God."[40] Because the revelation of God in nature remains objectively valid, Christian proclamation may include eristics as a proper threshold to the *kerygma*:

> Since Paul and Barnabas were preaching to Gentiles, it would have been useless for them to attempt to bring them to Christ at once. Therefore they had to begin from some other point, not so remote from common understanding, so that, when assent was given to them, they could pass over to Christ. The minds of the men of Lystra were possessed by the error that there are many gods. Paul and Barnabas show, on the other hand, that there is one Creator of the world. With the removal of that fictitious crowd of deities the way was open for the second step, to teach them what that God, the Creator of heaven and earth was like.[41]

Again, in Paul's preaching at Athens, "he shows by arguments from nature who God is, what he is like, and how he is to be worshipped properly...And he certainly does not deal in a subtle way with the secret essence of God, but shows from his works what profitable knowledge of him is."[42]

At Thessalonica, before a Jewish congregation, Paul was able to begin with argumentation from the Scriptures concerning Christ. But "if Paul had been dealing with Gentiles it would have been necessary for him to start further back, because they had heard nothing about the Christ; and profane men do not think that they need any mediator."[43] In this hypothetical case, Calvin implies, the truth about God as the unique Creator of heaven and earth, and the inexcusability of humans for their ignorance of God, would have been the starting place.

Furthermore, a remarkable situation arises in the case of the God-fearers adhering to the synagogue at Thessalonica. These "devout Greeks" are those "who had some taste of the true and legitimate worship of God, so that they were no longer devoted to crass idolatries." However, "their taste was only vague and light, so that it was removed from true instruction." These were devout not in the full sense of faith but in so far as they "had taken farewell to idols and were beginning to acknowledge the one God."[44] Thus, there is a case in which "such docility was an entrance to faith, and indeed, a kind of beginning of faith."[45] While this docility cannot be faith itself, and while the God-fearers are so distinguished only in order "that the whole of the world's religion might be reduced to nothing," Calvin seems to regard these gentiles as occupying a station intermediate between idolatry and faith, a state produced through argumentation from the creation. They have renounced idolatry and superstition on the basis of a true but not yet intimate (saving) knowledge of God.

Calvin rejects the medieval notion of implicit or unformed faith if the term is used to cloak "ignorance tempered by humility" in the garb of faith. But he does admit "that so long as we dwell as strangers in this world there is such a thing as implicit faith; not only because many things are as yet hidden from us, but because, surrounded by many clouds of errors, we do not comprehend everything." (*Inst.* III.2.4) The disciples' slowness to believe is attributed to the gradual passage from ignorance to enlightenment, and they are said to possess "a true but implicit faith," proof that "unbelief is, in all men, always mixed with faith." (*Inst.* III.2.4) Even the reprobate may experience a "transitory faith," tasting the divine goodness, and even Christ, but "without the Spirit of adoption." (*Inst.* III.2.11)

As well as recognizing generally that faith entails growth, Calvin finds acceptable the specific definition of implicit faith as "preparation of faith," faith which is nascent. The Scripture records that even without "a trace of the gospel teaching," there have been individuals like the court official mentioned at John 4.46 who accepted Christ's authority to heal and to teach. "Such reverent attention, which disposed them to submit themselves willingly to Christ, is graced with the title 'faith'; yet it was only the beginning of faith." (*Inst.* III.2.5) Naaman, Cornelius, and the Ethiopian eunuch, because of their ignorance of the Mediator, are also instances of faith which is "in some part implicit." (*Inst.* III.2.32)

While, properly speaking, faith is always the correlate of the Word and clings only to the divine promise of mercy in Christ, in missionary endeavor there appears an identifiable moment of transition between idolatry and faith, an intermediate stage constituting both a preparation for faith and a positive inclination toward it. There exists a theonomous intelligibility in the natural order from which a critique of idolatry and superstition may be mounted and a preparation for faith established. The general knowledge of God thus derived is always imperfect and highly vulnerable, inevitably succumbing to the distortions of idolatry and superstition unless the impress of the gospel is brought to bear upon it. However, this knowledge is not identical with idolatry; idolatry is a corruption of it.[46]

In sum, Calvin holds together the following double set of recognitions: first, that the inadequacy of existing forms of natural religion may be demonstrated on the basis of the natural order and natural reason, but that such argumentation is possible only on the part of one who knows and bears the light of the redemptive Word; second, that argumentation from nature can engender nascent faith, or receptivity to the gospel, but that the proclamation of the gospel will awaken its hearers to their fallen nature and to the predicament of culpability for which the gospel is the sole availing answer. The integrity of these recognitions is assured when it is remembered that for Calvin any implied contrast between Christ and the order of nature can only be provisional. Since Christ is mediator of creation as well as of redemption, the truly natural is that which is ordered from him and to him as the eternal Word. Therefore, the unnatural may be defined as that which has degenerated from its origin and goal in Christ. And by reason of both inconstancy or sin, it is this degeneration of the natural knowledge of God which makes the additional record of Scripture indispensable.

Scripture and the Opera Dei

Calvin's doctrine of Scripture reflects his characteristic emphasis on the positivity of revelation. Concerning the interpretation of Scripture he observes that the "one rule of modesty and sobriety" is "not to speak, or guess, or even to seek to know, concerning obscure matters anything except what has been imparted to us in God's Word." (*Inst.* I.14.4) While lesser *indicia* of the credibility of Scripture may be adduced, "the highest proof of Scripture derives in general from the fact that God in person speaks in it....For as God alone is a fit witness of himself in his Word, so also the Word will not find acceptance in men's hearts before it is sealed by the inward testimony of the Spirit." (*Inst.* I.7.4) Objectively and subjectively, revelation is God's work: "It would profit us little to have the divine law sounding in our ears or to have it exhibited in writing before our eyes, and to have it expounded by the voice of man, did not God correct our slowness of apprehension, and render us docile by the secret testimony of his Spirit."[47]

Scripture is credible and possesses authority because of the illumination of the Spirit. Against Spiritualist teaching, Calvin insists that "the Spirit, promised to us, has not the task of inventing new and unheard-of revelations, or of forging a new kind of doctrine of the gospel, but of sealing our minds with that very doctrine which is commanded by the gospel." (*Inst.* I.9.1) The Holy Spirit is sent to give certainty as to the divine origin of the Word and thus to confirm it: "God did not bring forth his Word among men for the sake of a momentary display, intending at the coming of his Spirit to abolish it. Rather he sent down the same Spirit by whose power he had dispensed the Word, to complete his work by the efficacious confirmation of the Word." Spiritualists may teach that the written Word constitutes a "dead letter," "but if through the Spirit it is really branded upon hearts, if it shows forth Christ, it is the Word of life. (*Inst.* I.9.3)

The connection between Calvin's doctrines of Scripture and of faith is thus established through the indispensable work of the Holy Spirit in validating the authority of Scripture. Nonetheless, it is important to recognize that he does not conceive of the Scriptures as containing essentially the history of redemption with only minor reference to the knowledge of God in creation. The theater of creation is not simply a back-drop for humanity's history with God. According to Calvin, humans will not only act in this theater; we are also summoned to behold its tacit message for us. "After the world had been created, man was placed in it as in a theater, that he, beholding above him and beneath the wonderful works of God, might reverently adore their Author."[48] "The intention of Moses, in beginning his Book with the creation of the world is to render God, as it were, visible to us in his works."[49] In the *Institutes* especially, Calvin considers Scripture as pre-eminently a witness to the *opera Dei* and therefore as an important additional source of the knowledge of God the Creator. For this reason, he places his doctrine of Scripture in Book I.

As related to the knowledge of God in the *opera*, Scripture functions first of all to **confirm** this knowledge. This is done through its re-presentation in written form as the revelation in creation is attested "more intimately and also more vividly." (*Inst.* I.10.1) E.A. Dowey suggests that a better title than that supplied for Chapter 10 of Book I would be: "The Agreement of the Knowledge of God the Creator Revealed in Creation with That Revealed in Scripture."[50] As Calvin himself says at *Inst.* I.10.2: "Indeed, the knowledge of God set forth for us in Scripture is destined for the very same goal as the knowledge whose imprint shines in his creatures, in that it invites us first to fear God, then to trust him." Scripture may add to our incidental knowledge of God's works but there is nothing essential lacking in the witness of the creation itself:

> Scripture, indeed, makes known to us the time and manner of the creation; but the heavens themselves, although God should say nothing on the subject, proclaim loudly and distinctly enough that they have been fashioned by his hands: and this of itself abundantly suffices to bear testimony to men of his glory.[51]

Scripture also **clarifies** the revelation in creation by bringing it into sharper focus, as is evident from Calvin's celebrated image of spectacles: "For just as eyes, when dimmed with age or weakness, or by some other defect, unless aided by spectacles, discern nothing distinctly; so, such is our feebleness, unless Scripture guides us in seeking God, we are immediately confused." (*Inst.* I.14.1) [52] In adopting this metaphor Calvin makes clear that the Scriptures are not a theater of their own. With respect to the functions of confirming and clarifying the revelation in creation, the Scriptures are for looking through, not at. Gerald J. Postema observes:

> The metaphor of the spectacles is a good one, for I believe (and this is Calvin's point too), that we do not and will not find God in the Bible, but, rather, that it is from the Bible that we discover where to look for God in our own experience, in history, in the creation, and in our own moral life. To put it crassly, the Bible is a do-it-yourself book which gives instructions on how to gain knowledge of—i.e., become committed to—God, in order to respond in a proper way to him. [53]

Calvin views Scripture as assisting our sight not only because of sin, but also because of human finitude and the ever-present danger of inconstancy. In discussing the use of Scripture as spectacles, Calvin observes that even the restored believer never escapes the need for their testimony:

> Such is the slowness and dullness of our wit that, to prevent believers from deserting to the fabrications of the heathen, we must depict the true God more distinctly than they do. Since the notion of God as the mind of the universe (in the philosopher's eyes a most acceptable description) is ephemeral, it is important for us to know him more intimately, lest we always waver in doubt. (*Inst.* I.14.1)

Again, in commenting on Christ's conversation with the Samaritan woman at the well, Calvin appears to attribute the need for the correction of Samaritan worship through revelation to the mind's natural imperfection and inconstancy rather than to its depravity:

> For since the human mind because of its feebleness can in no way attain to God unless it be aided and assisted by his sacred Word, all mortals at that time—except for the Jews—because they were seeking God without the Word, had of necessity to stagger about in vanity and error. (*Inst.* I.6.4)

Only the Word, which has been committed to writing in the Bible, can carry humans beyond the conjectural conception of deity and its ensuing deterioration into superstition. Through Scripture, "Not only does he teach the elect to look upon a god, but also shows himself as the God upon whom they are to look." (*Inst.* I.6.1)

Degrees of Knowledge

The spectacles of Scripture function to assist the constancy of restored believers by making knowledge of God the Creator clear and distinct. The Word sustains the believer's knowledge of God by providing an "intimate knowledge" (*familiarem notitiam*) of God, the enjoyment of which distinguished the Old Testament saints from unbelievers, although it was not the "inner knowledge" (*interior notitia*) whereby the elect are "illumined unto the hope of eternal life" in the Mediator. (*Inst.* I.6.1) The chief effect of this "intimate knowledge" as differentiated from the "interior knowledge" of faith, is that its recipients are enabled to discern between authentic and idolatrous conceptions of deity, since "Scripture, gathering up the otherwise confused knowledge of God in our minds, having dispersed our dullness, clearly shows us the true God." (*Inst.* I.6.1)

Calvin's point is that all people have need of Scripture in some way, just as all people in some way know God. To be sure, not all are "inner" or "saving" kinds of knowledge (faith focused on the redemptive Christ), but it is possible to speak of degrees of the knowledge of God. The spectrum ranges from the idolater's vague notion of deity; through the nascent faith of the conscientized God-fearer; to the true knowledge of God possessed by the Hebrew saint (who nonetheless can behold the incarnate Redeemer only in prospect); and finally to the knowledge of God in Christ which includes forgiveness of sin and eternal life. It is interesting that the same Calvin who describes the human mind as a "factory of idols" can also describe gentile docility as "an entrance to faith." Regarded from one perspective (the evangelical), the forms of the knowledge of God which are less than saving knowledge are but degrees of adulteration.[54] But from another (the sapiential), they can be seen to be degrees of integrity, stages along the way from ignorance to enlightenment. However limited it may be, and however distorted it may become, Calvin believes that the instinct for truth is integral to human understanding.[55]

Excursus on "Saving Knowledge"

The fact that Calvin regards the Scriptures as a corrective to human finitude as well as sin generates an ambiguity: would humans in their integrity, because finite and mutable, also have needed the spectacles of the revealing Word? In an important passage in the "Argument" to the *Commentary on Genesis* he says:

> Now in describing the world as a mirror in which we ought to behold God, I would not be understood to assert, either that our eyes are sufficiently clear-sighted to discern what the fabric of heaven and earth represents, or that the knowledge to be hence attained is sufficient for salvation. And whereas the Lord invites us to himself by means of created things, with no other effect than that of rendering us inexcusable, he has added (as was necessary) a new remedy, or at least by a new aid he had assisted the ignorance of our mind. For by Scripture as our guide and teacher, he not only makes those things plain which would otherwise escape our notice, but almost compels us to behold them; as if he had assisted our dull sight with spectacles. On this point (as we have already observed), Moses insists. For if the mute instruction of the heaven and the earth were sufficient, the teaching of Moses would have been superfluous.[56]

Elsewhere, Calvin takes up the positive insight of Heb. 11.3, that it is "by faith we understand that the world was created by the Word of God." Thus, "faith is not conceived by the bare observation of heaven and earth, but by the hearing of the Word (*ex verbi auditu*). It follows from this that man cannot be brought to a saving knowledge of God except by the direction of the Word."[57] In these two statements Calvin appears to regard the inadequacy of the revelation in creation for salvation as stemming from more than a subjective vitiation. Is he thereby denying that the revelation in creation ever would have sufficed to lead humans to a knowledge of the true God and ultimately to eternal life?

T. H. L. Parker argues so, maintaining that only a single sentence in the *Institutes* (at II.6.1) supports the view that the revelation in creation once sufficed for salvation.[58] There is, however, multiple attestation of this view both in the *Institutio* and elsewhere. The "single sentence" at *Inst.* II.6.1 (quoted in full and in context earlier at p. 91) describes "the frame of the universe as a school in which we were to learn piety, and from it to pass over to eternal life and perfect felicity." At *Inst.* I.15.8, Calvin avers that through the excellent endowments of their first condition "men mounted up to God and eternal bliss . . . In this integrity man by his free will had the power if he so willed, to attain eternal life." At *Comm. I Cor.* 1.21 he also says: "The right order of things was surely this, that man, contemplating the wisdom of God in his works, by aid of the innate light of his own natural ability might come to a knowledge of him." Summing up at *Comm. Rom.* 1.20, he asserts: "We must, therefore, make this distinction, that the manifestation of God by which he makes his glory known among his creatures is sufficiently clear as far as its own light is concerned."

The question of whether humans in their created integrity could have come to a saving knowledge of God on the basis of the revelation in creation is hypothetical for us today, both because of the actual and universally obtaining corruption of the race, and also because we regard the existence of fore-parents in Eden as an-historical. Thus, it may not matter greatly if we cannot make Calvin's teaching on this matter fully consistent. But Calvin did regard the paradisal existence and the occurrence of the fall as historical events shaping all ensuing experience. For this reason it is worth pursuing the question to gain a fuller understanding of Calvin's teaching.

The nub of the problem may be the ambiguity which attaches to the notion of *saving* knowledge. Loosely employed, it may refer to faith which is sufficient, through grace, to attain the estate of glory; i.e., to enjoy the bliss of beholding God in the heavenly existence. This is the intended end for believing humans whether in their integrity or as the redeemed elect. Strictly employed, however, the term's reference is to the redeemed elect only, those who can come to glory no other way than through the forgiveness of sin. In the nature of the case, humanity in its integrity does not need to be saved, but to be "elevated," lifted above the potential for inconstancy and defection that belongs to a mutable nature. In the condition of original rectitude, to be alive was to be innocent, to see God's perfections in the lineaments of created nature, and to enjoy a filial communion with the Eternal on earth. The original human condition was paradisal. Misconstructions of Calvin's teaching on this matter thus arise from the mistaken premise that even a clear knowledge of God's character and perfections would not be enough to "save" humanity. But this "clear-sighted" humanity, grateful and obedient in the state of rectitude, would not need to be saved, i. e., redeemed from sin.

Careful attention to the two passages cited above (p. 106) shows that they both assume the condition of humanity as fallen and in need of salvation. In the lengthy passage from the Genesis commentary, what is denied is that "the knowledge to be hence attained is sufficient for *salvation*." The instruction of Moses is necessary as a result of a complex in which, because of the fallen character of the perceivers and its noetic effects, the unfailing testimony of nature functions only to render them without excuse. In a similar fashion, the shorter passage from the Hebrews commentary magnifies the role of the Scriptural word because, without its direction, we "cannot be brought to a *saving* knowledge of God." In both cases we have reference to humans in the fallen state; it is as regards their need for salvation that the testimony of creation is insufficient.

The answer to the original question, then, is Yes: humans in their integrity could come to a knowledge of God sufficient to lead to perfection in glory without the interposition of the incarnate Mediator.

We remind ourselves, however, that it must be a qualified Yes, because the order of creation presupposes an incompleteness requiring fulfillment through grace. Even in their integrity humans would need the steadying and perfecting grace of Christ the eternal Word, and the knowledge of God attained from the creation would not automatically confer the gift of eternal life, as if God were obliged thereby. Gift is gift, and Calvin reminds us that in the state of rectitude human blessedness is "only earthly," lacking in the settled constancy which is the life "celestial" and which only Christ can bestow.[59]

"THE CHIEF GIFT OF GOD IN THIS WORLD"

"The chief gift of God in this world" (*praecipuum in hoc mundo Dei donum*)—this is how Calvin describes human reason at *Comm. I Cor.* 1.20. Yet in light of the incursion of sin, the mind is that aspect of human nature most responsible for, and most in need of redemption from, the corrupting effects of the fall. As noted in Chapter Three, what has been destroyed is not the rational capacity as such, but its integrity. "I readily allow that a certain judgment of life remains in man's soul, for understanding and judgment and will and all the senses are so many parts of life." But one power of the mind is utterly compromised: "since there is no part which aspires to the heavenly life, it is not surprising if the whole man is accounted dead so far as the Kingdom of God is concerned."[60] "Man's keenness of mind is mere blindness as far as the knowledge of God is concerned. Flesh is not capable of such lofty wisdom as to conceive God and what is God's, unless it be illumined by the Spirit of God." (*Inst.* II.2.19) Again at *Comm. I Cor.* 1.20, Calvin says: "Paul does not utterly condemn either the natural insight of men, or wisdom gained by practice and experience, or education of the mind through learning; but what he affirms is that all these things are useless for obtaining spiritual wisdom."

Replying to criticism that he pays more deference to reason than to the Word of God in his sacramental theology, Calvin defends himself by distinguishing among three principal uses of reason.[61] First, there is reason as it is constitutive of human nature, "reason naturally implanted which cannot be condemned without insult to God, but it has its limits which it cannot overstep without being immediately lost." This use is appropriate in earthly understanding and is evidence of a common grace. "There is another kind of reason which is vicious, especially in a corrupt nature, and is manifested when mortal man, instead of receiving divine things with reverence, would subject them to his own judgment." In this case, human reason actually opposes itself to the divine wisdom in proud rebellion. "But there is a third kind of reason, which both the Spirit of God and Scripture endorse." This last employment of reason occurs in the regenerate as they are transformed by the renewal of their minds, according to Rom. 12.2, and learn to think in accordance with the redemptive purpose of God fully disclosed in Jesus Christ and recorded in Scripture.

Authentic knowledge of God is impossible without the regenerative influence of the Holy Sprit; at the same time neither is it possible without the rationality which is common to the regenerate and natural uses of reason alike. Calvin is able to say with precision in what spiritual insight consists: "(1) knowing God; (2) knowing his fatherly favour on our behalf, in which salvation consists; and (3) knowing how to frame our life according to the rule of his law." (*Inst.* II.2.18) These three headings refer to the content of spiritual knowledge which cannot be attained without benefit of regeneration. But it is more difficult to say just how the actual process of ratiocination is affected by regeneration. Since reason is one and the same in its power as a gift of God the Creator, the actual processes of thought do not vary from the earthly to the spiritual exercise. This means that there is an area of overlap in which common rationality serves as an instrument of the regenerate mind in theological expression. In what way, then, does Calvin conceive of the relationship between the preserved natural capacity of thought and its specific exercise in spiritual understanding?

Natural Reason and Logic

Without a capacity for ratiocination, no thought of any kind would be possible. Natural reason and its axiomatic operations (logic) thus constitute a *conditio sine qua non* for theology as much as for any intellectual discipline. In objecting to the "*minutiae* of Aristotle" and the "nagging riddles" of the scholastics,[62] Calvin impugns not rationality itself but this capacity arrogantly ignoring its own limits. Natural reason provides us with self-evident truths prescribing, among other things, that prayer should be in one's native tongue,[63] that "what is supernatural is beyond the capacity of our abilities," [64] and that "he who is the Author of all things must necessarily be without beginning and self-created."[65]

There are also logical principles without whose observance only confusion and senseless babbling could result. These include the principles of non-contradiction and of identity. Calvin assumes this latter principle in his arguments against the supposed ubiquity of Christ's body. Christ's body cannot be real unless it continues to exhibit the properties of a physical body:

> Such is the condition of the flesh that it must subsist in one definite place, with its own size and form . . . But these trencher men think no power of God exists unless the whole order of nature be overturned . . . They object that it is wrong for the nature of the glorious body to submit to the laws of common nature.[66]

Calvin takes the principle of causality for granted also, and is perfectly at home in applying it according to its traditional medieval divisions. Giving an account of the cause of salvation and the relation of the persons of the Trinity to it, he writes:

> There is, perhaps, no passage in the whole of Scripture which more strikingly illustrates the efficacy of righteousness, for it shows that the mercy of God is the efficient cause, Christ with his blood the material cause, faith conceived by the Word the formal or instrumental cause, and the glory of both the divine justice and goodness the final cause.[67]

Furthermore, contrary to the extremes of Luther's polemic, Calvin does not repudiate the syllogism, since its proper use is merely the expression of the rules of logic in succinct form. In several notable instances he attempts to clinch crucial arguments in the interpretation of Scripture through the explicit form of a syllogism. At *Comm. Phil.* 1.6, for example, he states:

> Therefore let believers exercise themselves in constant meditation upon the benefits of God, that they may encourage and confirm hope for the future, and always ponder in their mind this syllogism: God does not forsake the work which his own hands have begun, as the prophet bears witness.(Ps.138.8; Isa. 64.8) We are the work of his hands. Therefore he will complete what he has begun in us.[68]

While Calvin nowhere argues that the satisfaction of the intellect is a primary goal in theological statement, as does Aquinas,[69] he puts the capacities of the intellect to full use in pursuing his goal of evangelical restatement. Calvin uses "reason, and its tool semiotics, [as] an important aid in the task of faith seeking understanding. In this respect, Calvin stands in the tradition of Augustine and Aquinas."[70]

Calvin's capacity for rhetorical and literary criticism represents the use of logic in the service of interpretation in still another way. In his comments on the first chapter of John alone he resolves ambiguous or difficult points through consideration of metaphor, hypallage, analogy, synecdoche, metonymy, implied comparison, and a comparison between major and minor premises.[71] The editors of the Seneca commentary find the use of fifty such figures in the course of Calvin's work there.[72]

Experience and Common Sense

As remarked in Chapter Two, Calvin finds evidence for a double decree of predestination in the observed fact that "the covenant of life is not preached equally among all men, and among those to whom it is preached it does not gain the same acceptance either constantly or in equal degree." (*Inst.* III.21.1) Parallel to this diversity in election is the very diversity of the created order. That not all are blessed with offspring, for instance, he adjudges testimony to the secret ordinance of providence. (*Inst.* I.16.8) Of God's providence, he remarks further at *Inst.* II.4.7: "Whether you will or not, daily experience compels you to realize that your mind is guided by God's prompting rather than your own freedom to choose." In these inferences, Calvin is relying upon experience or observation as an adjunct to, and confirmation of, the testimony of Scripture.

It is the argument of Charles Partee that *experientia* ("knowledge gained from experience") is ultimately understood by Calvin to be Christian experience, or the experience of faith.[73] In the "Catechism of the Church of Geneva," for example, Calvin teaches that the nature of faith as a special gift from God is confirmed by experience. The minister goes on to ask: "Tell me what experience you mean." The catechumen answers: "The Holy Spirit by his illumination makes us capable of understanding those things which would otherwise far exceed our grasp, and brings us to a sure persuasion by sealing the promises of salvation in our hearts."[74] As Partee observes, *experientia* here serves as a synonym for "assurance." Thus, only understood as experience of Jesus Christ through the illumination of the Holy Spirit can *experientia* be a source of sound spiritual knowledge.

However, Calvin also uses and appeals to experience as a phenomenon common to humans, whether regenerate or reprobate. Such is the case when he remarks that "experience teaches that the seed of religion has been implanted in all men." (*Inst.* I.4.1) Again, acknowledging awareness of God from natural experience, he writes that "the secular poets, out of a common feeling, called him the 'Father of all men.' " (*Inst.* I.5.3) In the political context, experience indicates "an aristocracy bordering on democracy as the best form of government." (*Inst.* IV.20.8)

Closely associated with experience is common sense, the exercise of reason in drawing conclusions from past repeated experience. In qualifying what he means by the corruption of human reason through the fall, he observes that "When we condemn human understanding for its perpetual blindness so as to leave it no perception of any object whatsoever, we not only go against God's word but also run counter to the experience of common sense." (*Inst.* II.2.12) Reflection upon life's daily occurrences is sufficient to refute the extravagant theory of the obliteration of man's rational capacity.

In the case of experience and common sense, there appears the same kind of overlapping as is present in the natural and regenerate exercises of reason in general: Calvin uses *experientia* in both a natural and regenerate sense. Thus, there are two distinct classes of experiential knowledge only one of which could bear scrutiny as a source for knowledge of God; yet the faculty for gaining knowledge through experience is one and the same. Generally, Calvin uses neither experience and common sense, nor natural reason and logic, as principal, much less autonomous, sources of spiritual knowledge. These serve, rather, to provide, from humanity's common life in the world, confirmation of doctrines taught uniquely in Scripture. They are allies in argumentation.

Calvin believes that experience always will prove a strong ally of faith since the God who engenders faith is the same One who rules the world providentially. With such confidence in mind, he dryly remarks of the pagan philosophers that, "sometimes, convinced by experience itself, they do not deny the great difficulty with which man establishes the rule of reason a kingdom within himself." (*Inst.* II.2.3) "In this sense, experience is the arena of human life where events occur which properly understood show that man deals with God in everything."[75] Just as the Holy Spirit is the Author, through "common grace," of the apparently natural illumination of unregenerate scholars and artists, so the trustworthiness of the teaching of experience must be attributed to this same Spirit.

What is notable about Calvin's use of experience and common sense as allies in theological argument is that he does not reflect upon its methodological significance. The glaring instance of this, of course, is his reliance on his own experience as a pastor, and on logical inference, to interpret and buttress the Scriptural warrants he finds for double predestination. From the point of vantage of his remarks on the futility of natural reason in understanding spiritual knowledge, one hardly would have expected to see natural reason and experience appear, without further explanation, in the theologian's arsenal.

By contrast, it is no surprise to find natural reason an ally of evangelical faith in the theology of Aquinas, since he announces this to be fundamental to his method. At *ST, Ia.* 2.2 *ad* 1, Aquinas observes that faith presupposes natural knowledge as grace presupposes nature. Again, at *Ia.*1.8 *ad* 2, he states: "Since grace does not supplant nature, but perfects it, reason ought to be the servant of faith in the same way as the natural inclination of the will is the servant of charity—'bringing every thought to the obedience of Christ', as the Apostle says in II Cor. 10.5." Interestingly, there is nothing in these general definitions of Aquinas which Calvin's use of reason and experience would contradict. The main difference between them becomes evident in the concrete: Calvin does not grant any independent theological use to reason, as does Aquinas, for instance, in the proofs for the existence of God. Thus, as respects spiritual knowledge, Calvin's sapiential breadth admits their universal and continuing relevance, while his evangelical aim prohibits their use except in the task of confirming the tenets of revealed truth.

"The Christian Philosophy"

Calvin intimates to the reader of the final French edition of the *Institutes* that what he has to communicate is "the sum of what God meant to teach us in his Word. Now that cannot be better done through the Scriptures than to treat the chief and weightiest matters comprised in the Christian philosophy."[76] Perhaps no term used by Calvin is more suggestive of the sapiential than the phrase, *philosophia Christiana*, and yet in using it, he has no intention of endorsing any kind of philosophic wisdom. On the contrary, it is short-hand for the practical wisdom derivable from the revealed Word. "For our wisdom ought to be nothing else than to embrace with humble teachableness, and at least without finding fault, whatever is taught in sacred Scripture." (*Inst.* I.18.4) The *philosophia Christiana* is a distillate of the content of Scripture which expresses,in nuce, the nature of Christian faith as it takes shape in the lives of the elect.

In the rectorial address of inauguration given by Nicolas Cop on All Saints' Day, 1533, and in which Calvin had some hand,[77] the Christian philosophy is defined as "a philosophy divinely given by Christ to man, to show forth the true and surest felicity," or alternatively, "the philosophy of Christ." It is contrasted with the effort of pagan philosophers who "long sought, but never found, the will of God," and with that of the Sorbonne "sophists" who "argue interminably over goat's wool" and "read the divine philosophy through a net." [78]

To embrace the Christian philosophy is to set oneself in opposition to conventional philosophic wisdom: "no one can be fit to learn the first principles of the Gospel, except the man who has first renounced that wisdom."[79] This is so because the primary Christian exercise of reason is its self-critique: "The Christian philosophy bids reason give way to, submit, and subject itself to, the Holy Spirit, so that the man himself may no longer live but bear Christ living and reigning within him." (*Inst.* III.7.1) A draught of similar vintage is offered at *Comm. II Cor.* 10.5: "Thus have we first to accept that he who would be wise must first become a fool; that is, we must give up our understanding and renounce the wisdom of the flesh and offer to Christ empty minds that he might fill them."

In his commentary on the Sermon on the Mount, Calvin specifically relates the philosophy of the disciples of Christ to their identification with Christ in cross-bearing:

> We know that it is not only the common crowd, but philosophers who are caught in this error: that the happy man is he who, relieved from all troubles, in possession of all he asks, leads a quiet and happy life...So Christ to accustom his men to bear the cross corrects the common idea that these are the happy ones who have it all good and prosperous...I admit

> that this doctrine is far from the general opinion, but it should be the philosophy of Christ's disciples, that they may set their happiness beyond the world, and above the desire of the flesh.[80]

In the end, paradoxically, the willingness to bear the cross leads us from misery to abiding happiness, as we find in Christ "hidden treasures," and all that the wise could desire:000 "This, indeed, is that secret and hidden philosophy which cannot be wrested from syllogisms." (*Inst.* III.20.1)

Because of sin and of the appointment of Christ to be redemptive Mediator, the Christian philosophy takes the concrete shape of emptying oneself of one's own wisdom in order to be filled with the apparent folly of a crucified Lord. Moreover, it issues in the practical response of discipleship to this same Lord. In both these senses, Calvin's evangelical intent is to the fore. However, there are also occasions on which he speaks of this philosophy without explicit focus on Jesus Christ who is its foundation and unique proponent. In these instances, Calvin may only be neglecting to make explicit what he trusts his readers to understand. But it is also possible that he conceives of the *philosophia Christiana* also as an expression of true wisdom in the context of a proper creature-Creator relationship. In this case, the spiritual wisdom arising out of the experience of grace would consist not only in recognition of mercy extended to undeserving sinners, but also in recognition of the sheer gratuitousness by which God ordains and sustains creaturely existence.[81]

Used without explicit christological focus, and thus more generally conceived, the Christian philosophy is an exposition of the sentence with which, in its varying forms, Calvin begins every edition of the *Institutes*: "Nearly all the wisdom we possess, that is to say, true and sound wisdom, consists of two parts: the knowledge of God and of ourselves." This knowledge consists in a humanity's humble acknowledgment of its utter dependence upon God:

> Now in summarizing what is required for the true knowledge of God, we have taught that we cannot conceive him in his greatness without being immediately confronted by his majesty, and so compelled to worship him. In our discussion of the knowledge of ourselves we have set forth this chief point: that empty of all opinion of our own virtue, and shorn of all assurance of our own righteousness—in fact, broken and crushed by the awareness of our own utter poverty—we may learn genuine humility and self-abasement.[82]

Humility is the watchword:

> A saying of Chrysostom's has always pleased me very much, that the foundation of our philosophy is humility. But that of Augustine pleases me more: "When a certain rhetorician was asked what was the chief rule in eloquence, he replied, 'Delivery'; what was the second rule, 'Delivery'; what was the third rule, 'Delivery'; so if you ask me concerning the precepts of the Christian religion, first, second, third, and always, I would answer, 'Humility' "...As our humility is his loftiness, so the confession of our humility has a ready remedy in his mercy.[83]

Taking up Paul's sentence at Romans 3.4, "Yea, let God be true and every man a liar," he underscores the juxtaposition of divine honor and human deceit: "The first proposition is the primary axiom of the Christian philosophy. The latter is taken from Ps. 116.11, where David confesses that there is no certainty from or in man."[84] In sum, "Nothing, however slight, can be credited to man without depriving God of his honor." (*Inst.* II.2.1) The pith of the Christian philosophy as understood by Calvin is ably expressed by T. F. Torrance: "We know God only in the inverse proportion of our poverty to his grace and glory."[85]

It is interesting to note that the elusive concept of *analogia fidei* proves to be another expression of this pith of the Christian philosophy. Precise definition of the analogy of faith is difficult to find in either the primary or secondary sources, but Calvin does add accompanying explanation to its mention on at least one occasion:

> When Paul wished all prophecy to be made to accord with the analogy of faith, he set forth a very clear rule to test all interpretations of Scripture. Now if our interpretation be measured by this rule of faith, victory is in our hands. For what is more consonant with faith than to recognize that we are naked of all virtue in order to be clothed by God?[86]

In so far as faith is an empty vessel to be filled from the sovereign sufficiency of God, the whole of sacred doctrine must conform, in its various parts, to this fundamental pattern. At *Inst.* IV.17.32, reference to the analogy of faith suggests that it is a rule governing Scriptural interpretation according to which no more than what God has actually committed to the text by revelation is to be found in it. At *Comm. Rom.* 12.6, the analogy of faith appears as a rule governing the exercise of the gifts of the Holy Spirit so as to keep this exercise within the bounds of what God has actually ordained. The idea common to both of these subsidiary passages is the circumscription of human "powers": we are empowered only in that degree to which we have been appointed.

The analogy of faith is thus more than a rubric permitting to theology only those analogies to God which are proposed in Scripture.[87] It concerns and reflects the Christian philosophy, the overall attitude of humble dependence that is the key to understanding the human condition before God. With respect to our need as both creatures and sinners, and in the face of the gifts given out of the sovereign sufficiency of God in both creation and redemption, our one true response is grateful humility. We are "naked of all virtue in order to be clothed by God."

CHRIST AS MEDIATOR OF THE KNOWLEDGE OF GOD THE CREATOR

Because of the effects of sin, humans cannot correctly perceive the revelation of God in creation without first experiencing the redemptive revelation in the incarnation and cross of Christ. In the "Argument" to the Commentary on Genesis, Calvin announces this noetic priority, and ascribes to the revelation in creation the function of confirming the knowledge of God previously gained by the believer in the redemptive revelation.

> Nothing shall we find, I say, above or below, which can raise us up to God, until Christ shall have instructed us in his own school... Yet this does not prevent us from applying our senses to the consideration of heaven and earth, that we may thence seek confirmation in the true knowledge of God.[88]

Having clarified the relationship between the two orders of knowing, he goes on immediately to explain that Christ is the ground of their unity:

> For Christ is that image in which God presents to our view, not only his heart, but also his hands and feet. I give the name of his heart to that secret love with which he embraces us in Christ: by his hands and feet I understand those works of his which are displayed before our eyes. As soon as ever we depart from Christ, there is nothing, be it ever so gross or insignificant in itself, respecting which we are not necessarily deceived.[89]

A more explicitly christocentric focussing of the doctrine of creation could scarcely be found, and for this reason its arresting metaphors require careful examination.

Christ's "hands and feet" are defined as "those works of his displayed before our eyes." They are the *opera Dei* which together constitute the original visibility of the character and perfections of God.

Under the rubric of the knowledge of God the Redeemer, Calvin regards Christ as the image of God in virtue of his humanity through the incarnation. Now we are clearly informed that Christ is also the image of the invisible God through the *opera Dei*. With respect to God's activity in creation, these works play a parallel revelatory function to the flesh of Christ in the divine activity of redemption.

But how widely does Calvin conceive that the *opera* reveal God *through Christ*? Does he mean, for instance, that prior to the fall, the authentic order of nature would have attested its christological origin and goal? In this case, how would Christ be recognizable, or, more precisely, what would be the content of the knowledge of Christ from the testimony of creation prior to the fall? From a strictly evangelical perspective, there is only one Christ to be known—the One who is *Jesus* Christ, the incarnate Redeemer. That there can be only one Christ is not in doubt: the eternal Word of creation is the One destined to take flesh for the salvation of humanity. And, this side of Eden, all that we know of the eternal Christ we know through the flesh of Jesus. We have no other access to a cognitive content for the vocable "Christ" than what is given us in the ministry of Jesus according to the prophetic and apostolic witness of Scripture.

As Calvin points out, however, it is the nature of the case that before the fall Christ could not be so known by creatures; only God could have such knowledge. Pondering the mystery of iniquity, he says:

> The question occurs, what had impelled Satan to contrive the destruction of man? Curious sophists have feigned that he burned with envy when he foresaw that the Son of God was to be clothed in human flesh; but the speculation is frivolous. For since the Son of God was made man in order to restore us, who were already lost, from our miserable overthrow, how could that be foreseen which never would have happened unless man had sinned?[90]

This means that if Adam and Eve in their integrity recognized the christological ordering of the creation, then this ordering must be construed as pertaining to Christ as the sustaining and perfecting Mediator of creation rather than as *Christus verus*.

From this perspective, light is thrown on two passages from the Commentary on John which strongly imply that humans in their integrity did recognize the ordering of creation to Christ. Thus Calvin writes at *Comm. Jn.* 1.10 concerning the light of reason:

> He was in the world. He accuses men of ingratitude, in that they were, so to say, voluntarily blinded; blinded in such a way that they did not know how the light they enjoyed was caused. And this is true of every age. Even before Christ was manifest in the

> flesh he revealed his power everywhere. Therefore, those daily effects ought to correct men's sluggishness; for what could be more unreasonable than to draw water from a running stream and never think of the spring it flows from? Accordingly, the world cannot plead ignorance as a legitimate excuse for not knowing Christ before he was manifest in the flesh. For it came from slackness and a sort of malignant dulness in those who always had him present in his power. The sum of it is that Christ was never so absent from the world that men ought not to have been awakened by his rays and to have looked up to him.

Earlier, at *Comm. Jn.* 1.4, he observes of the light of reason: "And since this light streamed forth to us from the Word its source, it should be as a mirror in which we may see clearly the divine power of the Word."

The implication is that, if fallen humans are guilty of failing to acknowledge Christ as the instrumental Author of their intelligence through the light of reason, then humans in their integrity must have recognized the ordering of their intelligence to Christ, not as the destined Redeemer but as eternal Wisdom. So the question remains: just what was the content of this knowledge; in what sense did Adam and Eve know Christ?

It is clear that for Calvin what is actually known of the divine character through Christ in creation and in redemption is one and the same thing. While the redemptive revelation offers the gifts of forgiveness, regeneration and eternal life ("that secret love"), it does not offer more cognitively. What Christ reveals of God in his incarnate ministry are the very perfections which we have seen to be manifested by the *opera Dei*. Commenting on the text, "Who is the image of the invisible God" at *Comm. Col.* 1.15, Calvin says:

> For Paul is not concerned here with those things which by communication belong also to creatures, but with the perfect wisdom, goodness, righteousness and power of God. . . For in Christ, he shows us his righteousness, goodness, wisdom, power, in short, his entire self.

This correspondence is indicated also in the following passage:

> To whatever subjects men apply their minds, there is none from which they will derive greater advantage than from continual meditation on his wisdom, goodness, righteousness and mercy....Accordingly Paul, in Eph. 3.18, declares that our height, length, breadth and depth, consists in knowing the unspeakable riches of grace, which have been manifested to us in Christ.[91]

If, then, Calvin means to assign to the content of the knowledge of Christ known through the *genuinus ordo naturae* precisely those perfections of deity revealed by the creation, our question becomes: how is it that these perfections are seen to be *mediated* perfections, mediated through the *persona* of the Word? The closest we may be able to come to an answer is to infer that for Calvin the presence of God to humans in the condition of rectitude (a paradisal estate) was so transparent that the character and perfections of deity attested by the creation were recognizably trinitarian. We may recall that at *Inst.* I.13.18, in distinguishing "economically" among the *personae* of the Trinity, he attributes "to the Son, wisdom, counsel and the ordered disposition of all things." Then he goes on to assert that there is in humans a natural disposition to perceive the divine in trinitarian terms: "For the mind of each human being is naturally inclined to contemplate God first, then the wisdom coming forth from him, and lastly the power whereby he executes the decrees of his plan." Human intelligence, of all the gifts of the Creator, is intimately related to eternal Wisdom.

While Calvin does not make explicit any dependence, it is also reasonable to suppose that he simply assumed the Stoic definition of the Logos as this definition was taken over and developed by the western theological tradition. In Stoic discourse, "the generative word" (*spermatikos logos*) is the instrument of creation, and as the principle of the order of the cosmos is also "Reason" or "Law." In his own doctrine of Christ as the instrumental author of creation, Calvin was following in the steps of others who found the Stoic doctrine insightful, including the evangelist John, Philo, and second-century apologists like Justin Martyr, Theophilus, and Clement of Alexandria. The Word incarnate in Jesus Christ is that very Word which is eternally with God, the wisdom immanent in deity, and which went forth in the act of creation.

CONCLUSION

There are two distinct sources of the knowledge of God—in creation and in redemption—but, properly speaking, only one knowledge. The unique image of God is also one in Christ, for Christ is also the *scopus* of the witness of creation to God's character and perfections. But there are two different ways in which he images God. According to his power as the Mediator of creation, he does it through the *opera* which exist from him, through him and unto him (his "hands and feet"). According to his power as the redemptive Mediator, he does it through his own incarnate flesh (his "heart"). Thus does Calvin claim an essential place for Christ in the content of the knowledge of God from creation.

This knowledge, however, now avails only for the opened eyes of faith, and thus the continuing significance of the revelation in creation is dependent on its relationship to the redemptive knowledge of Jesus Christ. On the one hand, the revelation in creation can function in the case of sinful humanity only to condemn its unbelief. "On the other hand believers to whom he has given eyes to see discern the sparks of his glory as it were shining out in every individual creature."[92] The revelation in creation comes into its own again with the illumination of faith assisted by the spectacles of Scripture. This restored and positive function of the revelation in creation is most clearly expressed in Calvin's summons to continual contemplation of the creation. For the believer, knowledge of God the Creator from "the dazzling theater" of the universe means increased awareness of God's goodness and glory, and affords greater opportunity for praise. Only so may we "recognize God's powers" and express true gratitude for the divine beneficence. In sum, without the content of the knowledge of God gained from the creation, a huge gap would exist in our appreciation and acknowledgement of God's greatness.

Recognition of Calvin's appreciation of the continuing significance of the knowledge of God deriving from creation, an appreciation which evidences his sapiential breadth, leads to consideration of our question in its ethical dimension. Given the Reformer's appreciation of the significance of the natural for knowledge of God, what place does he allow in his theology of creation, as it is related to Christ, for a concept of natural law?

NOTES

1. See also *Inst.* I.13.21.
2. Ibid., 62.
3. *Comm. Gen.*, "Argument," 59f.
4. *Comm. Ps.* 104. 1.
5. Ibid., 60.
6. Iain Paul, *Knowledge of God: Calvin, Einstein and Polanyi*, viii .
7. The title page of the 1536 edition announces: "*Christianae Religionis Institutio. totam fere pietatis summa.*"
8. Arvin Vos argues that "Calvin's 'firm and certain knowledge' is in substance identical with Aquinas, view that faith is a firm belief." *Aquinas, Calvin and Contemporary Protestant Thought: a Critique of Protestant Views on the Thought of Thomas Aquinas*, 4.
9. Op. cit., 3-40.
10. God's "beneficence" in creation is repeatedly mentioned in the *Institutes*, e.g., at I.5.7; I.10.1; I.14.6; I.14.11, 22.
11. E. A. Dowey, *The Knowledge of God in Calvin's Theology*, 72.
12. *Comm. Gen.*, "Argument," 63.
13. *Comm. Jn.* 1.13.
14. *Inst.* I.3.1. See also *Comm. Ps.* 40.6; *Comm. Jn.* 1.5, 9.
15. Ibid.
16. *Comm. Jonah* 1.5.
17. *Comm. Jonah* 1.7.
18. *Comm. Jonah* 1.6.

19. *Comm. Jonah* 1.6.
20. *Comm. Acts* 17. 28.
21. *Inst.* I.3.1.
22. *Comm. Heb.* 11. 3.
23. *Inst.* I.5.8; 6.2; 14.20; II.6.1; III.9.2; *Comm. Acts* 17. 26; *Comm. I Cor.* 1. 21; etc.
24. *Inst.* I.5.1, 11; *Comm. Heb.* 11. 3; *Comm. Ps.* 19. 4.
25. *Comm. Acts* 17. 27.
26. Ibid. See also *Inst.* I.5.3.
27. *Comm. Ps.* 19. 1.
28. *Comm. Acts* 17. 24.
29. These particular attributes can be found, with minor variations, throughout Calvin's writing on creation—e. g. at *Comm. Ps.* 19. 1; 86. 15; 103. 8; *Comm. Heb.* 11. 3.
30. *Comm. Ps.* 8. 1.
31. *Comm. Heb.* 11. 3.
32. *Comm. Acts* 17. 24.
33. Ibid.
34. *Comm. Acts* 17. 18.
35. *The Epistle to the Romans*, 240-57.
36. *Comm. Acts* 17. 37.
37. *Comm. Acts* 17. 31.
38. *Comm. Acts* 17. 30.
39. *Comm. Acts* 14. 16.
40. *Comm. Acts* 14. 17.
41. *Comm. Acts* 14. 15.
42. *Comm. Acts* 17. 22, 24.
43. *Comm. Acts* 17. 3.
44. *Comm. Acts* 17. 4
45. *Comm. Acts* 17. 17.
46. In this regard, Benjamin Milner comments on the argument of Karl Barth developed in *No: Answer to Emil Brunner*: "Barth...forces upon Calvin his own inability to distinguish between an imperfect and a saving knowledge of God (82), when he twists Calvin's assertion that such knowledge is the source of idolatry to mean an equation of such knowledge with idolatry (107), and when he apparently forgets that only real knowledge—and no mere possibility—'justifies the wrath of God and his judgment upon man'" (108). Benjamin Milner, *Calvin's Doctrine of the Church*, 28n6. The page references in brackets are to the Fraenkel translation of Barth's essay.
47. *Comm. Ps.* 119. 125. See also *Inst.* I.8.13.
48. *Comm. Gen.*, "Argument," 64.
49. Ibid., 58.
50. Op. cit. 87.
51. *Comm. Ps.* 19. 1.
52. See also *Inst.* I.6.1
53. Gerald Postema, "Calvin's Alleged Rejection of Natural Theology," *Scottish Journal of Theology*, 24 (1971), 429.
54. "Scripture, to direct us to the true God, distinctly excludes and rejects all the gods of the heathen, for religion was commonly adulterated throughout almost all the ages." (*Inst.* I.10.3)

55. "For we see implanted in human nature some sort of desire to search out the truth to which man would not at all aspire if he had not already savoured it." *Inst.* II.2.12.

56. *Comm. Gen.*, "Argument," 62.

57. *Comm. Acts* 14. 17.

58. T. H. L. Parker, *Calvin's Doctrine of the Knowledge of God,* 55. Parker maintains that the witness of the creation was never sufficient because "it does not bring us to the forgiveness of sins and eternal life." This is to overlook the facts that in the condition of rectitude no forgiveness of sin was necessary and that eternal life was already enjoyed in earthly though mutable form.

59. See Chapter Two, 36-41.

60. *Comm. Jn.* 5. 25. See also *Comm. Matt.* 11. 25.

61. "The True Partaking of the Flesh and Blood of Christ in the Holy Supper," in T. F. Torrance, ed., *Tracts and Treatises by John Calvin,* II, 512.

62. "Reply to Sadolet," in J.K.S. Reid, *Calvin: Theological Treatises,* 233.

63. "Necessity of Reforming the Church," in J.K.S. Reid, *Calvin: Theological Treatises,* 196.

64. *Comm. Eph.* 5. 28-32.

65. *Comm. Rom.* 1. 20.

66. *Inst.* IV.17.24; 25; and 29 respectively.

67. *Comm. Rom.* 3. 24. See also *Comm. Eph.* 1. 5. Writes Louis Goumaz, in *La Doctrine du Salut d'apres les Commentaires de Jean Calvin sur le Nouveau Testament,* 430: "*La doctrine du salut, moulée dans les categoires de cause efficiente, materielle, instrumentale, et finale, porte nettement, comme on voit, le cachet de la philosophie de l'époque.*"

68. See also *Comm. Gal.* 3. 10, 4. 6; and *Comm. Eph.* 2. 14.

69. *ST IIa IIae.* 2. 10.

70. From the abstract, Robert H. Ayers, "Language, Logic and Reason in Calvin's *Institutes.*" *Religious Studies* 16.

71. *Comm. Jn.* 1. 18; 1. 14; 1. 17; 1. 32; 1. 29; 1. 32; 1. 11; 1. 18, respectively.

72. F. L. Battles and André Malan Hugo, eds., *Calvin's Commentary on Seneca's "De clementia,"* 80.

73. Charles Partee, *Calvin and Classical Philosophy,* 36.

74. J. K. S. Reid, ed., *Calvin: Theological Treatises,* 105.

75. Charles Partee, op. cit., 38.

76. *Inst.* "Subject Matter of the Present Work," 6.

77. If Calvin did not actually write it, he certainly felt closely enough associated with its content to flee Paris along with Cop.

78. F. L. Battles, ed. and trans., "Academic Discourse on All Saints' Day," *Hartford Quarterly,* 6 (1965), 77f.

79. *Comm. Acts* 17. 18.

80. *Comm. Matt.* 5. 2.

81. E.A. Dowey, op. cit., 207, says: " 'Gratuitousness' is a word indicating God's Godhood, his otherness, his transcendence, his unconditionedness, his absolute freedom or sovereignty, his final incomprehensibility, his holiness—all these expressed as will." One is also reminded of Karl Barth's monograph, *Resurrection of the Dead,* wherein he argues that the theme uniting the disparate interests of I Corinthians is this very Godness of God: "Without any doubt at all, the words 'resurrection of the dead' are for him [Paul] nothing else

than a paraphrase of the word 'God.' What else could the Easter gospel be except the gospel become perfectly concrete that God is the Lord?" 202.

82. *Inst.* II.8.1. See also II.2.10.

83. *Inst.* II.2.11 See also II.1.1-3 and II.2.1.

84. *Comm. Rom.* 3. 4.

85. *Calvin's Doctrine of Man*, 143.

86. *Inst.* "Prefatory Address to King Francis," 12f. He writes also at II.1.2: "Here then is what God's truth requires us to seek in examining ourselves: it requires the kind of knowledge that will strip us of all confidence in our own ability, deprive us of all occasion for boasting, and lead us to submission. We ought to keep this rule if we wish to reach the true goal of both wisdom and action."

87. As T. F. Torrance argues, op. cit., 149.

88. *Comm. Gen.*, "Argument," 63f.

89. Ibid., 64.

90. *Comm. Gen.* 3. 1.

91. *Comm. Ps.* 103. 8.

92. *Comm. Heb.* 11. 3.

5

JESUS CHRIST AND THE NATURAL LAW

The concept of a natural law is suspect for evangelical theology because it implies an imperative existing and known independently of the revelation focused in Jesus Christ. If such an imperative is given in and with creaturely existence, then questions arise as to whether this law could itself constitute a valid basis for Christian decision-making and action, and what relationship would obtain between this law and the revealed law. Calvin speaks of several sources of authority for Christian obedience including the natural law, the moral law and conformity to the image of Christ. On the basis of his evangelical restatement, and in discourse primarily concerned with the life of the regenerate, he makes it clear that Christ is the scopus of revealed law and of all Christian action. Yet in surveying the breadth of human experience in the world, he will often refer ethical and moral questions, even if provisionally, to adjudication by "what nature teaches" or "the natural law." Calvin does not always make explicit the nature of the relationship obtaining among the three sources of the divine law, but it is abundantly clear that they are expressions of one law and that this one law is known in specifically Christian form as published, and also universally, according to natural light.[1]

THE NATURAL LAW AS EXPRESSION OF THE DIVINE WILL

Calvin refers to the structure of created being as "nature" and as the "*ordo naturae*," but these concepts do not imply independence from divine direction. "Nature is rather the order prescribed by God." (*Inst.* I.5.5) "Nature is not some blind impulse, but a law settled by the will of God. God then ever regulates by his own counsel and hand whatever happens."[2] "The whole order of nature depends solely on the commandment or decree of God."[3] By extraordinary acts or miracles God teaches us "that what he freely confers upon us, is entirely the result of his own will." The occurrence of the flood in Noah's time, the reversal of the rule of primogeniture in the case of Jacob's sons, and the adaption of the serpent's tongue such that Satan speaks by it, are examples of God "purposely chang[ing] the law of nature."[4] The radical dependence of the *ordo naturae* on God is further emphasized by its temporal limitation: in the consummation, the ordinary provisions of nature, such as progeny and food, will not be required to sustain life. (*Inst.* III.25.11). "Life is not (as they commonly speak) an intrinsic good, but proceeds from God. "[5]

Yet to assert the radical dependence of the natural order on the divine will does not imply an arbitrary and changing order—in effect, disorder—but its opposite. Because the order of nature arises from the *ordinatio dei* and is maintained by God, the order is firm and trustworthy.[6] "God, the maker of the world, will by no means neglect the order which he has established."[7] Without God's continual preservation and superintendence, nature would collapse and dissolve into nothing.[8] It is one thing for God to set aside the law of nature to demonstrate the gratuitousness of divine blessing; it is another for humans to do so. Since the ordinary activity of God is to uphold the order of nature divinely established, humans who go against it violate not merely an arrangement of the physical universe, but God's enduring will for the creation. Thus "nature is for Calvin both a concept of being and a concept of a norm."[9] The order of nature is divinely mandated and as such is to be regarded as tacitly legislating. For this reason, Calvin speaks of nature as guide and teacher ("*natura duce et magistra*") and of the *lex naturae*.

In his "Third Sermon on Deuteronomy19.14,15," Calvin makes repeated reference to this legislative function. Without the principle of boundaries being drawn and maintained, "which nature had unendingly taught," "there would be a horrible confusion among men and no laws would ever be observed." When princes undertake wars through ambition or greed, "it is like an insult to God to pervert the order of nature which he has established and would have observed as sacred." Of the law of Moses requiring more than one witness to convict of crime, Calvin says that "this law has been received by men without them ever having heard that Moses had spoken."[10] Among other precepts taught by nature are the inviolability of marriage, the futility of an imposed celibacy, the necessity of obedience to magistrates, the vanity of idleness, and the abhorrent character of fratricide, slavery and incest.[11]

Calvin not only speaks of natural law as obtaining universally in the creation, but also directs attention to the inner awareness of the law possessed by human beings. Natural law is present to human consciousness in much the same way as innate awareness of God: it is an "inward law...written, even engraved, upon the hearts of all." (*Inst.* II.8.1) As in the case of the *sensus divinitatis*, Calvin draws this conclusion about natural law from its evident universality. Since all societies "are disposed to make laws for themselves of their own accord, and without being instructed to do so, it is beyond all doubt that they have certain ideas of justice and rectitude...which are implanted by nature in the hearts of men."[12]

> They prove that there is imprinted on their hearts a discrimination and judgment, by which they distinguish between justice and injustice, honesty and dishonesty...There is, therefore, a certain natural knowledge of the law, which states that one action is good and worthy of being followed, while another is to be shunned with horror. (*Comm. Rom.* 2.15)

Closely associated with this innate awareness of divine law is conscience. Calvin defines conscience on the basis of its etymology, as "a witness joined to [humans], which does not allow them to hide their sins from being accused before the judge's tribunal." It is the "awareness which hales man before God's judgement."[13] Sometimes it is difficult to discern any difference between the functions of the inward law and human conscience, as when he says: "Natural law is that apprehension of the conscience which distinguishes sufficiently between just and unjust, and which deprives men of the excuse of ignorance, while it proves them guilty by their own testimony." (*Inst.* II.2.22) Whenever natural law is considered with particular reference to human nature, as a law engraved upon the hearts of all, a virtual equivalence of function appears to obtain between it and conscience. David Willis makes this observation: "Calvin is not consistent in the way he describes the relation between conscience and natural law. Sometimes he seems to equate natural law with conscience, and sometimes he defines one as a testimony of the other's existence."[14] This inconsistency creates ambiguity about the relationship between the natural order and the natural law.

Arthur Cochrane sought to resolve the inconsistency by identifying natural law strictly with conscience, regarding it as corrupt and variable as Calvin will say that conscience is. This interpretation leads to the corollary that one must distinguish sharply between the *ordo naturae* and the *lex naturae* in the following manner: "The order of nature—man's being with and for his fellowman—is a constant that remains in spite of sin and the fall. By contrast, natural law is man's variable and fallible apprehension of the order of his being."[15] The observation that human apprehension of the order of our being is fallible is well taken. However, the identification of this fallible apprehension with the natural law leads to greater interpretive difficulties than the one it seeks to resolve.

In so far as Calvin regards natural law as the order of nature tacitly legislating, the "law" is a function of the order and, as such, an invariable expression of the divine will for the creation. The testimony of the *ordo naturae* and the command of the *lex naturae* are integral to each other. For Calvin, the "law of nature" does not refer only to a law engraved on the human heart, but also to the ordered subjection of the whole world to God's command. The observed regularity and efficiency of the various parts of the physical world are evidence of this lawful obedience, and against an obstinate and rebellious humanity, "dumb and lifeless creatures bear testimony."[16] Indeed, Isaiah sends humans to oxen and asses to learn their duty:

> Nor ought we to wonder at this; for the beasts frequently observe the order of nature more correctly, and display greater kindness, than men themselves .. .What is the reason why all animals commonly bestow so much care in rearing their young, while it frequently happens that mothers, forgetful of the voice of nature and humanity, forsake their children?[17]

The contemplation of the unfailing order in other life forms can be described as a painting in which God shows us our duty.[18] In sum, the "inconsistency" evident in Calvin's definition of natural law arises from the fact that it is dictated not only from within human consciousness, but also from without; it is an imperative which arises, with regard to human nature, both intrinsically and extrinsically.[19] Thus, it is our apprehension of the law (based on reason and conscience), not the law itself, which is variable and fallible. The natural law "impressed" upon nature and human nature alike represents God's unchanging will.

Like the testimony of the *ordo naturae*, though, the positive import of the testimony of the *lex naturae* is vitiated through human sin. Its primary theological use, like that of the revealed law, is to obviate all human excuse before God. Even though "there is nothing more common than for a man to be sufficiently instructed in a right standard of conduct by the natural law," its teaching is now unavailing: "The purpose of the natural law, therefore, is to render man inexcusable." (*Inst.* II.2.22) The command of natural law extends everywhere and is sufficient in itself to condemn us: "The knowledge of good and evil is indeed imprinted by nature on men, whereby they are rendered inexcusable; nor has any amount of barbarism ever so extinguished this light that no form of law should exist."[20]

A calamitous result of human disobedience through sin is that conscience ceases to be a constructive "witness with us."

> There are two main parts of that light which yet remain in corrupt nature. Some seed of religion is sown in all: and also, the distinction between good and evil is engraven in their consciences. But what is the fruition at last, save that religion comes to monstrous birth in a thousand superstitions, and conscience corrupts all judgment, confounding vice with virtue?[21]

The mere fact of the testimony of conscience concerning the law does not guarantee action in accord with its warning voice. A shadow falls whenever we attempt to apply recognized principle to our own concrete circumstance:

> Every man will affirm that murder is evil. But he who is plotting the death of an enemy contemplates murder as something good. The adulterer will condemn adultery in general, but will privately flatter himself in his own adultery. Herein is man's ignorance: when he comes to a particular case, he forgets the general principle that he has just laid down. (*Inst.* II.2.23)[22]

While the deliberate choice of vice entails culpability for sin, here again Calvin's description of the human condition suggests that ignorance and adversity also play their part in confounding human judgment. Despite good intention, "our reason is overwhelmed by so many forms of deceptions, is subject to so many errors, dashes against so many obstacles, is caught in so many difficulties, that it is far from directing us aright." (*Inst.* II.2.25) Philosophers teach that "all things seek good through a natural instinct...But man does not choose by reason and pursue with zeal what is truly good for himself according to the excellence of his immortal nature; nor does he use reason in deliberation or bend his mind to it." *(Inst.* II.2.26)

In the fallen state, therefore, conscience is neither sufficiently trustworthy or powerful to keep us from wrong-doing. Its positive import is vitiated subjectively, in the same way as is the efficacy of the testimony of creation for knowledge of God. It now functions to arraign our guilt and even to add to its burden: "There is no doubt that the more clearly the conscience is struck with awareness of its sin the more the iniquity grows. For stubborn disobedience against the Lawgiver is then added to transgression." (*Inst.* II.7.1) Knowledge of the law in this circumstance can only bind the conscience with a curse. (*Inst.* II.7.14, 15) However, it is possible for humans to enjoy a conscience set free from condemnation: this follows upon the redemption and restoration that occurs through the justification of the ungodly. The imputed righteousness of Christ is the only refuge for awakened consciences. (*Inst.* III.12.3)

The important chapter on Christian freedom in the *Institutes* (III.19) is essentially an account of the nature of conscience as restored; Calvin notes three aspects of its liberty. Taking courage from its justification before God, the conscience is free to set aside all legal righteousness (*Inst.* III.19.2), and also to regard all humanly devised obligations in religion as *adiaphora*, matters indifferent (*Inst.* III.19.7). The third aspect is more immediately positive in its significance: the consciences of believers can now observe the law not from necessity, but from a joyful readiness, as "freed from the law's yoke, they willingly obey God's will." (*Inst.* III.19.4)

"A good conscience, then, is nothing but inward integrity of heart. In this sense, Paul writes that the fulfilment of the law is love from a clear conscience and sincere faith." (*Inst.* III.19.16) As redeemed and regenerate, believers may strengthen themselves "by remembering their own innocence and uprightness," since "the purity of their own conscience brings them some comfort and confidence." On this basis, good works serve as a secondary testimony of election: "A conscience so founded, erected, and established is established also in the consideration of works, so far, that is, as these are testimonies of God dwelling and ruling in us." (*Inst.* III.14.18) The conscience thus "indicts or acquits, depending on the degree of free obedience,"[23] and, grace upon grace, imputed righteousness becomes actual wherever Christian freedom obtains.

The difference between the condemned and the freed conscience also makes for a difference in the function of the natural law. As in the case of the revelatory capacity of the order of nature, the effects of redemption and restoration allow the natural law to come into its own again. What occurs with the publication of the moral law by Moses is that "the authority of God is conjoined to what we already should have known beforehand."[24] "Accordingly (because it is necessary both for our dullness and for our arrogance), the Lord has provided us with a written law to give us clearer witness of what was too obscure in the natural law, shake off our listlessness, and strike more vigorously our mind and memory." (*Inst.* II.8.13) "It is a fact that the law of God which we call the moral law is nothing else than a testimony of natural law and of that conscience which God has engraved upon the minds of men." (*Inst.* IV.20.16) The testimony of Scripture is required to clarify and confirm the imperative of the law for the regenerate, but its commands are seen to originate in the will of God and to be perpetually valid. Knowledge of God's law in nature as well as in Scripture intensifies the believer's sense of assurance and clean conscience. As with the revealed law, the pre-eminent use (*usus praecipius*) of natural law is fundamentally positive, the direction of the faithful life.

François Wendel states that Calvin's teaching on the natural law constitutes a "foreign body" in his theology.[25] While Wendel is correct in perceiving Calvin's dependence on the tradition before him, his assessment is insufficiently dialectical to do justice to the complexity of the Reformer's position. Calvin cannot consign the idea of natural law to the category of the sub-evangelical when his goal is to produce a definition of it complementary to his evangelical restatement. He is not advocating an unrefracted concept of the *lex naturae*, as if it obtained irrespective of the fall. Rather, he is offering a rationale for the extension of the imperatives of the revealed law into the world of experience and action outside the Church, thereby asserting the inescapable relevance to all life of standards which belong uniquely but not solely to the household of faith. What is explicitly commanded in the revealed law also obtains universally, though in a tacit way.

Furthermore, Calvin's teaching is distinguished from that of the medievals in its emphasis on the connection of natural law with conscience rather than directly with reason. To be sure, he views conscience as a major constituent of the "light of nature," but, as has been observed, the natural law cannot be regarded simply as either as a function of reason or as equivalent to conscience. In contrast, according to the teaching of Aquinas, the natural law is to be viewed properly and essentially as a function of reason in its practical use and is actually constituted by it.[26] "This is to say that natural law appears to be less an extrinsic principle of human action than an intrinsic one. It is not so much a law (*lex*) imposed from without as a person's own realization of what is right (*ius*)."[27] For Calvin, however, the emphasis falls on a concept of natural law that is constituted autonomously from reason, though human reason is ordered to it; it is "implanted" by God and is apprehended by conscience. In sum, it is a conception more focused on human responsibility than on human capacity; on relationship rather than being.

While Calvin thus maintains his evangelical focus, he is aware that with respect to observance of the law there are pagans whose obedience sometimes puts so-called Christians to shame. For instance, pagans are aware of the natural law commanding the sanctity of monogamous marriage, "as nature itself taught Plato, and others of the sounder class of philosophers."[28] In the bizarre case of Abraham's jeopardizing Sarah through presenting her as his sister, Calvin extols the conduct of Abimelech who is both repentant for his intended sin against Sarah and also angry with Abraham's deception. "The king of Gerar could not indeed have spoken thus, had he not acknowledged the sacred right of marriage." Although Calvin manages to exonerate Abraham by construing his cowardice as a prudent concern to secure the perpetuity of God's chosen seed, it is ironic that it is a pagan who "was a herald of that divine judgment which miserable men in vain endeavour to elude by their cavils." [29] On the other hand, such exemplary conduct serves as the basis for a critique of Christian libertinism rather than for an endorsement of pagan rectitude.

In particular, it is with respect to the content of the first table of the law that humans generally are at the farthest remove from perceiving naturally what divine law requires. "Man is so shrouded in the darkness of errors that he hardly begins to grasp through this natural law what worship is acceptable to God." (*Inst.* II.8.2) Again, with respect to the principal points of the first table, including putting our trust in God and observing the sabbath, Calvin says: "What soul, relying on natural perception, ever had an inkling that the lawful worship of God consists in these and like matters?" In contrast, "Men have somewhat more understanding of the precepts of the second table because those are more closely concerned with the preservation of civil society among them." (*Inst.* II.2.24)

As far as the natural law concerns matters of the second table—that is, justice in human society rather than justification before God—there is greater possibility of approximation to the standards of divine law, even if they are known in a confused and inadequate way. In other words, there are degrees of clarity in the perception of natural law, just as there are degrees of clarity in the knowledge of God from the natural order. None of the degrees along the spectrum, of course, is sufficient for filial communion with God. There is not to be found in any human "a full knowledge of the law," only "some seeds of justice implanted in their nature."[30] Yet the distinctions produced by these seeds as they generate obedience on varied soil are not inconsequential.

Positively, Calvin can attribute the wisdom and achievements of the unregenerate to the anonymous work of the Spirit of God. Negatively, he maintains that without explicit faith these noble pagans fail to attain true righteousness "because duties are weighed not by deeds but by ends":

> For even though they are God's instruments for the preservation of human society in righteousness, continence, friendship, temperance, fortitude, and prudence, yet they carry out these good works of God very badly. For they are restrained from evil-doing not by genuine zeal for good, but either by mere ambition or by self-love, or some other perverse motive. (*Inst.* III.14.3)

One wishes that Calvin had stuck to the high road in guarding evangelical truth and avoided such a dismissive tone. One wonders also whether he really has valued at full significance what he himself acknowledges, namely, that there are pagans who know the law in some degree, and obey what they know of it, sometimes putting Christians to shame. Their partial obedience certainly does not provide any ground for (theological) justification before God since they have no inkling of right worship, let alone saving faith in the Redeemer. But does it not please God that their conduct is in some measure in harmony with the prescription of social duties in the law?

The problem is not unrelated to Bonhoeffer's question about the status of the (ethically) good man. What has the gospel to say to the non-believer who nevertheless is not failing in his fundamental human responsibilities and whose company, compared to that of many of the "pious," one might prefer? The chasm between the present-day interpreter of Calvin and Calvin himself at this point is very wide. For us today, the existence of "noble pagans" in our midst is a challenge and a mystery. Ultimately, we too may ascribe their wisdom and work to the anonymous gifts of the Holy Spirit, but not so neatly (and dismissively) as Calvin, and not without acknowledging the courageous nature of their response to what remains for them unacknowledged grace.

THE NATURE AND FORMS OF THE DIVINE LAW

LAW AS THE PRINCIPLE OF ORDER

Among Calvin's major contributions to theology is his thoroughly positive conception of law, a conception deriving from the fact that, for him, law is ultimately a synonym for order, the universal order willed by God for the creation. In its narrower definition, law is associated with prescription and proscription, and with negative notions of judgement, restraint and accusation. But more generously conceived, law is essentially positive, setting forth the structure of right relationships between Creator and creatures. Writes E. A. Dowey: "It is not something that comes in between God and man, destructive of a personal relation, but is the mode of that relation."[31] Moreover, as John H. Leith observes, it belongs to Calvin's high estimation of law that he understands it "not in an impersonal sense but as the personal presence and claim of God."[32] Thus Calvin remarks that "the true and pure religion was so handed on in the law that God's countenance in a manner shone forth therein."[33] "In the law God shows us what is pleasing to him. Those, therefore, who wish to examine properly how far they agree with God, test all their purposes and practices by this standard."[34]

Regarding law as essentially the expression of proper submission and obedience to the Creator, Calvin avers that even before the fall, a law was established in Eden. In the prohibition of one tree in the garden "God designed that the whole human race should be accustomed from the beginning to reverence his deity . . . and [be] subject to his authority."[35] Yet the purpose is emphatically positive: "Here is the object of the teaching of the law: to join man by holiness of life to his God, and as Moses elsewhere says, to make him cleave to God." (*Inst.* II.8.51)

Good Hebrew scholar that he was, Calvin knew that "law" is "Torah," a gift of relationship, shaped by grace. "I understand by the word 'law' not only the Ten Commandments, which set forth a godly and righteous rule of living, but the form of religion handed down by God to Moses."[36] Thus, the law is not the denial of the covenant with Abraham but its renewal, and believers grasp in the law not only its commands, but the accompanying promises of grace. When David commends the law so highly,

> he does not speak simply of the precepts of the Moral Law, but comprehends the whole covenant by which God has adopted the descendants of Abraham to be his peculiar people; and, therefore, to the moral law—the law of living well—he joins the free promises of salvation, or rather Christ himself, in whom and upon whom this adoption was founded.[37]

"Now from the grace offered the Jews we can surely deduce that the law was not devoid of reference to Christ." (*Inst.* II.7.1)

For Calvin there can never be a stark contrast between law and gospel. There is only one covenant between God and the elect—founded, expressed, and finally to be consummated in Jesus Christ. Calvin never tires of affirming that the basis of the covenant of life is the same for patriarchs and apostles: Jesus Christ.[38] "The God who of old appeared to the patriarchs was no other than Christ."[39] After the fall, the basis of our salvation is by grace, such that "the fathers (according to the offer made them through the word of God) are by faith made partakers of this life; that this word itself was founded upon Jesus Christ; and that all the pious who have since lived were sustained by the very same promise of salvation by which Adam was first raised from the fall."[40] The patriarchs have "a common salvation with us by the grace of the same Mediator." (*Inst.* II.10.2) For Calvin, law entails covenant, covenant entails grace, and grace entails the Mediator. Christ is the scopus of the revealed law. "Indeed, every doctrine of the law, every command, every promise, always points to Christ."[41]

Calvin's view of the law as positive ordering principle and expression of covenantal relationship issues in his description of it as life-giving. It follows that its condemnatory character is purely accidental:

> For since the law is the perfect rule for leading a godly and holy life, and makes plain the righteousness of God, it is justifiably regarded as the teaching of life and salvation...The law therefore holds life itself... Its description as the "ministration of death" is something that is accidental to it on account of man's corrupt nature. For the law does not create sin, but finds it in us. The law offers life; but because of our corruption we ourselves receive nothing but death from it.[42]

Calvin draws the corollary that for anyone capable of observing the law in all its commands, whether in its natural or published form, "the reward of eternal life is not promised in vain."[43] Yet, because of the universal incursion of sin, the law now functions to convict everyone of unrighteousness. (*Inst.* II.7.6) This is the first and "theological" use of the law.

Second, the law also serves the civil community by restraining "certain men who are untouched by any care for what is just and right unless compelled by hearing the dire threats in the law." (*Inst.* II.7.10) But its third and pre-eminent use (*usus praecipius*) is to confirm the regenerate in their understanding of the divine will and to encourage them in an aroused obedience. "In this perfection to which it exhorts us, the law points out the goal toward which throughout life we are to strive." (*Inst.* II.7.13) This third use is identical in function with the original use of the law in Eden. "The law of God contains in itself that newness by which his image can be restored in us." (*Inst.* III.6.1)

One Law, Diverse Forms

Whether expressed as the natural law, the moral law (contained in the Mosaic commandments and the teaching of Christ), or conformity to the image of Christ, there is only one divine law variously apprehended, the unity of which consists in identity of content. Calvin observes of the relationship between the law known through natural light and through revelation: "Now that inward law, which we have above described as written, even engraved, upon the hearts of all, in a sense asserts the very same things that are to be learned from the two Tables." (*Inst.* II.8.1) Again, he writes: "It is a fact that the law of God which we call the moral law is nothing else than a testimony of natural law and of that conscience which God has engraved upon the minds of men." (*Inst.* IV.20.16) While Moses eulogizes the revealed law at length, "it prescribes nothing which nature does not itself dictate to be most certain and most just, and nothing which experience itself does not show us to be more profitable or more desirable than anything else."[44]

The fact that the publication of the law by Moses came about because of human sin does not make the content of the law adventitious, nor invite the conclusion that its imperative is abrogated for those regenerate in Christ. There is an essential content in the Mosaic commandments which Calvin denominates "the moral law," which possesses perpetual validity: "For it is his eternal and unchangeable will that he himself indeed be worshipped by us all, and that we love one another." (*Inst.* IV.20.15)[45] While the ceremonial laws of the Old Testament cultus are abrogated at the coming of Christ, this is not the case for the moral law. Calvin strongly rejects the point of view that Christ's appearance in history implies either a deficiency in the law or its abrogation. Of Christ's word in the Sermon on the Mount, "Ye have heard that it was said," he avers: "So let us have no more of that error, that here a defect of the Law is corrected by Christ: Christ is not made into a new law-giver, adding anything to the everlasting righteousness of his Father, but is to be given the attention of a faithful interpreter, teaching us the nature of the law, its object, and its scope."[46]

The challenge presented by Christ is not to Moses, but to scribal glosses, "which had vitiated the purity of the divine law."[47] "Christ prescribed no other rule of pious and upright life than that handed down in the Mosaic Law, for perfect love of God and of the neighbor is altogether perfect righteousness."[48] Nor does the apostolic witness to Christ add anything to the law: "The writings of the apostles contain nothing but a simple and natural explanation of the law and the prophets along with a clear description of the things expressed in them."[49]

"There are not many rules, but one everlasting and unchangeable rule to live by." (*Inst.* II.7.13) As Calvin never ceased to say, the gospel abrogates the law only in its rigour and curse, not in its validity.[50]

Conformity to the Image of Christ

As observed earlier, law is essentially an expression of divine order and covenantal relationship, both entailing grace; accordingly, Jesus Christ is its scopus. While this concept of Christ as *scopus* refers to the law in its published form (the moral law), it is not irrelevant to the law as naturally known. Since the divine law is one in all its forms, and, since the natural law, no less than the revealed law, functions now to condemn fallen humanity, it will also find in the reconciling and redeeming work of Christ its liberating key. As the revealed law is restored to its pre-eminent and original use through the effects of regeneration, so is the natural. Conceived apart from Christ, it ministers only condemnation but, as restored, it accomplishes its proper life-maintaining work.

Integral to a full account of Calvin's teaching on the divine law is his concept of conformity to the image of Christ, his particular version of *imitatio Christi.* He begins with the evangelical insight that the ethical significance of Christ is founded on his work in justification and sanctification. This work not only rescues believers from condemnation before the law but also sets them on their feet so that we can act in willing obedience to God's rule. "The object of regeneration . . . is to manifest in the life of believers a harmony and agreement between God's righteousness and their obedience, and thus to confirm the adoption that they have received as sons." *(Inst.* III.6.1) From an evangelical perspective, no human is in a position to consider what it means to do justly and to love mercy, or to follow Christ, except through the grace of regeneration flowing from Christ's vicarious work.

Pagan philosophers exhort humans to virtue by encouraging them to live in accordance with nature. But given human mutability and corruption, greater motivation and greater explicitness are required. The greater source of motivation is found in grateful recognition of the unparalleled benefits deriving from divine love in the redemptive grace of Jesus Christ:

> Ever since God revealed himself as a Father to us, we must prove our ungratefulness to him if we did not in turn show ourselves his sons. Ever since Christ cleansed us with the washing of his blood, and imparted this cleansing through baptism, it would be unfitting to befoul ourselves with new pollutions. Ever since he engrafted us into his body, we must take special care not to disfigure ourselves, who are his members, with any spot of blemish. Ever since Christ him-

> self, who is our Head, ascended into heaven, it behooves us, having laid aside love of earthly things, wholeheartedly to aspire heavenward. Ever since the Holy Spirit dedicated us as temples to God, we must take care that God's glory shine through us, and must not commit anything to defile ourselves with the filthiness of sin. Ever since both our souls and bodies were destined for heavenly incorruption and an unfading crown, we ought to strive manfully to keep them pure and uncorrupted until the day of the Lord. These, I say, are the most auspicious foundations upon which to establish one's life. One would look in vain for the like of these among the philosophers, who, in their commendation of virtue, never rise above the natural dignity of man. (*Inst.* III.6.3)

The "more" in regeneration includes emphatic awareness of the lengths to which God's benevolence extends itself to meet our need.

If the greater motivation derives from Christ's work, the greater explicitness derives from the fact that Christ is the sovereign exemplar of that conduct taught by divine law. The content of Christ's teaching, as we have seen, is identical with the moral law as published by Moses and adds nothing to it. The "more" that Christ offers ethically stems from his own active obedience which constitutes an image to which "all the godly must be conformed."[51] According to Calvin, Paul does not simply say that believers "should be conformed to Christ, but to the image of Christ, in order to teach us that in Christ there is a living and conspicuous exemplar which is set before all the sons of God for their imitation."[52] Ingrafting into Christ must issue in an ethical dynamic:

> Scripture shows that God the Father, as he has reconciled us to himself in his Christ has in him stamped for us the likeness (*imaginem*) to which he would have us conform . . . Christ, through whom we return into favour with God, has been set before us as an example (*exemplar*) whose pattern we ought to express in our life . . . For we have been adopted as sons by the Lord with this one aim: that our life express Christ, the bond of our adoption. (*Inst.* III.6.3)

The crucial content of the image to which we are called to conform "is that denial of self which Christ enjoins with such great earnestness upon his disciples at the outset of their service." (*Inst.* III.7.2) Conformity to Christ is ultimately cruciform: members of his body must be willing to accept suffering like his and also to suffer for his sake in accordance with his "example of patience." Cross-bearing is an essential part of the life of the elect because it was an essential part of Christ's earthly life; "his whole life was nothing but a sort of perpetual cross." Believers must bear the cross also because "It is the heavenly Father's will thus to exercise them so as to put his children to a definite test." As Christ undertook the bearing of the cross for no other purpose than "to attest and prove his obedience to the Father," so our patience and obedience are being refined in affliction. The cross also "strikes at our perilous confidence in the flesh" in order that our trust might be transferred to God.[53] And in times of relative ease, unruly desires to indulge the flesh can only be resisted by voluntarily submitting to the discipline of Christ's yoke, "putting on meekness and being conformed to Christ."[54]

Conformity to the image of Christ attested in the New Testament thus constitutes the most compelling form of divine law. But the radical nature of the summons of Christ to cross-bearing raises a question: does the concept of self-denial and of the willing acceptance of suffering constitute an overplus in the one form of divine law (conformity to Christ), a content not taught by nature? To take the example of injustice and oppression, it seems natural not to accept suffering in the face of injustice but rather to seek the restoration of just conditions, if need be, by force. In this case, the pattern of conformity to Christ's suffering would be paradoxical in the face of natural law, if not a contradiction of it.

Luther maintains just as strongly as Calvin that the content of the natural law is the same as that of Scriptural law.[55] But he also emphasizes that there is a "law of Christ and of the gospel" which is binding on the believer but not on the heathens.[56] "For no matter how right you are, it is not right for a Christian to appeal to law or to fight, but rather to suffer wrong and endure evil, and there is no other way . . . We have all we need in our Lord, who will not leave us, as he has promised. Suffering! suffering! Cross! cross! This and nothing else is the Christian law!"[57]

Calvin also, though less dramatically, counsels patient endurance in the face of oppression. He admits that it is natural to oppose a tyrant: "No deed is considered more noble, even among philosophers, than to free one's country from tyranny. Yet a private citizen who lays his hand upon a tyrant is openly condemned by the heavenly Judge." (*Inst.* III.11.6) Only those who bear an equivalent status to that of the ancient Spartan ephors, that is, those to whom responsibility for checking the wilfulness of chief magistrates has been committed, may oppose a tyrant with God's blessing. (*Inst.* IV.20.31)

The appeal to a law of Christ beyond the natural is, however, only apparent in Calvin's case. The willingness to suffer injustice patiently belongs as much to his concern for a proper order as to his understanding of evangelical imperatives. The argument that no private person may oppose a ruler without divine condemnation comes also from his belief that each individual should "look to his own calling": "Each individual has his own kind of living assigned to him by the

Lord as a sort of sentry post so that he may not heedlessly wander about through life." (*Inst.* II.11.6) Only those possessing the proper calling of ephors may challenge a tyrant because others doing so would violate the order of nature represented in callings.

In Calvin's mind, the imperatives of revealed and natural law, love and justice, coincide. While Luther acknowledges an area of overlap between these two expressions of divine law, he nonetheless maintains a sharp distinction between the imperatives as they obtain in the sphere of church and gospel, and in that of state and society. Calvin observes the distinctions but ultimately regards the commonality between them as more significant. Because of his conception of law as the order of right relationship, love and justice (or equity) go hand in hand in his theology, and he finds it congenial to ground love of the neighbor upon law. The love which the regenerate willingly express toward God and neighbor is, at the same time, a duty they owe. To love the neighbor is precisely to recognize her standing and therefore her rights as a child of God, "since all should be contemplated in God, not in themselves." (*Inst.* II.8.55) "He who loves will render to every man his right, will do injury or harm to no man and will, so far as he can, do good to all."[58] The fulfillment of social duty, which is evidently commanded in natural law, ultimately is seen to coincide with the gospel imperative of self-denial, since to seek the well-being of other men and women involves nothing less than the redirection of love away from ourselves to others. (*Inst.* II.8.54) Away, then, with the scholastic notion that the evangelical command to love is an (optional) counsel of perfection: "God's eternal law" is "that we are to love our neighbor." (*Inst.* II.8.56)

The Content of Divine Law and the Imago Dei

Calvin's insistence on the unity of the various forms of divine law through identity of content has been noted and he identifies this single content as the prescription of fundamental equity among men. Thus he argues that, while the constitutions and positive laws of different societies may vary widely, they are all legitimate "provided all equally press toward the same goal of equity." "Equity, because it is natural, cannot but be the same for all, and, therefore, this same purpose ought to apply to all laws, whatever their object." (*Inst.* IV.20.16) Natural law offers "this precept, wherein the people are commanded to cultivate equity toward all without exception."[59] The concept of equity as fundamental to social relations pushes the believing community beyond the mere enumeration of rights and duties. In his exposition of the revealed law, Calvin points out that the Ten Commandments actually prescribe as well as proscribe. True obedience to them, as an obedience rendered to the Lawgiver, involves more than the avoidance of vice:

> We say that the virtue goes beyond this to contrary duties and deeds. Therefore in this commandment,

> "You shall not kill," men's common sense will see only that we must abstain from wronging anyone or desiring to do so. Besides this, it contains, I say, the requirement that we give our neighbor's life all the help we can. To prove that I am not speaking unreasonably: God forbids us to hurt or harm a brother unjustly, because he wills that the brother's life be dear and precious to us. So at the same time he requires those duties of love which can apply to its preservation. (*Inst.* II.8.9)

This active benevolence is at the heart of the natural law also. Thus Calvin writes that the brotherly love of the neighbor espoused in the Sermon on the Mount is "the course which nature herself dictates."[60] Love of the neighbor is not only rooted in the *ecclesia* but also in the common nature of humankind:

> To keep us in a fraternal bond of love, God testifies that our neighbors are all men in general, for the common tie of nature unites us. As often as I see a man, who is my bone and my flesh, I must necessarily see myself, as reflected in a glass. Though the majority may recoil from an association in holy things, yet the natural order is not ruined by this grievous fault of theirs, for we must consider God the Author of the union.[61]

The evangelical commands do not contradict or supersede, but rather confirm, natural fellow-feeling. Even within the household of faith an appropriate sharing of responsibility is naturally mandated: "Now the sharing of tasks among members is believed to have nothing gratuitous about it, but, rather, to be a payment of that which, due by the law of nature, it would be monstrous to refuse." (*Inst.* III.7.7)

Since natural law is the tacit imperative of the order willed by God for the creation, the failure to observe the law of love involves the disfigurement of the *ordo naturae*. God has so connected us together that to fail in the duty to assist those in need is to "pervert the order of nature."[62] In this unity is found "a sacred bond by which the whole of society is bound together" so as to preclude violence: "For man cannot injure man, but he becomes an enemy to his own flesh, and violates and perverts the whole order of nature."[63] In his reading of Acts 13.36, Calvin discerns the natural basis of mutual assistance in society:

> We are taught by this how men are to live in the world, viz., helping each other in their mutual dealings. For each man is not born to live for himself; but the human race is bound together by a sacred chain. Therefore unless our intention is to overthrow the

> laws of nature, let us remember that we must not live privately for ourselves, but for our neighbors.[64]

Crucial to Calvin's understanding of the natural imperative is his concept of the *imago Dei*. It is significant that the atrocity of murder is characterized as an offence against God not because each human being is one to whom the offer of salvation in Jesus Christ is made—a possible move on evangelical premise—but because of the engraved *imago*: "Men are indeed unworthy of God's care, if respect be had only to themselves; but since they bear the image of God engraven on them, he deems himself violated in their person."[65] "Take note, therefore, that God bears us such love as to consider himself wounded and violated in our persons, the more so because he has created us in his image."[66] "Whosoever then uses violence against the life of man, destroys as far as he can, the image of the eternal God."[67] Again, the rigor of the master-servant relationship is to be moderated because "we have been joined together as in one flesh, and are all formed in the image of God."[68] Furthermore, the distinction between friend and foe can be only provisional, "for the wickedness of men cannot annul the right of nature."[69] And of those beyond the household of faith, Calvin says: "Love is, indeed, extended to those outside, for we are all of the same flesh and are all created in the image of God."[70]

Calvin's teaching on the *imago Dei* represents an especially evident instance of the complementarity of the evangelical and sapiential dimensions in his theology, since, as we have seen (in Chapter Three), he offers both "dynamic-christological" and "static-ontological" definitions of it. This has consequences for the interpretation of Calvin's ethic, as, for example, in the question of whether fallen humans can perceive the image of God in their fellows. If Calvin held only the dynamic conception, the answer would be an emphatic No: the image has been so disfigured by the fall that such recognition is not possible naturally. Only as that image is restored in Christ can it be perceived as such.[71] Objectively, the true image of God can be perceived through a transformation that will be complete only at the consummation and through both the saving and perfecting work of Christ. Thus Calvin writes that through the gospel "we should be transformed into God's image...By continual progress we increase both in the knowledge of God and in conformity to his image."[72]

On the dynamic conception, therefore, the *imago* is perceived variably, shining forth whenever righteousness is fulfilled. Moreover, it is focussed on Christ: "Now we see how Christ is the most perfect image of God: if we are conformed to it, we are so restored that with true piety, righteousness, purity and intelligence we bear God's image." (*Inst.* I.15.4) The christological nature of the transformation into the image of God is especially evident when Calvin situates discussion of the *imago* within the church: "it is among members of the household of faith that this same image is more carefully to be noted, in so far as it has been renewed through the Spirit of Christ." (*Inst.* II.7.6)

That it is within the household of faith that the image of God in humanity is most to be noted alerts us to the fact that, subjectively, it is only the regenerate who can perceive the *imago* for what it truly is. This is not only a privilege for the believer, but a singular responsibility, as Calvin notes in referring to the pagan sailors who took compassion on Jonah and whose obedience the Christian's must excel: "we ought not only to imitate these sailors, but to go far beyond them."[73] Our duty to the fellow human is clear enough. But our duty to each other within the body of Christ is clearer still. In a powerful image Calvin asserts that to fail in the duty of love here is to "tear Jesus Christ in pieces."[74] "Love is, indeed, extended to those outside, for we are all created in the image of God. But because the image of God shines more brightly in the regenerate, it is proper that the bond of love be much closer among the disciples of Christ."[75]

To give an unqualified No as the answer to our question, however, is not dialectical enough to do justice to Calvin. If there were no natural perception of the *imago*, then what is it that the unregenerate perceive such that they treat the other as a neighbor, as in the case of the sailors who, "taught by nature," showed compassion on Jonah? It appears that while they cannot know the law in the sense of clear perception or whole-hearted observance, they can know that there is an order and a law instituted throughout the creation by divine power, an order and law before which they are accountable, though their knowledge is imperfect and confused. "Heathen authors also saw this, although not with sufficient clearness, that since all men are born for the sake of each other, human society is not properly maintained, except by an interchange of good offices."[76] The entire human race belongs in a single body and membership in this body entails inescapable responsibilities of mutual affection and aid.[77]

Unregenerate humanity not only perceives a common bond uniting the race, but in some measure also recognizes its root in the *imago*. In "The First Sermon on Deuteronomy 2.1-7," for example, Calvin states "that all men must regard themselves as formed in the image of God, as possessing a common nature among themselves. And pagans have clearly recognized this fact."[78] In another sermon on Deuteronomy, Calvin asserts that the divine prohibition of murder is naturally imprinted on the heart: "Men recognize themselves to be of one nature and each one sees the image of God in his neighbor."[79] In these cases, Calvin's assumption is that the *imago* is not so defaced as to be unrecognizable to an unregenerate humanity. On the ontological conception of the *imago*, a remnant of humanity's original integrity is always present and at least partially visible, since the image of God is indelibly imprinted, or engraved, upon human nature. Sometimes, in fact, Calvin speaks so confidently of the content of the *imago* that one would think it directly and eminently visible. Thus, at *Comm. Ps*. 8.5, he summarizes "the distinguished endowments which clearly manifest that men were formed after the image of God":

> The reason with which they are endued, and by which they can distinguish between good and evil; the principle of religion which is planted in them; their intercourse with each other, which is preserved from being broken up by certain sacred bonds; the regard to what is becoming, and the sense of shame which guilt awakens in them, as well as their continuing to be governed by laws; all these things are clear indications of pre-eminent and celestial wisdom.

On the one hand, therefore, Calvin holds that the *imago* is being restored through a progressive transformation occurring under the aegis of the Holy Spirit; its existing disfigurement is a sign of human guilt and inexcusability. Only through Christ, who is the image of God in humanity fully visible, and to the eyes of the regenerate is the *imago* truly known. On the other hand, the disfigurement does not leave the *imago* in eclipse; unregenerate humanity recognizes a common human nature which is God-originated and experiences an innate imperative to honour it. Some pagans, without knowing the full significance of this God-ordained nature and imperative, are exemplary in their response and are said to "see the image of God" in their neighbors. Yet what they see is the *imago* disfigured, and they cannot grasp its origin in an integrity that once perfectly reflected the divine glory, or its perfect restoration in Jesus Christ.[80]

CIVIL GOVERNMENT AND THE LORDSHIP OF JESUS CHRIST

A major remaining area of investigation in Calvin's ethic, and one that could scarcely be overlooked, is the Reformer's doctrine of civil government. Two fundamental questions are relevant in this regard. First, what does Calvin conceive to be the theological basis for the existence of the state; does it derive its justification from God's eternal purpose in Jesus Christ or from the *ordo naturae*, or from some combination of the two? Second, what kind of relationship is conceived to exist between civil government and the spiritual government of Christ; what is the nature and degree of autonomy of the one from the other?

The Positive Basis of Civil Government

After the fall, civil government functions as a part of the provision of God's preserving grace. From this point of view the state's *raison d'être* is to restrain human society from bringing destruction upon itself. This is the tenor of Calvin's remarks at *Comm. Rom.* 13.3:

> The usefulness of rulers is that the Lord has designed by this means to provide for the peace of the good, and to restrain the waywardness of the wicked. In these two ways the safety of mankind is secured. Unless the fury of the wicked is opposed and the innocent protected from their wilfulness, there will be universal destruction. If this, therefore, is the only remedy by which mankind can be protected from destruction, we ought to preserve it with care, unless we want to admit that we are public enemies of the human race.

As well as providing for "a quiet life," ordered government also offers other benefits, including the "preservation of godliness" and "the care of public gravity."[81] It is clear that Calvin regards other ordinances, including both labour and marriage, as divine institutions originating with humanity's condition as created.[82] Interpretation concerning the state is less certain. Emil Brunner has argued that civil government is an "ordinance of preservation" (not "of creation," like labour and marriage), occasioned by sin.[83] However, Calvin's teaching on civil government is not always dominated by this negative character. In further remarks on Rom. 13, for example, he dismisses the notion that human government might have arisen as a divinely-ordained punitive discipline, and gives no hint that he regards it as primarily occasioned by sin:

> The reason why we ought to be subject to magistrates is that they have been appointed by God's ordination. If it is the will of God to govern the world in this manner, any who despise his power are striving to overturn the order of God, and are therefore resisting God himself, since to despise the providence of the One who is the author of civil government (*uris politici*) is to wage war against him. We should understand, furthermore, that the powers of magistrates are from God, not as pestilence, famine, war, and other punishments are said to be from him, but because he has appointed them for the just and lawful government of the world.[84]

It is the positive principle of order in the creation which actually controls Calvin's understanding of civil government, not the negative principle of the restraint of evil: "It has not come about by human perversity that the authority over all things on earth is in the hands of kings and other rulers, but by divine providence and holy ordinance." (*Inst.* IV.20.4) It is as instruments of providence that magistrates are called "vicars of God." (*Inst.* IV.20.6) "Magistrates are appointed by

God for the protection of religion and of the public peace and decency, just as the earth has been ordained to produce food."[85] "Its function among men is no less than that of bread, water, sun, and air. (*Inst.* IV.20.3)

Even the arrogant rule of a tyrant must be endured: "Although dictatorships and unjust authorities are not ordained governments, yet the right of government [as such] is ordained by God for the well-being of mankind."[86] While the tyrant's regime is immoral and under divine judgment, it is not, strictly speaking, illegitimate. The existence of political order is an *ordinatio Dei* and "human depravity is no reason for not cherishing something instituted by God."[87] Christians are obliged to observe God's ordinance even under the odious circumstance of government by enemies of the gospel.[88]

A key to Calvin's positive estimate of civil government is his belief that to be human is to be a "social animal" (*sociale animal*); this is the general principle underlying that most important of all social institutions, marriage.[89] It is also the basis of the Christian's revulsion against slavery: in its institution "the order of nature was violently infringed," "because men were created for the purpose of cultivating mutual society between each other."[90] The concept of an ordered society belongs to human nature as such:

> Since man is by nature a social animal, he tends through natural instinct to foster and preserve society. Consequently, we observe that there exist in all men's minds universal impressions of a certain civic fair dealing and order. Hence no man is to be found who does not understand that every sort of human organization must be regulated by laws, and who does not comprehend the principles of those laws. Hence arises that unvarying consent of all nations and of individual mortals with regard to laws. For their seeds have without teacher or lawgiver, been implanted in all men. (*Inst.* II.2.13)

Furthermore, the seeds of political order are an essential component of human nature, evidence of the image of God[91] and "ample proof that in the arrangement of this life no man is without the light of reason." (*Inst.* II.2.13)

While Calvin nowhere employs the terminology, government is an order of creation, not preservation. Its primarily positive character derives from its place in the *ordo naturae*.[92] Like the law, its negative function of restraining evil arises only accidentally; originally and essentially it exists to enable social intercourse through ordered relationships willed by God. And just as, in the intact state, the preserving and perfecting grace of Christ would be necessary for humans to enter an eternal felicity, so the authority of government would be necessary even "if Adam had remained upright." Because of sin, the positive ordering principle of government must be taken up and integrated in the urgent need of government to preserve public safety and decency through the restraint of evil.

The Twofold Government

As had Luther, Calvin had to contend with the perfectionist arguments of the radical reformers and his doctrine of the state reflects this fact. In rejecting the perfectionist political ethic and its unsettling corollary, Christian anarchism, Calvin also had to avoid the opposite danger of endorsing erastianism. It is for this reason, if for no other, that we find in Calvin's writings, as much as in Luther's, a doctrine of two kingdoms or governments. The word "government," with a few exceptions, is Calvin's preference. He uses the singular form, "twofold government" (*duplex regimen*) on at least one occasion, as well as the more usual, "two governments." (*Inst.* IV.20.1) In Calvin's hands, the two-governments doctrine does posit an important distinction in the manner of God's rule, but it does not carry the connotation that civil government or political power is outside the sphere of evangelical obedience.[93]

In his chapter on Christian freedom in the *Institutes*, Calvin meets Anabaptist extremism by insisting "that we are not to misapply to the political order the gospel teaching on spiritual freedom." (*Inst.* III.19.15) Calvin observes that "there is a twofold government in man: one aspect is spiritual, whereby the conscience is instructed in piety and in reverencing God; the second is political, whereby man is educated for the duties of humanity and citizenship that must be maintained among men." The one government pertains to the life of the soul and therefore impinges on conscience, while the other pertains to regulating outward behaviour, including "laying down laws whereby a man may live his life among other men holily, honourably, and temperately," and from the observance of which no man may claim exemption on grounds of conscience.[94]

It is noteworthy that in the above-mentioned passage from the *Institutes* Calvin locates the two governments in humanity (*duplex in homine regimen*) rather than outside it. This derivation of the legitimate authority of the state from the *ordo naturae* expressed in human nature reminds us of the part that the irreducible remnant of the *imago Dei* continues to play in Calvin's theology. "There are in man, so to speak, two worlds, over which different kings and different laws have authority." (Ibid.) In grounding the distinction between the spiritual and civil governments within human nature itself, Calvin links the social and political order to the order of nature originally intended by the Creator.

In the extended discussion of civil government at *Inst.* IV.20,

Calvin maintains "that Christ's spiritual kingdom and the civil jurisdiction are things completely distinct," yet in such a way that these two jurisdictions are seen to be "not at variance." Civil government must not intrude in the realm of inner piety or conscience; indeed, conscience has to do with God alone and therefore is neither encouraged nor discouraged by civil righteousness, or lack of it. But it does have responsibility not only to remove any obstruction to those expressions of Christian faith which are public, but also to support these public forms. Calvin makes it clear that magistrates are called by God to enforce the first table of the Law as well as the second, and that this is the case according to natural as well as revealed law. "If Scripture did not teach that it extends to both tables of the law, we would learn this from secular writers: for no one has discussed the office of magistrates, the making of laws, and public welfare, without beginning at religion and divine worship." (*Inst.* IV.20.9) Although the positive support of the kingdom of Christ by the magistracy arises only "incidentally" (because of sin), this support extends to the power of the sword.[95]

According to Calvin, the responsibility of civil authorities to God is not merely a matter of maintaining the ethical standards of the Christian religion under a religiously neutral concept of equity. In his preface to Olivétan's translation of the New Testament, he challenges princes to endorse and promote the explicit doctrines of Christian faith and especially the lordship of Jesus Christ.

> It is unthinkable that Jesus Christ, in whom God wills to be glorified and exalted, should not have dominion over you; and in fact it is reasonable enough that you should be the ones to give him this pre-eminence, provided your own power is founded in him alone. Otherwise what an ingratitude it would be that you should want to shut out him who has established you in the power you possess, and maintains and keeps you in it . . . Let each of you engage himself by his own hand to magnify and exalt him who is God's true and glorious image, in whom he fully represents himself to us. Moreover, to do this, it is not enough merely to confess Jesus Christ, and to profess to be his own, so that you have the title without the truth and reality of the matter; you must give place to his holy gospel and receive it with obedience and humility. This is an office every man must fulfill; but it belongs to you especially to see to it that the gospel is heard, to have it published in your lands, in order that it may be known by the people who have been committed to your charge; in order that they may know you as servants and ministers of this great King, and may serve and honour him, by obeying you under his hand and under his guidance.[96]

With a like temerity, Calvin appeals to Sigismund Augustus, the King of Poland, to submit to Christ as supreme governor and to show proper gratitude to him as the source of all regal power. This gratitude will involve "the fact that you recognize, Your Majesty, that for Christ to take full possession of his kingdom there must needs be a complete purge of all superstitions."[97]

With regard to Christ's lordship in the offices and institutions of secular society Paul Althaus makes the claim that "Jesus and the New Testament agree with Luther":

> [Luther] does not claim that Christ is lord within the orders as such but only in men who act within these orders. Thus the secular kingdom does not stand under the lordship of Christ in the same way that the kingdom of Christ or Christendom does . . . The New Testament itself speaks of the lordship of Christ only as his lordship in persons, that is, in their faith. [98]

Calvin agrees that the spiritual lordship of Christ is exercised directly in "the spiritual government by which Jesus Christ keeps us in obedience until he has entirely reformed us to his image, and having robbed us of this mortal body, he places us in heaven."[99] But Christ does exercise an indirect lordship over civil society and its offices no less real than that over the Church and its offices. "For when princes are commanded to kiss the Son of God, not only are they enjoined to submit to His authority in their private position but also to use all the power they possess in defending the Church and maintaining godliness."[100]

In contrast to Luther, Calvin believes that Christ is lord not only of individuals who may happen to be rulers also, but of these rulers in their governing office. He clearly appeals to magistrates and rulers as individuals who must first of all be won to the cause of Christ as private persons before public policies in their constituencies will be formulated in accordance with that cause. But Christ's lordship is an objective fact, altogether independent of the personal faith of individual rulers. The actions of a government committed to the cause of Christ do not bring Christ's lordship into existence in that realm but rather constitute a recognition of it.

While in his earthly ministry Christ rejected the demand of the multitude to make him a king (John 6.15), Calvin willingly applies Prov. 8.15 to him. Christ is king of kings: "It is said (Prov. 8.15) that it is he who gives grace to magistrates to make laws and statutes, and to govern the peoples in equity. Jesus Christ is not a king in his own right, but he is the defender of all kingdoms, since he has founded and instituted them."[101] All secular principalities are figures of the kingdom of Christ and for this reason, if no other, we are obliged to pray for them.[102] "If magistrates properly exercise their office, we see that there exists between their actions and the order deriving from the reign of our

Saviour Jesus Christ a felicitous unity."[103]

In this forthright way, Calvin asserts that Christ is the source of all authority, both spiritual and civil. What is it in his thinking that leads him to take this approach as compared to Luther's? In his discussion of the relationship between civil government and Christ's spiritual lordship, there is no doubt that Calvin is always referring to Christ as incarnate Mediator, ascended and reigning. But reference to Christ as the author and perfecter of the created order is implied in his teaching that human government belongs to the *genuinus ordo naturae* and that participation in an ordered society of mutual assistance is integral to human nature. While Calvin nowhere says so explicitly, it may be that his teaching is different from Luther's because of the "extra" dimension: the Christ known in the incarnate ministry of the Mediator is always, for Calvin, the One who never ceases to uphold the universe by divine right and power. The order of nature has never passed out of the domain of Christ as eternal Word and putatively autonomous "orders of creation" cannot be separated from it. Political authority derives its ultimate legitimacy from Christ who as the eternal Word is one with the Creator of the natural order. And now, as ascended and reigning, the human nature of Christ shares in this rule of the triune God. In Calvin's thought, there can be no radical *caesura* between the secular and the sacred realms because there can be no radical *caesura* between Christ as incarnate and as *logos*.

CONCLUSION

For Calvin, the concept of natural law does not represent an order of creation that exists independently of the order of God's electing purpose in Jesus Christ. The *lex naturae* is one with all divine law and is nothing other than the order of nature tacitly legislating, while the *genuinus ordo naturae* is nothing other than the order prescribed by God in the work of creation. Natural law is distinguished from other forms of law in that knowledge of it is given in and with creaturely existence, though, without the clarifying influence of revealed law and the regenerative influence of the Holy Spirit, its initial function in human experience is only to arraign and condemn. While examples can be found of pagans who not only know the law of nature, but also obey it, such noble behavior is qualified by the fact that these pagans perceive the law only through "the mists of confusion and disorder" (Milner) and obey it only from compromised, if not perverse, motives. Yet Calvin is aware that there are degrees of clarity and obedience among the unregenerate, just as there are degrees of clarity and obedience implicit in the life-long aspiration and growth of believers.

Nature, the moral law published in the Mosaic commandments and the teaching of Christ, and the evangelical summons to conformity with the image of Christ all attest an identical content, namely, fundamental equity, which Calvin regards as convertible with love. In the light of Calvin's evangelical intent, the basis of the coincidence of the imperatives of justice and love is Jesus Christ, through whom God has once for all brought about justification for believing humanity and in whom we see the image of God perfectly restored. Only the justified can enjoy a freed conscience before the law since only to them has righteousness been imputed through faith in Jesus Christ; only incorporation into Christ (conformity to Christ through adoption) can issue in conduct on the pattern of Christ's obedience (conformity to the image of Christ).

On the other hand, from a sapiential perspective, the basis of the coincidence is also the fact that Christ's redeeming work is the restoration of the world's divinely intended order, an order characterized by obedience to God and mutual assistance and care among neighbors. The Christian's freedom of conscience is not a freedom from law, excepting the canonical or humanly devised; it is a freedom for law, a freedom for willing and whole-hearted obedience to the One who is the law's giver and the faithful keeper of covenant. Love is the fulfilling of the law because the law commands nothing else than right relationships, relationships in which the aggrandizing self is humbled and remade through encounter with divine grace, and tested through self-denial for the sake of others.

The essentially positive character of law as expressive of divine order is nowhere more evident than in Calvin's doctrine of civil government. Government belongs to the very order of nature since it is God's will that humans should be "social animals," and that mutual society should be cultivated among them. While, in harmony with Luther, Calvin teaches a doctrine of two governments, in contrast he holds that Christ is lord not only of individuals who are rulers but also of these rulers in their realms. *Christus verus* is also the One who now reigns at the right hand of Majesty and fully exercises the being and power that is his eternally as the Logos.

The degree to which Calvin sees the functions of church and state intertwining under a single sovereign sway is evident in his reluctance to claim too much for the church. In particular, he does not take up the (obvious?) opportunity to see in the fellowship of the church an eschatological sign of the perfection of humanity's social nature. While on earth, the life of the visible church is not only inextricably connected to civil society and government, but it also falls short of being a particularly exemplary society: for Calvin, the true church, the exemplary society, is the invisible church, the society of believers whose identity and number will be known only in eternity. In the present world in which wheat and tares grow together, sometimes it is pagans who are exemplary and who shame "Christians" by their conduct.

NOTES

1. In *Calvin und das Recht*, 1934, Josef Bohatec argued that Calvin studies had neglected "a description of nature as the source and origin of natural law." He observed that "a clear demarcation is lacking between the purely natural elements and those determined and limited by Christian knowledge, and a presentation of the synthesis of both attempted by Calvin." 2f.

2. *Comm. Jon.* 4. 6-8.

3. *Comm. Ps.* 119. 91.

4. *Comm. II Pet.* 3. 5; *Comm. Gen.* 48. 17; and *Comm. Gen.* 3.7 respectively. The quotes are from the second source.

5. *Comm. Gen.* 2. 9.

6. Benjamin Charles Milner, Jr., *Calvin's Doctrine of the Church*, 16.

7. *Comm. Ps.* 11. 4.

8. *Comm. Gen.* 2. 2; *Comm. Ps.* 104. 29; *Comm. Jn.* 5. 17.

9. Emil Brunner, "Nature and Grace," in Karl Barth and Emil Brunner, *Natural Theology*, 37, says: "Calvin uses 'nature' to designate the original creation in so far as it is still recognizable as such, i.e., the God-given form of all created being."

10. *CO* 27, 566; 566f.; and 568, respectively.

11. *Comm. Gen.* 2. 24; *Inst.* II.8.43; *Inst.* II.8.6; *Comm. Gen.* 2. 15; *Comm. Gen.* 4. 15; 37. 18; *Comm. Gen.* 12. 15; *Comm. Gen.* 35. 22; 38. 26, respectively. E. A. Dowey, *The Knowledge of God in Calvin's Theology*, 71, adds to the list: the office of parents as divine instruments for preserving order in society (*Comm. Ex.* 20.12), property rights (*Comm. Ex.* 21.1), helping the needy (*Comm. Isa.* 58.7), respecting the aged (*Comm. Lev.* 19.32) and preserving human life (*Inst.* II.8.39-40). Dowey notes that Doumergue's catalogue from *Jean Calvin—les Hommes et les Choses de Son Temps*, V, 467-9, also lists the rejection of magic, simplicity in food and clothing, the condemnation of counterfeiting, and the evil of drunkenness.

12. *Comm. Rom.* 2. 14.

13. *Inst.* III.19.15 and parallel at IV.10.3.

14. David E. Willis, *Calvin's Catholic Christology*, 148.

15. Arthur Cochrane, "Natural Law in Calvin," in Elwyn A. Smith, ed., *Church State Relations in Ecumenical Perspective*, 197.

16. *Comm. Isa.* 1. 2.

17. *Comm. Isa.* 1. 3.

18. "Sermon CXXVI on Deuteronomy 22," *CO* 38, 24.

19. Aquinas deals with the natural law as also "extrinsic" to human nature by differentiating among three aspects of its observance in humanity. The first is the tendency we have in common with all other creatures to preserve our own being by fulfilling the elementary requirements of life. Secondly, we have instincts in common with other

animals: this is the natural law expressed in such forms as the coupling of male and female and the nurturing of offspring. The third aspect concerns our instinct for the good, or our nature as rational. This includes the natural commands that we should shun ignorance and live civilly with each other. Only this last is intrinsic to human nature as such. *ST, Ia IIae*. 94.2.

20. "The Use of the Law" in *Harmony of Exodus* etc., 3, 196. See also "Sermon CXXIV on Job 33," *CO* 35, 74.

21. *Comm. Jn.* 1. 5.

22. Calvin's teaching here bears a strong resemblance to the teaching of Aquinas. At *ST, Ia IIae*. 94.4, Aquinas observes that "although there is some necessity in general principles, the more we get down to particular cases, the more we can be mistaken....Knowledge of what is right also may be distorted by passion or bad custom or even by radical proclivity...."

23. E. David Willis, op. cit., 149.

24. "Sermon on Deuteronomy 5.17," *CO* 26, 324.

25. François Wendel, Calvin: T*he Origins and Development of His Religious Thought*, 208. This judgment has been shared by other major commentators, notably Ernst Troeltsch. Paul Lehmann quotes Troeltsch in *Gesammelte Schriften* (Tübingen: Mohr, 1922), 1, 442, as follows: "Obviously, the continuation of the analogy between the Decalogue, natural law and Christian law means the infiltration of the infra-worldly ethic into the Christian, as had been the case for the whole of patristic and medieval ethics." Paul Lehmann, "Toward a Protestant Analysis of the Ethical Problem," *The Journal of Religion*, 24 (1944),1. In contrast, David Willis observes: "If natural law is engraved on man as created, thereby being a part of his original righteousness, and if regeneration constitutes some sort of restoration of that original condition, then the natural law has a positive function for the communion of saints." Op. cit., 149f.

26. *ST, Ia IIae* 90.1; 91.1; and 94.1.

27. Michael Strasser, "Natural Law in the Teachings of St. Thomas Aquinas," in Elwyn A. Smith, ed., *Church-State Relations in Ecumenical Perspective*, 170.

28. *Comm. Gen.* 2. 18.

29. *Comm. Gen.* 20. 9.

30. *Comm. Rom.* 2. 15.

31. E. A. Dowey, *The Knowledge of God in Calvin's Theology*, 225.

32. John Haddon Leith, "Creation and Redemption; Law and Gospel in the Theology of John Calvin," in Paul C. Empie and James I. McCord, eds., *Marburg Revisited*, 148.

33. *Comm. Deut.* 5.3. *CO* 24, 262.

34. *Comm. Rom.* 8. 7.

35. *Comm. Gen.* 2. 16.

36. *Inst.* II.7.1. See also *Comm. Gal.* 3. 23.
37. *Comm. Ps.* 19. 8.
38. E.g., at *Inst.* II.6.3; 7.1; 10.2.
39. *Inst.* I.13.27. See also *Comm. Isa.* 16. 5; 43. 8; *Comm. Jer.* 23. 5; *Comm. Heb.* 1. 5.
40. *Comm. Gen.*, "Argument," 65.
41. *Comm. Rom.* 10. 4.
42. *Comm. Acts* 7. 38. See also *Comm. II Cor.* 3. 7; *Comm. Rom.* 7. 10,11; *Comm. Gen.* 2. 16.
43. *Comm. Deut.* 30. 15.
44. *Comm. Deut.* 10. 12.
45. See also *Inst.* II.8.5; *Comm. Matt.* 5. 17,21; *Comm. Tit.* 2. 12; *Comm. Jer.* 26. 4,5.
46. *Comm. Matt.* 5. 21.
47. *Comm. Matt.* 5. 43. See also *Inst.* II.8.7.
48. *Comm. Lk.* 10. 26. See also *Comm. Matt.* 5. 21.
49. *Comm. II Tim.* 3. 17.
50. E.g., at "*Contre Le Secte des Libertines,*" *CO* 7, 206f.
51. *Comm. Jn.* 15. 10.
52. *Comm. Rom.* 8. 29.
53. The four middle quotations in this paragraph are from *Inst.* III.8.1-4.
54. *Comm. Matt.* 11. 28.
55. E.g., Luther says that the natural law teaches the golden rule (*LW* 46, 114) and a Sabbath rest (*LW* 40, 98).
56. *LW* 46, 28.
57. *LW* 46, 31.
58. *Comm. Gal.* 5. 14.
59. *Comm. Lev.* 19. 33.
60. *Comm. Matt.* 5. 43.
61. Ibid.
62. "Sermon on Gal. 6.9-11," *CO* 51, 100.
63. *Comm. Gen.* 37. 25.
64. *Comm. Acts* 13. 36.
65. *Comm. Gen.* 9. 6.
66. "Sermon on Deut. 4.39-43," *CO* 26, 227.
67. *Comm Jon.* 1. 13,14.
68. "The Fifth Sermon on Deut. 5.13-15," *CO* 26, 304.
69. *Comm. Gal.* 5. 14.
70. *Comm. Jn.* 13. 34.
71. "Our whole duty towards our neighbor is really based on one fact that we can know only in Christ—that all men are made in the image of God." Ronald Wallace, *Calvin's Doctrine of the Christian Life*, 148.
72. *Comm. II Cor.* 3. 18.
73. *Comm. Jon.* 1. 13,14.

74. "Eleventh Sermon on Deut. 2," *CO* 26, 9.

75. *Comm. Jn.* 13. 34.

76. *Comm. Deut.* 23. 19,20; parallels at Ex. 22.25 and Lev. 25.35 ff.

77. "Sermon on Job 1.6-8," *CO* 33, 66; and "The Eleventh Sermon on Deut. 4.39-43," *CO* 26, 229.

78. *CO* 26, 9.

79. "The Seventh Sermon on Deut. 5.17," *CO* 26, 324.

80. Emil Brunner accounts for the duality in Calvin's teaching in the following manner. Calvin has a "formal definition" of the *imago* according to which humans are distinguished as man from all other creatures; in this sense the *imago* is inalienable since it confers upon humans their very nature as a responsible subjects. Then there is the "material definition" of the *imago* according to which humanity's actual condition as sinful is acknowledged, such that there is nothing in humankind that has not been vitiated by sin. Emil Brunner, "Nature and Grace," in Karl Barth and Emil Brunner, *Natural Theology*, 23f.

81. *Comm. I Tim.* 2. 2.

82. Before the fall, labor was "pleasant and full of delight," entirely exempt from all trouble and weariness" (*Comm. Gen.* 2. 5), while afterward it became servile, as if humans "were condemned to the mines" (*Comm. Gen.* 3. 17). At *Comm. Gen.* 2. 22, he tells us that marriage is a divine institution, and at *Comm. Gen.* 2. 24, "that among the offices pertaining to human society, this is the principal, and as it were the most sacred, that a man should cleave to his wife."

83. Emil Brunner, op. cit., 44. This position is also taken by David Willis, op. cit., 147. In disagreement are: Dowey, op. cit., 63n93; Benjamin Milner, op. cit., 30; and Ernst Troeltsch, *The Social Teaching of the Christian Churches*, II, 163f. These latter interpreters see Calvin's doctrine of the state as essentially positive.

84. *Comm. Rom.* 13. 1.

85. *Comm. I. Tim.* 2. 2.

86. *Comm. Rom.* 13. 1.

87. *Comm. I. Tim.* 2. 2.

88. "Sermon XIV on the Epistle to Titus," *CO* 54, 557.

89. *Comm. Gen.* 2. 18.

90. *Comm. Gen.* 12. 5.

91. *Comm. Ps.* 8. 5 includes in the list of the "distinguished endowments which clearly manifest that men were formed after the image of God" the following: "their intercourse with each other, which is preserved from being broken up by certain sacred bonds...as well as their being governed by laws."

92. "On the whole Calvin looks not to the fall of man but to the order of nature for the origin and basis of all offices involving superiority and subordination. Such order is necessary, not merely to avoid confusion, but to enable society and man to express that true in-

tegrity and humanity which are part of the image of God in which man was originally made." Ronald Wallace, op. cit., 159f.

93. Even Luther may never have maintained this. Paul Althaus observes that the basis of Luther's distinction of the two governments is to be found in the Reformer's discovery in Scripture of two types of paranesis, the one commanding evangelical obedience without concern for social consequence and the other affirming the divinely instituted power of the state to maintain the social order. *The Ethics of Martin Luther*, 43-5. What differentiates Calvin's conception from Luther's is the boldness of his understanding of the state as a part of the created *ordo naturae*, and as deriving from the nature of humanity as the "social animal."

94. *Inst.* III. 19. 15. See also *Comm. Matt.* 22. 21.

95. *Comm. Jn.* 18.36 and "Dedication to the Second Part," *Comm. Acts*, 16.

96. *CO* 9, 791ff. This translation is from Joseph Haroutunian and Louise Pettibone Smith, eds., *Calvin: Commentaries*, 71f.

97. Dedication to *Comm. Heb.*, x.

98. *The Ethics of Martin Luther*, 79.

99. "First Sermon on the Ascension of Our Lord Jesus Christ," in Leroy Nixon, ed. and trans., *The Deity of Christ and Other Sermons*, 200. (*CO* 48, 588) See also *Comm. I Cor.* 8. 6.

100. *Comm. Jn.* 18. 36.

101. "*Contre les Anabaptistes*," *CO* 7, 89.

102. "Sermon XI on I Tim. 2.1-2," *CO* 53, 132. The call to pray for those in authority indicates that the Church has a reciprocal responsibility toward the state. André Bieler has called this the "*mission politique de l'Eglise.*" Bieler indicates four facets of this political mission: to pray for those in civil authority; to interpret to and for them the nature of their office as divinely ordained and their inescapable responsibility before God for whatever injustice they allow to go unchecked in their realms; to champion the cause of the poor and the weak against the rich and powerful; to appeal to the state for appropriate civil injunctions in maintaining Church discipline. *La Pensée Économique et Sociale de Calvin*, 295-300.

103. "Sermon XII on I Tim. 2.1-2," *CO* 53, 137.

AFTERWORD

While extended study of any shaper of the history of religious ideas is intellectually stimulating and a privileged opportunity, the nature of Calvin's thought pushes its student to respond to the question, To what end? What is there in Calvin's christology that speaks to the present moment and the needs of the church today? There may be many potential responses to the question; reflecting on my own study, I wish to offer three.

1. The first concerns the way that Calvin's christology goes against the stream and presents a challenge to the shibboleths of the present hour. In a time when transcendence can be defined as nothing more than the transpersonal spirit of mutual relationship, Calvin's insistence on the majesty and sovereign power of God offers towering perspective. There is no doubt that we need to incorporate new images of God's relationship to the world and human subjects. Culturally-conditioned images of divine *apatheia* and predominantly coercive power ought not to blind us to the Bible's clear witness: God has a relationship of vulnerability with the world and with people of the covenant. Yet vital faith is born of reverence and awe before the greatness of God, and if we allow our conception of transcendence to become only a function of creaturely relationships, something essential is lost in our doctrine of God and of the eternal Word. Even Calvin's flawed account of the atonement serves us as he wrestles with the height and depth that is the holiness of God.

Again, in a time when the Jesus of history again is being presented as the only authentic Jesus, Calvin's conception of *Deus manifestatus in carnem* shows us a Christ who is the risking reach of God's own self. What we can discover of the "historical Jesus" is always important: we ought not to teach and preach a Christ whom we know to be incongruous with the Jesus who actually lived and ministered in Palestine. More positively put, we need to have confidence that what we teach about Jesus is as historically grounded as possible. Yet, as Schillebeeckx has observed, the Jesus of history is as much a human construct as the Christ of faith. None of us has direct access to the earthly Jesus, and the hypothesis of a Mediterranean peasant-sage need have no more authority than Schweitzer's of an eschatological visionary. The historical Jesus of the present moment has a gospel, of course, and a liberating one, but unless it is "God manifest in the flesh" who bears it, why give allegiance to Jesus rather than some other liberating figure? Simply because he is part and parcel of our cultural inheritance? The risk and commitment entailed in faith calls for a Jesus who is finally the revelation of the character of God.

To offer one further brief example, when essays in christology turn increasingly to disclaiming images of atonement and sacrifice, those of us who know folly and failure in our lives can find in *Christus verus* a love that will not let us go. We may be in search of new images here also, to express the reconciling character of Jesus' work, but can any pull be stronger than that of One who lays down his life for his friends? Thus, encounter with Calvin's thought recalls for us the benchmarks of historic faith, a faith in which many of us were nurtured and still find strength, and provides depth of field and needed balance in viewing the present theological scene.

2. A second response concerns the way in which Calvin's christology and method also provide for us clues and openings relevant to the present moment, and thus can be seen to go with the stream. In particular, his intense awareness of the beauty and revelatory character of the natural world (the creation-intoxicated theologian!) finds resonance in the mandates of eco-theology. Whatever religiously unaffiliated people find in the natural order, Christians can find more. The world about us and within us is not only wondrous, beautiful and imperilled, but the handiwork and gift of God, and, still more, the theatre of the divine glory. Wherever people of faith are found among those imagining, and working for, the healing of the earth, none ought to be more committed than those who have learned from Calvin.

In this appreciation of the natural order, Calvin draws special attention to the role of Christ as the instrumental author and perfecter of creation. Our time calls for a "whole-world ecumenism," an ecumenism that will enable us to make common cause not only with other Christian bodies and individuals, but also with other faiths, indeed with all individuals and groups who are concerned for the well-being of the creation. Christians can undertake such a risky and fulfilling mandate as Christians when the One who gives us our distinctive identity is seen to be the source and goal of all that is natural. From the beginning, the Word and Wisdom of God once incarnate in Jesus Christ has never ceased to play its sustaining and healing role throughout the universe.

Calvin's teaching on the transcendence of Christ's ministry of reconciliation beyond the conditions of fleshly existence also has potential to assist us in global religious dialogue. The Word of God incarnate in Jesus Christ is the source of life and light for all intelligent creatures. Thus, the Christian may be in a position to acknowledge, and affirm, insights and gifts offered from other families of faith precisely because they originate with the One who is known to us as the Word incarnate. Though Calvin never takes the step of affirming the value of any other religion than the Christian, he is aware of the frailty of Christian profession and faithfulness, and of the existence of varying degrees of awareness of God, and of obedience to the divine law, in all humans. Even idolatrous religion and confused obedience recall for us the universality of God's rule and care, and can serve to humble "Christian" arrogance.

3. Finally, if it is true that Calvin aimed at a balanced approach in which evangelical focus and sapiential perspective each have a role, then he provides us with a model for doing theology in a transitional age. Undertaking his theological task in another century of wide-ranging change, Calvin may appear to us as a scribe trained for the kingdom of heaven, able to bring out of his treasure both the new and the old (Matt.13.52). While underscoring the new insight of *Christus verus*, he did not fail to think deeply about the relationship of the mediatorial Christ to the whole of God's wisdom and work, and to set knowledge of God the Redeemer alongside knowledge of God the Creator. Calvin's christology is an essay in method from which we might learn wisely today.

BIBLIOGRAPHY

PRIMARY SOURCES

Ante-Nicene Fathers, The. Edited by Alexander Roberts and James Donaldson. Vol. 1. Buffalo: The Christian Literature Publishing Company, 1885.

Aquinas, Thomas. *Nature and Grace: Selections from the Summa Theologiae of Thomas Aquinas.* Vol. 11 of *The Library of Christian Classics.* Translated and edited by A. M. Fairweather. Philadelphia: Westminster, 1954.

--------. *Opera Omnia.* Vols., 7, 10, 13. New York: Musurgia Publishers, 1949.

--------. *Summa Theologiae.* Edited by Thomas Gilby. 60 Vols. Oxford: Blackfriars, 1964ff.

Barth, Karl. *Church Dogmatics.* Edited by G. W. Bromiley and Thomas F. Torrance. 13 Half-vols. Edinburgh: T&T Clark, 1936-69.

--------. *The Epistle to the Romans.* Translated by Edwyn Hoskyns. London: Oxford University Press, 1933.

---------. *The Resurrection of the Dead.* Translated by H. J. Stenning. London: Hodder and Stoughton, 1933.

---------. *The Word of God and the Word of Man.* Translated by Douglas Horton. London: Hodder and Stoughton, 1928.

Book of Confessions. Part I of *The Constitution of the United Presbyterian Church of the U.S.A.* Philadelphia: Office of the General Assembly, 1966-7.

Calvin, John. "Academic Discourse on All Saints' Day, 1553". Translated and annotated by D. Cooper and Ford Lewis Battles. *Hartford Quarterly,* 6 (1965), 91-106.

--------. *Calvin: Theological Treatises.* Edited and with introductions and notes by J. K. S. Reid. Philadelphia: Westminster, 1954.

--------. *Calvin's Commentaries.* (Old Testament) Calvin Translation Society. Grand Rapids: Eerdmans, 1948-53.

--------. *Calvin's Commentaries.* Vol. 23 of *The Library of Christian Classics.* Translated and edited by Joseph Haroutunian, in collaboration with Louise Pettibone Smith. Philadelphia: Westminster, 1958.

--------. *Calvin's Commentary on Seneca's De clementia*. Vol. 3 of Rennaissance Text Series. Edited and with an introduction by F. L. Battles and André Malan Hugo. Leiden: E. J. Brill, 1969.

--------. *Concerning the Eternal Predestination of God*. Translated by J. K. S. Reid. London: Clarke, 1961.

--------. *The Deity of Christ and Other Sermons*. Translated by Leroy Nixon. Grand Rapids: Eerdmans, 1950.

--------. *Institutes of the Christian Religion*. Vols. 20, 21 of *The Library of Christian Classics*. Edited by John T. McNeill and translated by Ford Lewis Battles. Philadelphia: Westminister, 1960.

--------. *Institution of the Christian Religion; Facsimile of the 1536 Edition*. Translated and edited by Ford Lewis Battles. Pittsburgh: Pittsburgh Theological Seminary, 1969.

--------. *Ioannis Calvini Opera quae supersunt omnia*. Edited by William Baum, Edward Cunitz, and Edward Reuss. 59 Vols. Brunswick: C. A. Schwetschke and Son, 1863-1900.

--------. *The Mystery of Godliness and Other Selected Sermons*. Grand Rapids: Eerdmans, 1950.

--------. *New Testament Commentaries*. Edited by David W. Torrance and Thomas F. Torrance. 12 Vols. Grand Rapids: Eerdmans, 1959.

--------. *Sermons of Master John Calvin on Deuteronomy*. Translated by Arthur Golding. London: 1583.

--------. *Tracts and Treatises by John Calvin*. Translated by Henry Beveridge and edited by Thomas F. Torrance. 3 Vols. Grand Rapids: Eerdmans, 1959.

John Calvin: Selections from his Writings. Edited and with an introduction by John Dillenberger. Garden City: Anchor Books, 1977.

D. Martin Luthers Werke. 39/2 Band. Weimar: Bohlaus Nachfolgen, 1932.

Luther, Martin. *Luther's Works*. Edited by Jaroslav Pelikan (Vols. 1-30) and Helmut T. Lehmann (Vols. 31-55). St. Louis: Concordia, and Philadelphia: Muhlenberg, 1958-75.

Pannenberg, Wolfhart. *Jesus—God and Man*. Translated by Lewis L. Wilkins and Duane A. Priebe. London: SCM, 1968.

Scotus, John Duns. *Opera Omnia*. Vols. 10, 14, 22, 23. Paris: Ludovicum Vives, 1891-5.

SECONDARY SOURCES

A. Books and Pamphlets

Allegra, Gabriel M. *My Conversations with Teilhard de Chardin on the Primacy of Christ.* Translated and with an introduction by Bernardino Bonansea. Chicago: Franciscan Herald Press, 1971.

Althaus, Paul. *The Divine Command: A New Perspective on Law and Gospel.* Translated by Franklin Sherman, with an introduction by William Lazareth. Philadelphia: Fortress, 1966.

--------. *The Ethics of Martin Luther.* Translated and with a forward by Robert C. Schultz. Philadelphia: Fortress, 1972.

--------. *The Theology of Martin Luther.* Translated by Robert C. Schultz. Philadelphia: Fortress, 1966.

Anderson, Bernhard W. *Understanding the Old Testament.* Englewood Cliffs, N.J.: Prentice-Hall, 1957.

Babelotzky, Gerd. *Platonische Bilder und Gedankenganze in Calvins Lehre vom Menschen.* Wiesbaden: Franz Steiner, 1977.

Baillie, Donald. *God Was in Christ.* New York: Scribner's, 1948.

Bangs, Carl. *Arminius: A Study in the Dutch Reformation.* Nashville and New York: Abingdon, 1971.

Battles, Ford Lewis. *An Analysis of the Institutes of the Christian Religion of John Calvin.* Revised Edition. Pittsburgh: Pittsburgh Theological Seminary, 1970.

--------. *New Light on Calvin's Institutes: A Supplement to the McNeill-Battles Edition.* Hartford, 1966.

Barth, Karl and Emil Brunner. *Natural Theology.* Translated by Peter Fraenkel. London: Bles, 1946.

Bauke, Hermann. *Die Probleme der Theologie Calvins.* Leipzig: J. C. Hinrich'schen, 1922.

Baxter, J. H. and Charles Johnson. *Mediaeval Latin Word List.* London: Oxford, 1934.

Bieler, André. *La Pensée Économique et Sociale de Calvin.* Genève: Librairie de l'Université George et Cie., 1959.

Bohatec, Josef. *Calvin und das Recht.* Aslen: Scientia, 1971.

Bonhoeffer, Dietrich. *Christology*. Translated and introduced by Edwin H. Robertson. London: Collins, 1966.

Bornkamm, Heinrich. *Luther's Doctrine of the Two Kingdoms in the Context of His Theology*. Translated by Karl H. Hertz. Philadelphia: Fortress, 1966.

Bouwsma, William J. *John Calvin: A Sixteenth-Century Portrait*. New York and Oxford: Oxford U. P., 1988.

Boyle, Marjorie O'Rourke. *Erasmus on Language and Method in Theology*. Toronto and Buffalo: University of Toronto Press, 1977.

Breen, Quirinus. *John Calvin: A Study in French Humanism*. Grand Rapids: Eerdmans, 1931.

Brunner, Emil. *The Christian Doctrine of Creation and Redemption*. London: Lutterworth, 1952.

Chenu, Marie-Dominique. *The Scope of the Summa of St. Thomas*. Translated and adapted by Robert E. Brennan and Albert M. Landry. Washington: Thomist Press, 1958.

--------. *Toward Understanding St. Thomas*. Translated by Albert M. Landry and D. Hughes. Chicago: Henry Regnery, 1964.

Dillistone, Frederick. *The Structure of the Divine Society*. Philadelphia: Westminster, 1951.

Doumergue, Emile. *La Pensée Ecclésiastique et la Pensée Politique de Calvin*. Vol. 5 of *Jean Calvin -- Les Hommes et les Choses de Son Temps*. Lausanne: Bridel, 1917.

--------. *La Pensée Religieuse de Calvin*. Vol. 4 of *Jean Calvin—Les Hommes et les Choses de Son Temps*. Lausanne: Bridel, 1910.

Dowey, Edward A. *The Knowledge of God in Calvin's Theology*. New York: Columbia, 1952.

Eire, Carlos, M. N. *War against the Idols*. Cambridge U. P., 1986.

Fromm, Erich. *The Fear of Freedom*. London: Routledge and Kegan Paul, 1942.

Ganoczy, Alexandre. *The Young Calvin*. Translated by David Foxgrover and Wade Provo. Philadelphia: Westminster, 1987.

Gerrish, Brian A. *Grace and Gratitude; the Eucharistic Theology of John Calvin*. Minneapolis: Fortress, 1993.

Gilson, Etienne. *The Spirit of Medieval Philosophy*. New York: Scribner's, 1940.

Goumaz, Louis. *La Doctrine du Salut d'après les Commentaires de Jean Calvin sur le Nouveau Testament*. Nyon, Switzerland: Cherix, 1917.

Hall, Basil. *John Calvin: Humanist and Reformer*. London: The Historical Association, 1967.

Hancock, Ralph C. *Calvin and the Foundation of Modern Politics*. Ithaca and London: Cornell, 1989.

Handbook of Christian Theology, A. Edited by Maritn Halverson and Arthur A. Cohen. Cleveland: World, 1958.

Heppe, H. L. J. *Reformed Dogmatics*. Translated by G. T. Thompson. London: George Allen, 1950.

Hoogland, Marvin. *Calvin's Perspective on the Exaltation of Christ in comparison with the Post-Reformation Doctrine of the Two States*. Kampen: J. H. Bok, 1966.

Hopfl, Harro. *The Christian Polity of John Calvin*. Cambridge U. P., 1982.

Knowles, David. *The Evolution of Medieval Thought*. London: Longmans, Green, 1962.

Kuiper, H. *Calvin on Common Grace*. Grand Rapids: Eerdmans, 1930.

Leith, John Haddon. *An Introduction to the Reformed Tradition*. Atlanta: John Knox, 1977.

--------. *John Calvin's Doctrine of the Christian Life*. Louisville: Westminster/John Knox, 1989.

de Lubac, Henri. *The Mystery of the Supernatural*. Translated by Rosemary Sheed. Montreal: Palm, 1967.

McDonnell, Kilian. *John Calvin, the Church and the Eucharist*. Princeton U. P., 1967.

McGrath, Alister E. *A Life of John Calvin; A Study in the Shaping of Western Culture*. Oxford: Blackwell, 1990.

McNeill, John T. *The History and Character of Calvinism*. New York: Oxford, 1954.

Milner, Benjamin Charles, Jr. *Calvin's Doctrine of the Church*. Leiden: E. J. Brill, 1970.

Neeser, Maurice. *Le Dieu de Calvin*. Neuchatel: Secretariat de l'Université, 1956.

Niesel, Wilhelm. *The Theology of Calvin.* Translated by Harold Knight. London: Lutterworth, 1956.

Nixon, Leroy. *John Calvin's Teaching on Human Reason.* New York: Exposition, 1963.

Oberman, Heiko Augustinus. *The Harvest of Medieval Theology; Gabriel Biel and Late Medieval Nominalism.* Cambridge: Harvard U. P., 1963.

Parker, Thomas Henry Louis. *Calvin's Doctrine of the Knowledge of God.* Grand Rapids: Eerdmans, 1959.

--------. *John Calvin: A Biography.* London: Dent, 1975.

Partee, Charles. *Calvin and Calssical Philosophy.* Leiden: E. J. Brill, 1977.

Paul, Iain. *The Knowledge of God: Calvin, Einstein and Polanyi.* Edinburgh: Scottish Academic Press, 1987.

Pesch, Otto Hermann. *The God Question in Thomas Aquinas and Martin Luther.* Translated by Gottfried G. Krodel. Philadelphia: Fortress, 1972.

Portalie, Eugene. *A Guide to the Thought of St. Augustine..* With an introduction by Vernon J. Bourke and translated by Ralph J. Bastian. Westport, Conn.: Greenwood, 1960.

Quistorp, Heinrich. *Calvin's Doctrine of the Last Things.* Translated by Harold Knight. London: Lutterworth, 1955.

Rahner, Karl. *Nature and Grace: Dilemmas in the Modern Church.* Translated by Dinah Wharton. New York: Sheed and Ward, 1964.

Reumann, John. *Creation and New Creation; the Past, Present and Future of God's Creative Activity.* Minneapolis: Augsburg, 1973.

Reuter, Karl. *Das Grundverstandis der Theologie Calvins.* Neukirchen: Erziehungverein, 1963.

Scheffcyzk, Leo. *Creation and Providence.* Montreal: Palm, 1969.

Schmidt, Karl Theodore. *Rediscovering the Natural in Protestant Theology.* Minneapolis: Augsburg, 1962.

Selinger, Suzanne. *Calvin against Himself.* Hamden, Conn.: Archon, 1984.

Stauffer, Richard. *Dieu, la Création et la Providence dans la Predication de Calvin.* Berne: Peter Lang, 1978.

Strong, Augustus Hopkins. *Christ in Creation and Ethical Monotheism.* 2 Vols. Westwood, N.J.: F. H. Revell, 1899.

Taylor, Henry Osborn. *The Mediaeval Mind; A History of the Development of Thought and Emotion in the Middle Ages.* 2 Vols. London: MacMillan, 1930.

Tillich, Paul. *A History of Christian Thought.* London: SCM, 1968.

Torrance, Thomas F. *Calvin's Doctrine of Man.* London: Lutterworth, 1949.

--------. *The Hermeneutics of John Calvin.* Edinburgh: Scottish Academic Press, 1988.

Troelstch, Ernst. *The Social Teaching of the Christian Churches.* Translated by Olive Wyon. 2 Vols. New York: Harper, 1960.

Van Buren, Paul. *Christ in Our Place: the Substitutionary Character of Calvin's Doctrine of Reconciliation.* Grand Rapids: Eerdmans, 1957.

Van Til, C. *Common Grace.* Philadelphia: Presbyterian and Reformed, 1947.

Von Rad, Gerhard. *Genesis; A Commentary.* Translated by John H. Marks. Philadelphia: Westminster, 1961

--------. *Old Testament Theology.* 2 Vols. Translated by D. M. G. Stalker. New York and Evanston: Harper, 1962.

Vos, Armin. *Aquinas, Calvin and Contemporary Protestant Thought; a Critique of Protestant Views on the Thought of Thomas Aquinas.* Washington and Grand Rapids: Christian University Press, 1985.

Wallace, Ronald. *Calvin's Doctrine of the Christian Life.* Grand Rapids: Eerdmans, 1961.

--------. *Calvin, Geneva and the Reformation; a Study of Calvin as a Social Reformer, Churchman, Pastor and Theologian.* Edinburgh: Scottish Academic Press, 1988.

Walzer, Michael. *The Revolution of the Saints; a Study in the Origins of Radical Politics.* Cambridge: Harvard, U. P., 1965.

Warfield, Benjamin Breckenridge. *Calvin and Augustine.* Philadelphia: Presbyterian and Reformed, 1956.

--------. *Calvin and Calvinism.* New York: Oxford U. P., 1931.

Wendel, François. *Calvin et l'Humanisme.* Paris: Presses Universitaires de France, 1976.

--------. *Calvin: the Origin and Development of his Religious Thought.* Translated by Philip Mairet. London: Collins, 1963.

Westermann, Claus. *Creation*. Translated by John J. Sullivan. London: SPCK, 1971.

Willis, Edward David. *Calvin's Catholic Christology; the Function of the So-Called Extra-Calvinisticum in Calvin's Theology*. Leiden: E. J. Brill, 1966.

B. Articles

Ayers, Robert H. "Language, Logic and Reason in Calvin's Institutes", *Religious Studies*, 16 (1980), 283-297.

Bangs, Karl. "Arminius as a Reformed Theologian", in John H. Bratt, ed., *The Heritage of John Calvin*. Grand Rapids: Eerdmans, 1973.

Barth, Karl. "Thoughts on the Anniversary of Calvin's Death", in Martin Rumscheidt, ed., *Fragments Gay and Grave*. London: Fontana, 1971.

Battles, Ford Lewis. "Calculus Fidei", in Wilhelm Neusner, ed., *Calvinus Ecclesiae Doctor*. Kampen: J. H. Kok, 1978.

--------. "God Was Accommodating Himself to Human Capacity", in Donald K. McKim, ed., *Readings in Calvin's Theology*. Grand Rapids: Baker, 1984.

Bavinck, Hermann. "Calvin on Common Grace", in W. P. Armstrong, ed., *Calvin and the Reformation: Four Studies*. New York: Revell, 1909.

--------. "The Future of Calvinism", *The Presbyterian and Reformed Review*, 5 (1894), 1-24.

Bell, Charles M. "Was Calvin a Calvinist?", *Scottish Journal of Theology*, 36 (1983), 535-540.

Benoit, Jean-Daniel. "Calvin the Letter-Writer", in G. E. Duffield, ed., *John Calvin*. Appleford: Courtenay, 1966.

--------. "The History and Development of the *Institutio*", in G. E. Duffield, ed., *John Calvin*. Appleford: Courtenay, 1966.

Bouwsma, William. "Calvin and the Dilemma of Hypocrisy", in Peter de Klerk, ed., *Calvin and Christian Ethics; Papers Presented at the Fifth Colloquium on Calvin and Calvin Studies*. Grand Rapids: Calvin Studies Society, 1987.

--------. "Calvinism as Renaissance Artifact", in Timothy George, ed., *John Calvin and the Church; a Prism of Reform*. Louisville: Westminster/John Knox, 1990.

--------. "The Spirituality of John Calvin", in Jill Raitt, ed., in collaboration with Bernard McGinn and John Meyendorff, *Christian Spirituality: High Middle Ages and Reformation*. New York: Oxford U. P., 1989.

Breen, Quirinus. "John Calvin and Rhetorical Tradition", in Nelson Peter Ross, ed., *Christianity and Humanism.* Grand Rapids: Eerdmans, 1968.

--------. "St. Thomas and Calvin as Theologians", in John H. Bratt, ed., *The Heritage of John Calvin.* Grand Rapids: Eerdmans, 1973.

Cochrane, Arthur C. "Natural Law in the Teachings of John Calvin", in E. A. Smith, ed., *Church-State Relations in Ecumenical Perspective* . Pittsburgh: Duquesne U. P., 1966.

--------. "A Preliminary Aspect of Calvin's Epistemology", *University of Toron to Quarterly,* 14 (1944), 382-393.

Demson, David. "The Image of Calvin in Recent Research", in E. J. Furcha, ed., *In Honour of John Calvin; Papers from the 1986 International Calvin Symposium.* Montreal: ARC Supplement #3, Faculty of Religious Studies, McGill University, 1987.

DeWolf, Lutan Harold. "Theological Rejection of Natural Theology: an Evaluation", *Journal of Religious Thought,* 15 (1958), 91-106.

Douglass, Jane Dempsey. "Calvin's Use of Metaphorical Language for God: God as Enemy and God as Mother", *Archiv für Reformationsgeschichte,* 77 (1968), 126-140.

Dowey, Edward A. "The Structure of Calvin's Theological Thought as Influened by the Two-fold Knowledge of God", in Wilhelm Neusner, ed., *Calvinus Ecclesiae Genevensis Custor.* Bern: Peter Lang, 1984.

Duffield, G. E. "The Growth of Calvin's Institutio", in *Puritan and Reformed Studies,* Conference 15th., London, 1964.

Finlayson, R. A. "Calvin's Doctrine of God", in *Puritan and Reformed Studies,* Conference 15th., London, 1964.

Foxgrover, David. "The Humanity of Christ: within Proper Limits", in Robert V. Schnucker, ed., *Calviniana; Ideas and Influence of Jean Calvin.* Vol. 10, *Sixteenth Century Essays and Studies.* Kirksville, Missouri: Sixteenth Century Journal Publishers, 1988.

Gamble, Richard C. "Calvin's Theological Method: Word and Spirit, a Case Study", in Robert V. Schnucker, ed., *Calviniana; Ideas and Influence of Jean Calvin.* Kirksville: Sixteenth Century, 1988.

Gerrish, Brian Albert. "John Calvin on Luther", in Jaroslav Pelikan, ed., *Interpreters of Luther; Essays in Honor of Wilhelm Pauck.* Philadelphia: Fortress, 1968.

--------. "To an Unknown God; Luther and Calvin on the Hiddenness of God", *Journal of Religion,* 53 (1973), 263-292.

Gessert, Robert A. "The Integrity of Faith: an Inquiry into the Meaning of Law in the Thought of John Calvin", *Scottish Journal of Theology*, 13 (1960), 247-261.

Godbey, John C. "Arminius and Predestination", *Journal of Religion*, 52 (1953), 491-498.

Grislis, Egil. "Calvin's Use of Cicero in the Institutes, I.1-5: a Case Study in Theological Method", *Archiv für Reformationsgeschichte*, 62 (1971), 5-37.

Hall, Basil. "Calvin and the Calvinists", in G. E. Duffield, ed., *John Calvin*. Appleford: Courtenay, 1966.

Jansen, John F. "I Cor. 15.24-28 and the Future of Jesus Christ", *Scottish Journal of Theology*, 40 (1987), 543-570.

Kuizinga, Henry Bernard. "The Relation of God's Grace to His Honour in John Calvin", in Franklin H. Littell, ed., *Reformation Studies; Essays in Honour of Roland Bainton*. Richmond: John Knox, 1962.

Lane, A. N. S. "Calvin's Sources of St. Bernard", *Archiv fur Reformationsgeschichte*, 67 (1976), 253-283.

Lazareth, William H. "Luther's Two Kingdom Ethic Reconsidered", in Paul C. Empie and James I. McCord, eds., *Marburg Revisited*. Minneapolis: Augsburg, 1966.

Lehmann, Paul. "Towards a Protestant Analysis of the Ethical Problem", *The Journal of Religion*, 24 (1944), 1-16.

Leith, John Haddon. "Calvin's Doctrine of the Proclamation of the Word and its Significance for Today", in Timothy George, ed., *John Calvin and the Church; a Prism of Reform*. Louisville: Westminster/John Knox, 1990.

--------. "Calvin's Theological Method and the Ambiguity in His Theology", in Franklin H. Littell, ed., *Reformation Studies; Essays in Honour of Roland Bainton*. Richmond: John Knox, 1962.

--------. "Creation and Redemption; Law and Gospel in the Theology of John Calvin", in Paul C. Empie and James I. McCord, eds., *Marburg Revisited*. Minneapolis: Augsburg, 1966.

Little, David. "Calvin and the Prospects for a Christian Theory of Natural Law", in Gene Outka and Paul Ransey, eds., *Norm and Context in Christian Ethics*. New York: Scribner's, 1968.

McGrath, Alister E. "John Calvin and Late Medieval Thought; a Study in Late Medieval Influences upon Calvin's Theological Development", *Archiv für*

Reformationsgeschichte, 77 (1986), 58-78.
McNeill, John T. "Natural Law in the Teaching of John Calvin", *Journal of Religion,* 24 (1946), 168-182.

Oberman, Heiko Augustus. "The Extra Dimension in the Theology of Calvin", *Journal of Ecclesiastical History,* 21(1970), 43-64.

Packer, James I. "Calvin the Theologian", in G. E. Duffield, ed., *John Calvin.* Appleford: Courtenay, 1966.

Palmer, Ian S. "The Authority and Doctrine of Scripture in the Thought of John Calvin", *Evangelical Quarterly,* 49 (1977), 30-39.

Partee, Charles. "Calvin's Central Dogma Again", in John H, Letih, ed., *Calvin Studies III.*_Davidson, N. C.: Colloquium on Calvin Studies at Davidson College and Davidson College Presbyterian Chruch, 1986.

Pesch, Otto Hermann. "Existential and Sapiential Theology—the Theological Confrontation between Luther and Thomas Aquinas", in Jared Wicks, ed. and trans., *Catholic Scholars Dialogue with Luther.* Chicago: Loyola U. P., 1970.

Postema, Gerald J. "Calvin's Alleged Rejection of Natural Theology", *Scottish Journal ofTheology,* 24 (1971), 423-434.

Prins, Richard. "The Image of God in Adam and the Restoration of Man in Jesus Christ: a Study in Calvinism", *Scottish Journal ofTheology,* 25(1972), 32-44.

Raitt, Jill. "Calvin's Use of Bernard of Clairvaux", *Archiv für Reformationsge--schichte,* 72 (1981), 98-121.

Reardon, Patrick H . " Calvin on Providence: the Development of an Insight", *Scottish Journal ofTheology,* 27 (1974), 517-533.

Stob, Henry. "Calvin and Aquinas", *The Reformed Journal,* 24 (1974), 17-20.

Strasser, Michael. "Natural Law in the Teachings of St. Thomas Aquinas", in Elwyn A. Smith, ed., *Church-State Relations in Ecumenical Perspective.* Pittsburgh: Duquesne U. P., 1966.

Torrance, James. "Interpreting the Word by the Light of Christ or the Light of Nature? Calvin, Calvinism and Barth", in Robert V. Schnucker, ed., *Calviniana: Ideas and Influence of Jean Calvin.* Kirksville: Sixteenth Century, 1988.

Willis, E. David. "Persuasion in Calvin's Theology; Implications for his Ethics", in Peter de Klerk, ed., *Calvin and Christian Ethics: Papers presented at the Fifth Colloquium on Calvin and Calvin Studies.* Grand Rapids: Calvin Studies Society, 1987.

--------. "Rhetoric and Responsibility in Calvin's Theology", in Alexander J. McKelway and E . David Willis, eds ., *The Context of Contemporary Theology*. Atlanta: John Knox, 1974.